CHALLENGES
TO A
LIBERAL
POLITY

CHALLENGES
TO A
LIBERAL
POLITY

Human Rights, Citizenship
& Identity

M. HAMID ANSARI

PENGUIN
VIKING
An imprint of Penguin Random House

VIKING

USA I Canada I UK I Ireland I Australia
New Zealand I India I South Africa I China

Viking is part of the Penguin Random House group of companies
whose addresses can be found at global.penguinrandomhouse.com

Published by Penguin Random House India Pvt. Ltd
4th Floor, Capital Tower 1, MG Road,
Gurugram 122 002, Haryana, India

First published in Viking by Penguin Random House India 2022

10 9 8 7 6 5 4 3 2 1

ISBN 9780670096947

Typeset in Adobe Caslon Pro by Manipal Technologies Limited, Manipal
Printed at Thomson Press India Ltd, New Delhi

www.penguin.co.in

'I see no rule for people but the law
Of rulers, who themselves set up the law.'
—Iraqi poet Maruf al-Rusafi, in his poem
The Negative Truth about Me

Contents

SECTION THREE
INDIAN MUSLIM PERCEPTIONS &THE INDIAN
CONTRIBUTION TO THE CULTURE OF ISLAM

Introduction

I

These essays dwell on the performance of the Indian state in its existential plurality and in terms of its commitments to human and group rights pursuant to national and international norms. It is premised on, and is built, on the contours of the Indian society.

Written over a span of two decades, including a few during my longish tenure in a constitutional position (2007–2017), each of these essays presented me with an occasion to express my personal understanding of the subject. The present selection is essentially chronological. Each piece relates to an aspect of Indian polity; each was thus crafted for an occasion and by implication intended to stand alone.

The paper on Nehru sought to discount simplistic depictions of a statesman who focused on the consolidation of the Indian state in its infancy, on the avoidance of war and on the furtherance of cooperation with all to India's benefit. He was not devoid of statecraft and was aware that in certain eventualities no pious sentiments would stop India from using nuclear power for non-peaceful purposes.

Given my background of almost four decades in the profession of diplomacy, I could not be oblivious to the global context. My perceptions on the international system in the mid and late 1990s were in good measure reflective of the position I had held as India's Permanent Representative to the United Nations in New York. This was at a time when in the post–Cold War period and in the context of the optimism generated by *An Agenda for Peace*, the expectation was of meaningful reforms being established to bring forth 'moral sanction and political effectiveness' in the global system.[1] Our expectation of emphasis on both the *Purposes* and *Principles* of the Charter and for a more representative decision-making mechanism functioning democratically in an international organization that balances its State System Values and Human Rights Values were soon belied, and the former continued to prevail over the latter.

The folly of the approach of the United States, in what was proclaimed as the New American Century, to the Afghanistan and Iraq questions, and the wider failure to comprehend the resort to what Said Arjomand described as 'religiously conditioned political action' in the guise of 'politically conditioned religious action'[2] as a motivating factor of resistance was evident to all except the most myopic; its consequences in practice were graphically depicted, among others, by Bob Woodward in his *State of Denial* (2006). A doctrine of intervention nevertheless remains in place and has been dilated upon more recently by Gregory Gause III, Anthony H. Cordesman and Rory Stewart in their essays.[3]

II

In political literature, a polity in the best sense is a form of government for the common good of the public. Its antithesis is tyranny or some variant of it. It is liberal because it is based on Rule of Law that, as Professor Upendra Baxi has said, goes beyond a mere division of functions in modes of governance and 'links it for core notions: rights, development, governance and justice'.[4] This approach is upheld in judicial pronouncements. Rule of Law said the *Supreme Court in Dalmia Cement (Bharat) Ltd v Union of India* (1996) 'is a potent instrument of social justice to bring about equality in result'.

Some years back, a distinguished academic edited a collection of essays and dedicated it *to whom it may concern*. Its contents made it evident that the addressees are the people of India, an expression that is encapsulated in the first words of the Preamble to our Constitution.

Notwithstanding constitutional ideals and the creation of the National Human Rights Commission (NHRC) in 1993 and earlier of the National Minorities Commission, the mindset of segments of the Indian state apparatus hampered, and continues to hamper, the realization of the objectives visualized by the founding fathers in the wider norms of 'righteousness'.[5] The derailment in the thought process commenced earlier and popular imagination and political opportunism contributed to ideological compromises when confronted by a determined adversary, aided by trained cadres, to exploit the public's faith in its inherited cultural traditions and practices. I dwell upon this in the Fakhruddin Ali Ahmad Memorial Lecture (19 July 2019).

This impacted on the less privileged segments of society and on the minority groups. The debate in concrete terms should be about identity, security, equity and role in decision-making; its assessment too should be in terms of substantive equality achieved. Instead, the resort increasingly is to collective myth-making and emotive allusions to integration and mainstream. It ignores that integration is a function of inclusion and that in the Indian context the mainstream has to be sought in the existential reality of pluralism of our society and in the fraternity enjoined in the Preamble to the Constitution. Its import was spelt out unambiguously in 1995:

> Integration is not a process of conversion of diversities into a uniformity but a congruence of diversities leading to a unity in which both the varieties and similarities are maintained.

Adding that:

> In the semantics of functional politics, the term national integration means and ought to mean cohesion and not fusion, unity and not uniformity, reconciliation and not merger, accommodation and not annihilation, synthesis and not dissolution, solidarity and not regimentation of the people constituting the larger political community, that is the State.[6]

The unity of India lies in its diversity. This was a core ingredient of the freedom movement. Lately a belief system, and a segment of opinion, seeks to jettison it in favour of a manufactured uniformity premised on a cultural alterity of 'us' and 'them.' This is based on a jaundiced view of our history that reads into the past a political happening of recent times. This 'reading of history in terms of mutually exclusive religions' may serve a political purpose but is not and should not be taken as gospel truth.[7]

The derailment was part of a wider process. A constitutional authority, Goolam E. Vahanvati, had opined many years earlier that there were cancerous developments in each of the principal institutions of the state as a result of which Rule of Law was threatened.[8] It took a decade to fructify and has since continued downhill. Some of the lectures in Section 2 and the sources cited therein testify to it in good measure.

Constraints on freedom of expression in the media speak for themselves. A matter of wider concern is its implication for dissent. It has been rightly argued that non-violent dissent is an essential component of democracy. Yet,

> When nationalism yielded the nation state, a plurality of visions was reduced to a basic civics of citizenship and governance. Over time, with internal strife and frictions on the border, the nation state became a National Security State. The sense of violence and paranoia that accompanied it transformed the National Security State into a National Surveillance State where information became a commodity. We moved to create an India between the enclosure and what has been called the 'panopticon'. What facilitated this move and legitimized it was the emergence of a majoritarian society.[9]

This went hand in hand with a debate of wider dimension on the nature of the State and its purpose itself. Signs of this could be discerned after 2014 and assumed a sharper profile after the 2019 general election when both the style and contents of governance changed visibly. This vision of a new India is perceived to be 'a blend of new Hindutva and the political economy of a new variety'. In it, the former 'exhorts the followers to become Hindu politically and become "religious Hindus" by way of public manifestation of religiosity' resulting in a conflation of nationalism and Hindutva as the 'backbone of new ideological dominance'.[10]

The contents of Section 3 dwell on matters that are domestic but have at times external manifestations. Religious minorities constitute just over 20 per cent of our population; of these, 14.2 per cent (around 200 million) are citizens of Muslim faith with a long and diverse history. They have contributed to Indian culture and civilization[11] and in turn have benefited from it. In this sense, India is sui generis. Muslims are dispersed all over the country, are not homogenous in linguistic and socio-economic terms and reflect in good measure the diversities that characterize the people of India as a whole. The Mushawarat Anniversary lecture of August 2015 focused both on the policy and in-practice correctives of the government and autonomously by the community individually and collectively. Similarly, the September 2017 lecture dealt with the shortcoming arising from social prejudices and practices unrelated to religion that have impacted adversely on women's participation in the workforce.

Another constraining factor is caste. Since now there is an acceptance that the traditional caste system is pervasive and extends to all segments of our population, there is also an assertiveness in the Muslim demand that the 1950 Presidential Order excluding Muslims and Christians from the lists of Scheduled Castes (SCs) and Scheduled Tribes (STs) be appropriately rectified to include relevant Muslim (and Christian) segments. The politics of this demand is yet to surface fully.

III

The post-Independence landscape inflicted physical and psychological insecurity on Muslims in many parts of the country. Some of its implications came to be officially acknowledged only in 2006 through the Sachar Report that brought out the educational deprivation experienced by the Muslim community and pointed out that 'access to education is critical for benefiting from emerging opportunities that are accompanied by economic growth'. Two years later the Kundu Report said 'unequal economic opportunities lead to unequal outcomes which in turn lead to unequal access to political power. This creates a vicious circle since unequal power structure determines the nature and functioning of the institutions and their policies. All these result in persistence of initial conditions'.[12]

Despite these, the correctives are slow and patchy. The challenge now is to sustain the struggle for the actualization of legal and constitutional rights, to do so without being isolated from the wider community and to endeavour at the same for self-correctives and empowerment in a fast-changing world. The focus has to be on the principles enunciated in the Preamble: *Justice, Equality, Fraternity.* The latter, said Ambedkar, 'means a sense of common brotherhood of all Indians—"of Indians being one people". It is the principle which gives unity and solidarity to social life. It is a difficult thing to achieve'.[13]

Thus, legislative or administrative devices intended to dilute or deny any of these must be eschewed.

The last few years have shown that mere statements of foundational principles have little impact on state practice since the evident failure of institutions has allowed the resultant imbalance to manifest itself on rights of the citizen body and principally on dissent. A candid editorial comment makes this evident:

There is reason to fear that the State now uses the (UAPA) Act to silence dissent and imprison its critics. Among those booked in recent years under UAPA and denied bail include rights activists, lawyers and academicians imprisoned in the 2018 Bhima Koregaon-Elgar Parishad case, students and youth arrested in anti-CAA protests, human rights defenders, RTI activists.[14]

Since the traditional landscape of articulating grievances through political parties, regional or national, stands discredited, even disempowered, the search for alternatives is inevitable.

How and where? Objectively and otherwise, we have not reached the stage that might give credence to Trotsky's observation of 'the forcible entrance of the masses into the realm of ruler-ship over their own destiny'.[15] Yet, Maoist movements and insurgencies in different regions and peasant agitation in recent years do suggest that expressions of discontent are going beyond the traditional avenues of protest and are mutating into newer forms. The successfully concluded farmer's protest around Delhi and the anti-CAA protest of the year before that are good examples of these.

We do have a system of governance within the framework of a functioning Constitution but parts of it seem to be partially dysfunctional. A ray of hope now emerges in the shape of regional political parties holding their ground in regional elections. Euphoria apart, how will its impact manifest itself on different segments of public consciousness? Will it give new direction to national politics?

The partial functioning of principal institutions is one aspect of the matter; another, more substantive, is the quality of the output. Democracy has brought forth increasing representation but decreasing responsiveness of the state. Recent state elections have shown a marked preference for local causes and a search of alternatives. Greater social activism adds to it. These together highlight the idea of a pluralistic India and of more meaningful cooperative federalism that figures in political discourse from time to time.

It has been opined that in a new situation, the requirement may be an impulse 'for struggles around federal autonomy to be fought collectively around other states (apart from Tamil Nadu) that calls for credible political coalitions to strengthen federalism. The Indian variety of federalism— which is very flexible—can be sustained only by such a political coalition'.[16]

Such a prognosis, however, may be premature given political orientations elsewhere in the country.

A new global discourse has also taken shape in recent decades. It is global in character and its impact on national actors is uneven. In this process, the State Value System enshrined in the traditional doctrine of state sovereignty has been circumscribed by the Human Rights Values. The international system has inscribed this in a series of covenants in pursuance of Article 55 of the Charter and other provisions of its Chapter IX.[17] Its impact poses contradiction. One aspect was globalization or the closer integration of the economies of the world. This also narrowed the choices facing democracies: 'We can have a democracy with one person one vote, and still get outcomes that are more in accord with what we might expect in a system with one dollar one vote.'[18] By the same process, however, globalization has also 'heightened the role of human rights in two senses, on the one hand the processes of globalization have allowed to expand the reach of human rights across the globe, which in turn influenced the content and nature of globalization that we are witnessing'.[19]

Our stated national objective is to become an inclusive society. How far have we travelled towards it? Here we have to understand the meaning of social exclusion. It is understood to mean 'the inability of an individual to participate in the basic political, economic and social functioning of the society' and 'denial of equal access of opportunities for it'. Such exclusion can be active or passive, wilful or consequential. This, in relation to a group, would mean social exclusion from opportunities of participation in the work of the society and could be based on caste, ethnicity or religion. It results in covert or overt discrimination and leads to under-development, inequality and poverty.

Eminent sociologist T.K. Oommen identifies nine categories of people in our society who are deemed socially and/or politically and/or economically excluded. These are: Dalits; Adivasis; Other Backward Castes (OBCs); cultural minorities—both religious and linguistic; women; refugees, foreigners, outsiders; people from North-East India; the poor; and the disabled.[20]

Inclusiveness has been defined in the Preamble to the Constitution. In it *We the People of India* dedicated ourselves to the achievement of Justice (social, economic and political); Liberty (of thought, expressions, belief, faith and worship); Equality (of status and opportunity); and Fraternity (assuring the dignity of the individual and the unity and integrity of the Nation).

Successive governments over the past seven decades have dedicated themselves to this goal and have sought to achieve it. The result of this effort is to be sought less in policy statements, promissory notes and slogans, which are invariably positive and optimistic, but in the scorecard of the results obtained. In terms of quantification, the following shed much light on it:

- The United Nations Development Programme's (UNDP's) Human Development Index for 2017 places India at 131 amongst 188 countries.
- Reports of our National Human Rights Commission give details of Dalits who live below the poverty line as also of infant mortality, undernourishment, and illiteracy among them. Details are also available about other forms of discriminatory treatment.
- The condition of STs, who constitute 104 million of our population, has not improved. In fact, policies resulting in alienation of tribal lands are the single biggest source of their pauperization and resentment.
- Answering a question in the Rajya Sabha, on 10 March 2016, the Minister for Human Resource Development (HRD) said that in 2014, some 6.064 million children remained out of school. Of these, a massive 4.6 million or 76 per cent belonged to the SCs, STs and other religious minorities.
- Despite significant social and economic transformation, caste hierarchies remain deeply entrenched in the mind and in practice and caste relations often result in violent outcomes.
- Official and civil society reports clearly indicate that the principal problems confronting India's Muslims, constituting 14.5 per cent of the population, relate to (a) identity and security; (b) education and empowerment; (c) equitable share in the largesse of the state; and (d) fair share in decision-making.
- The Sachar Committee Report of 2006 had observed that only 17 per cent of Muslim children above the age of seventeen were found to have completed matriculation as compared to the general average of 26 per cent. Another report, in 2013, found that the level of matriculation education among Muslims both in rural and urban areas is lower than even SCs and STs. This is also evident in higher education.

- Despite all governmental and societal efforts, the overall literacy rate in the country in 2017 was 74 per cent, with female literacy at 65 per cent.
- The actual status of women and the treatment of the girl child belie our constitutional commitment to equality of status and opportunity. Workforce participation and social mobility, particularly among Muslim women, is abysmally low.
- Youth unemployment and rural distress have assumed acute dimensions and cannot but effect social peace.

Thus, the fault lines in our society are visible; even official economists speak of two Indias—'the urban rich India and the rural poor Bharat'. This continues to hurt and the numbers of the excluded add up to a high percentage of the citizen body. India is rated as the twelfth most inequitable economy in the world, with 45 per cent of wealth controlled by millionaires and almost half of India's total wealth is in the hands of the richest 1 per cent, while the top 10 per cent controlled about 74 per cent of it. The poorest 30 per cent, meanwhile, had just 1.4 per cent of the total wealth.[21]

Amartya Sen and Jean Dreze, eminent scholars of socio-economic development in modern India, have noted that 'the societal reach of economic progress in India has been remarkably limited'; they added that the agenda for political, economic and social democracy remains unfinished because of continued disparity between the lives of the privileged and the rest and because of persistent ineptitude and unaccountability in the way the economy and society are organized. Furthermore, the mutual reinforcement of the inequalities of caste and gender creates enormous disparities in our society, and these are aggravated by class dimensions.[22]

It is thus evident that while democratic mobilization has produced an intense struggle for power, it has not delivered millions of citizens from the abject dictates of poverty. Thus, the de jure 'WE, the People' in the first line of the Preamble is in reality a fragmented 'we', divided by yawning gaps that remain to be bridged.

Deprivation in our society takes diverse forms and, as the Kundu Report of 2008 pointed out, 'Unequal economic opportunities lead to unequal outcomes which in turn lead to unequal access to political power. This creates a vicious circle since an unequal power structure determines the nature and functioning of the institutions and their policies. All these result in persistence of initial conditions.'

The late George Verghese had written more than a decade earlier:

As India's multitudinous but hitherto dormant diversities come to life, identities are asserted and jostle for a place in the sun. Issues of majority and minority, centre and periphery, great and little traditions, rural and urban values, tradition and modernity and all of Naipaul's million mutinies have to be negotiated and managed.[23]

He suggested that 'we need instrumentalities of communication, education, institutions and policies to help negotiate the country's myriad diversities'.[24]

So, to what extent are we addressing these diversities and challenges? Some of the government programmes are slowly but surely making a difference to the lives of people in many states and there is enormous scope for extending these achievements to other states also. And yet, these will remain inadequate and insufficient unless conscious and concerted efforts are made to address the under-development of those who rightfully claim their rights as citizens but are socially and historically excluded.

Experience shows that in the final analysis, those claiming social justice as citizens and confronted with stated or unstated perceptions and practices of denial have to pay heed to what Dr Ambedkar suggested many years before Independence: 'My final words of advice to you are educate, agitate and organize, have faith in yourself, and never lose hope.'

IV

An unavoidable gap between democratic institutions and the reality of caste is both a historical truth of the Indian subcontinent and a reality of modern-day India. Its impact on a fragmented society was to convert the social scene into a vast battlefield for equality. To Ram Manohar Lohia, it was not class but caste and gender that provided the basis of an understanding of inequality since 'caste restricts opportunity (and) restricted opportunity constricts ability (and) constricted ability further restricts opportunity where caste prevails; opportunity and ability are restricted to ever-narrowing circles of the people'.

It has been opined that in regard to the question of castes, the sociological and judicial perceptions do not necessary tally, resulting in a distinction in reservations made in legislatures on the one hand and government jobs and seats in educational institutions on the other, since 'the first provide access to power while the second results in securing jobs, entry into various professions and for improving the quality of life in general'.[25]

In a contemporary introduction to Dr Ambedkar's *Annihilation of Caste*, it has been remarked that

> since caste is considered a potent instrument of socio-economic and political empowerment, the caste and sub-caste organizations are proliferating. There is a growing demand on the part of some castes, to get included in the OBC categories, and some OBCs into the STs (for example Jats in Haryana and Rajasthan) for economic benefits, while keeping their castes hierarchy, arrogance and other privileges intact. The wind is thus moving in the opposite direction.[26]

To give this shape, caste data was required; as a result, every census till 1931 had published data on castes. It was collected in 1941 but not published. From 1951 to 2011 only data on SCs and STs was published but not on other castes. In July this year it was announced in the Lok Sabha that 'the Government of India has decided as a matter of policy not to enumerate caste-wise population other than SCs, and STs in census'.[27]

The ongoing debate on this question makes evident the interplay of hard political interests.

V

How do these, and other practices, reflect on the liberal polity envisaged in the ideals and principles of the Constitution? The correctives must be conceptual and practical. For a liberal polity we need a clear understanding of what constitutes patriotism and nationalism in the context of the core values of the Indian Constitution.

We the Peoples of the United Nations live as citizens in nation states (except those under foreign occupation). Citizenship implies national obligations. It necessitates adherence to, and affection for, the nation in all its rich diversity. This is what nationalism means, and should mean, in a global community of nations. Liberal nationalism 'requires a state of mind characterized by tolerance and respect of diversity for members of one's own group and for others;' hence it is 'polycentric by definition' and 'celebrates the particularity of culture with the universality of human rights, the social and cultural embedded-ness of individuals together with their personal autonomy'. On the other hand, 'the version of nationalism that places cultural commitments at its core is usually perceived as the most conservative and illiberal form of nationalism. It promotes intolerance and arrogant patriotism'.[28]

Here a conceptual clarity is needed. Nationalism is often confused with patriotism and used interchangeably. Both are words of 'unstable and explosive content' as was pointed out by George Orwell in his essay 'Notes on Nationalism'. Nationalism means identifying oneself with a single nation, placing it beyond good and evil and recognizing no other duty than of advancing its interests; patriotism, on the other hand, is devotion to a particular place or way of life without wishing to force it on others.

What are, or could be, the implications of nationalism and its variants for pluralism and secularism? It is evident that both would be abridged since both require for their sustenance a climate of opinion and a state practice that eschews intolerance, distances itself from extremist and illiberal nationalism, subscribes in word and deed to the Constitution and its Preamble, and ensures that citizenship irrespective of caste, creed or ideological affiliation is the sole determinant of Indianness.

Thus, patriotism is of its nature defensive—both militarily and culturally—and nationalism is inseparable from the desire for power. Decades earlier Rabindranath Tagore had called nationalism 'a great menace', described it as 'one of the most powerful anesthetics that man has invented'. He had expressed himself against 'the idolatry of the nation', an 'ideological poison' that has no hesitation in transcending and transgressing individual rights.

In our plural secular democracy, therefore, the 'other' is to be none other than the 'self'. Any derogation of it would be detrimental to its core values.

A study of recent Election Manifestos of the Bharatiya Janata Party (BJP) is, therefore, instructive. The 2009 manifesto spoke about 'the civilisational consciousness of India (that) not only accepts diversity but respects it and even more celebrates it. Hindu or Bharatiya view of life seeks unity in diversity.' The 2014 manifesto spoke of the 'the civilisational consciousness of India'. The 2019 Sankalp Patra asserted, 'This election is not between two political parties; rather, it is an election to dissipate the negativity that makes us oblivious to our glorious past and our cultural roots and values . . . The election is to defeat dynasticism, casteism, communalism and corruption so that India's democracy can be infused with greater strength.' One consequence of it was the much-lauded acts of vandalism presented as 'cultural regeneration'. Its result will be to transform our political culture from an open democratic diversity to a narrow formalization of democracy and openness.

To sum up, the challenge to our liberal polity is both ideological and practical. The latter can be countered by a corrective administered by the electoral process as has been done from time to time. The former, on the other hand, requires a careful examination of the philosophic backdrop, ideological pronouncements and terminological sophistry of the political hypothesis that succeeded at the polls in 2014 and again in 2019, and which is optimistic about the immediate and foreseeable future. To this end it puts across a slanted view that while diversity is inherent in the Indian scheme of creation and is the manifestation of a cosmic entity in different forms, its acceptance in the context of the Hindu or Bharatiya view of life requires the exclusion of all alien views that impacted the Indian way of life or left a mark on them. In the process it seeks to erase other influences down the ages, including the existential reality of over a thousand years of Indian history, and to impose an imagined version of cultural homogeneity with all its political connotations, leading to what has been called an 'ethnic democracy' whose characteristics have been described by the sociologist Sammy Smooha[29] and more specifically by Indrajit Roy.[30]

The challenge is real; it is also urgent. It has to be met in terms of ideas, practices and day-to-day behaviour.

December 2021

SECTION ONE

HUMAN RIGHTS AND GROUP RIGHTS

1

Annual Conference of the
National Minorities Commission*

This indeed is a signal honour. It is the first occasion in twenty-eight years that the Commission has been privileged to welcome the Prime Minister. The gesture itself is significant: *dair ayad, durust ayad* (better late than never). Today we focus on the *durust* part of it. It signifies a purpose, suggests an approach, indicates a willingness to hear—in this case a cry in which anguish and expectations alternate—and to redress.

When the Minorities Commission was established, through a Resolution of the Government in 1978, its stated purpose was to 'safeguard the interests of Minorities'. At the time of the NCM Act of 1992, the Statement of Objects and Reasons said it would 'infuse confidence among the minorities'. The purpose on both occasions was to safeguard rights and to reassure. This indeed was the intention of the Constitution-makers. Sardar Patel urged the minorities 'to trust the good sense and the sense of fairness of the majority'. Jawaharlal Nehru called it an 'act of faith' for all, and particularly for the majority, to ensure behaviour that is 'generous, fair and just'. These perceptions were amply reflected in the Constitution.

Why then was there the felt need to reassure?

What was it that was not done?

What was done that should have been avoided?

The answers are disconcerting. They need to be addressed, not evaded.

The Minorities, Prime Minister, reflect an important aspect of the Indian reality:

---

* Address to the National Minorities Commission, 2 February 2006.

- They constitute 18.4 per cent of the population. Every sixth Indian, therefore, belongs to a religious minority.
- Credible data shows that considerable sections of minorities remain marginalized in terms of socio-economic development.
- The pace of progress of the minorities thus inevitably impacts on the all-round progress of the country.
- The minorities need assurance of physical security, of life with dignity, and of equality of treatment at the hands of the agents of the state.
- They stand in need of accelerated development, and of carefully calibrated affirmative action directed at achieving it, so that they can attain substantive equality and contribute in full measure to the national effort.

Attitudes in segments of our society aggravate the problem. Some tend to consider the minorities as a bothersome nuisance; some others would wish to assimilate them to the point of extinction. Unreasonable attitudes induce irrational reactions. Both sets of perceptions promote intolerance and harm national cohesion in a plural, secular and democratic polity. A corrective effort is imperative, and the state has to take the lead in the matter.

The Common Minimum Programme of the Government, Prime Minister, reflects awareness of these issues. The new 15-Point Programme, and your recent pronouncements, are expressive of a desire to apply correctives.[1] These commitments have been widely welcomed.

The critical question, however, is of implementation. Given past experience, the need of the hour is to supplement the official monitoring machinery with a civil society mechanism at central and state levels. Such a step would also help generate public awareness of minority questions, an awareness that is sadly lacking as is evident from the absence of debate within the Parliament and in the media.

The country has travelled a considerable distance in enforcing the human rights of individual citizens; a similar endeavour with regard to minority rights needs to be made since both form part of the charter of rights. Furthermore, and in the age of globalization, national standards of minority rights need to move in step with international norms.

The National Commission for Minorities has now functioned for thirteen years, under the Act of 1992. The human and financial resources given to it are inadequate for the totality of tasks assigned to it by the Act.

Experience shows that its monitoring responsibility cannot be discharged adequately unless it is equipped with an instrumentality of the type given to the NHRC and the Commission for Scheduled Castes. It is our hope that the Constitution (Amendment) Bill, aimed at giving constitutional status to the National Commission, would rectify these practical deficiencies.

The situation with regard to the State Minority Commissions is worse. More than half of the states do not see the need for them; others treat them either as part of the administrative machinery or as outcasts. Even in regard to the National Commission, the approach of the state governments tends to be evasive. This is a disturbing trend since, in the final analysis, effective protection of minority rights as of human rights is to be ensured on a day-to-day basis at the local and state levels.

2

India and the Contemporary International Norms on Group Rights*

Humans seek to live in society. The challenge posed by their interactions was enunciated by Rousseau: 'Taking men as they are and laws as they can be made, it is possible to establish some just and certain rule of administration in civil affairs . . . to reconcile what right permits and what interest prescribes'.[1] The concept of justice thus became central to the discourse on governance. The principle of justice is one aspect of the matter; dispensing justice is another.

Justice and Rights

Justice, wrote a modern political philosopher, is the first virtue of social institutions: 'Therefore in a just society the liberties of equal citizenship are taken as settled; the rights secured by justice are not subject to political bargaining or to the calculus of social interests'.[2] This doctrine of rights, enshrined in most modern constitutions and having universal acceptance, is the product of a long history. Kautilya wrote about the duties of kings towards his subjects but made no mention of the latter's rights except property rights.[3] For Manu, the dispensation of justice was the primary duty of the ruler.[4] In ancient Athens, the citizen had the right to share 'in the administration of justice, and in offices'.[5] In the Qur'an, the emphasis is on justice and Islamic jurisprudence highlights rights of man (*haqq al abd*) as a distinct category.[6] Europe in the Middle Ages approached the matter in a different paradigm: 'It is a distinctive trait of medieval doctrine that within every human group it decisively recognises an original and active

* *Indian Foreign Affairs Journal*, volume 2, number 2, April–June 2007.

Right of the group taken as a Whole'.[7] It, however, lacked the character of the universality of the modern world.[8] To John Locke who wrote to justify the English Revolution of 1688, every man had two birthrights: the right over his person, and the right to inherit.[9]

A century later new horizons unfolded in the *American Bill of Rights* of 1776 and the French *Declaration of the Rights of Man* of 1789. The focus of these was on individual rights. Over time, the efficacy and legitimacy of a state came to be judged in terms of its ability to secure rights for its citizens. As the debate developed, normative questions were raised: what rights a person *ought* to have, and what rights the state *ought* to protect and enforce. Such a system of rights could thus be considered from three positions: the viewpoint of the individual, of the group or groups to which he may belong, and of the community in which he and the groups are located. Furthermore, and in a democratic polity, the individual's choice could be at variance with that of the majority of his fellow citizens, giving rise to the question of majority and minority and to what John Stuart Mill termed the 'tyranny of the majority' emanating either from the government or from the social group, and threatening the liberty of the individual in a minority. This would hold good, in equal measure, for groups that find themselves in minority.

Minority Rights

The argument thus far was within the ambit of the territorial jurisdiction of states, and in the framework of individual rights. Independently, and in a parallel development, the question of rights of groups finding themselves as minorities surfaced in Europe in the 18th and the 19th centuries in the period of the emergence of nation states. The Treaty of Kutchuk–Kainardji between Russia and Turkey (1774), the declaration by the Netherlands in regard to Belgium (1814), the agreement between Great Britain, France and Russia on conditions of recognition of the independence of Greece (1830) and the Treaty of Berlin (1878), are good examples of it. The impact was telling:

> National minorities had lived under foreign rule long before the emergence of nation-states, but the 'problem of national minorities' surfaced in full force only in the aftermath of the First World War, following the dissolution of empires. The establishment of nation-states did increase

the number of people who came to be ruled by their fellow nationals. It also resulted in a considerable number of national minorities left to be ruled by others, and feeling deprived and threatened due to their failure to accomplish their national aims. In a world of nation-states, being a minority not only entails subjugation to foreign rule, but also forfeiting recognition as a distinct national group. The most palpable expression of disregard for stateless national groups was, and still is, that international institutions such as the League of Nations or the United Nations, in spite of their names, accept only states as members.

'National minorities found subjugation to the nation-states more oppressive than imperialist rule for a further reason. Empires had indeed been perceived as foreign ruling power, but had left cultural matters to the discretion of national groups. By contrast, the nation-state was not only assigned administrative, economic and strategic functions, but also adopted a particular cultural and national identity. Consequently, in order to be considered full-fledged citizens, individuals had to identify not only with the state and its institutions but also with the culture of the ruling nation. State involvement in cultural matters deeply affected the self-image of national minorities, which came to feel that the effort to shape all the citizens of the state into one homogenous nation destined them for erosion. Mobilisation of the masses, socialisation, cultural uniformity nation-building, assimilation, all the magic words of the modern nation-states, became the national minorities' nightmare'.[10]

Experience showed that the relationship between the State and its minorities could take any one of five different forms: elimination, assimilation, toleration, protection and promotion. The prospect of the first two of these became a matter of serious concern in the wake of World War I. To address these misgivings, the new European States were forced to pledge respect for religious, linguistic, cultural and political rights of the minorities. Good examples of these were the Protection of Minorities Treaties between the Principal Allied and Associated Powers and Poland and Romania signed on 28 June and 9 December 1919, respectively. Articles 8–11 of both the treaties guaranteed equality and political, cultural and linguistic rights to minorities. Article 12 stipulated that these rights were in the nature of international obligations under the guarantee of the League of Nations. Similar treaties were signed with Czechoslovakia, Greece and Yugoslavia and their entry into the League of Nations was made conditional on the grant of minority rights. Minority rights thus came within the purview of international law. The operative principles were laid down in two celebrated judgements of the Permanent Court of International Justice, first in the case of the Greco–Bulgarian community in 1930 and subsequently in the case of minority schools in Albania. The first, the Court observed, 'defined a community not in terms of numbers but in terms of shared religious, racial and linguistic traditions, traditions that the group wishes to preserve and perpetuate through ritual, education and socialization of the young. The existence of such a community, ruled the Court, is not dependent upon recognition by law'. In the Albanian case the Court commented on the Albania's Declaration on minority rights and said its objective was twofold: 'the objective of minority rights is to secure for minority groups the possibility of living peaceably alongside the rest of the population and cooperating amicably with them while at the same time preserving the characteristics which distinguish them from the majority and satisfying the ensuing special needs'. The Court held that:

> These two characteristics are indeed closely interlocked, for there would be no true equality between a majority and a minority if the latter were deprived of its own institutions and were consequently compelled to renounce that which constitutes the very essence of its being a minority . . . Equality in law precludes discrimination of any kind, whereas equality in fact may involve the necessity of different treatments in order to attain a result which establishes an equilibrium between different situations. It is easy to imagine cases in which, equality of treatment of the majority and the minority, whose situations and requirements are different, would result in inequality.[11]

Despite this early recognition, minority rights remained in the background in the early days of the United Nations. They find no explicit mention in the Charter (1945) and in the Universal Declaration of Human Rights (1948). The focus of both these seminal documents was on human rights of 'everyone'. The group per se tended to be overlooked. It was, however, soon realized that minority rights could not simply be subsumed in universal rights. The corrective took the shape of the International Covenant on Economic, Social and Cultural Rights and the International Covenant on Civil and Political Rights, both in December 1966. These resulted in specific obligations across a wide spectrum being accepted by the States

Parties to these Covenants. Two articles of the Covenant on Civil and Political Rights (CCPR) are of particular relevance:

> Article 26: all persons are equal before the law and are entitled without discrimination to the equal protection of the law. In this respect, the law shall prohibit any discrimination and guarantee to all persons equal and effective protection against discrimination on any ground such as race, colour, sex, language, religion, political and other opinion, national or social origin, property, birth or other status.

> Article 27: In those states in which ethnic, religious or linguistic minorities exist, persons belonging to such minorities shall not be denied the right, in community with other members of their group, to enjoy their own culture, to profess and practice their own religion, or to use their own language.[12]

These perceptions were amplified in the 1981 Declaration on the Elimination of All Forms of Discrimination Based on Religion or Belief, and in the 1992 Declaration on the Rights of Persons Belonging to National or Ethnic, Religious and Linguistic Minorities. These were reiterated and reinforced through the 1993 Vienna Declaration and Programme of Action adopted at the World Conference on Human Rights. The obligation undertaken in paragraph 19 of the Vienna Declaration was specific:

> Considering the importance of the promotion and protection of the rights of persons belonging to minorities and the contribution of such promotion and protection to the political and social stability of States in which such persons live, the World Conference on Human Rights reaffirms the obligation of States to ensure that persons belonging to minorities may exercise fully and effectively all human rights and fundamental freedoms without any discrimination and in full equality before the law in accordance with the Declaration on the Rights of Persons Belonging to National or Ethnic, Religious and Linguistic Minorities.
>
> The persons belonging to minorities have the right to enjoy their own culture, to profess and practice their own religion in private and in public, freely and without interference from any form of discrimination.[13]

India subscribed to each of these documents. Relevant in this context is Article 51C of the Constitution of India; it enjoins the State 'to foster respect for international law and treaty obligations in the dealings of organised people with one another'.

The meaning and implications of these agreements on the rights of religious minorities have been amplified through discussions in UN committees and in authoritative commentary. The Human Rights Committee of the UN commented at some length on the intent behind Article 27 of CCPR with a view to clarify concepts and 'educating world opinion':

- This right 'shall not be denied'. Article 27 'establishes and recognises a right which is conferred on individuals belonging to minority groups and which is distinct from, and additional to, all other rights which, as individuals in common with everyone else, they are already entitled to enjoy under the Covenant'.
- The enjoyment of this right 'does not prejudice the sovereignty and territorial integrity of a State party'.
- The right conferred under Article 27 is distinct from, and does not in any manner abridge, the rights conferred by Articles 2(1) and 26 of the Covenant.
- 'The terms used in Article 27 indicate that the persons designed to be protected are those who belong to a group and who share a common culture, a religion and/or a language. Those terms also indicate that the individuals designed to be protected need not be citizens of a State party.'
- 'Although Article 27 is expressed in negative terms, that article, nevertheless, does recognise the existence of a "right" and requires that it shall not be denied. Consequently, a State party is under an obligation to ensure that the existence and exercise of this right are protected against their denial or violation. Positive measures of protection are, therefore, required not only against the acts of the State party itself, whether through its legislative, judicial or administrative authorities, but also against the acts of other persons within the State party.'
- 'Although the rights protected under Article 27 are individual rights, they depend in turn on the ability of the minority group to maintain its culture, language or religion. Accordingly, positive measures by the State may also be necessary to protect the identity of a minority and the rights of its members to enjoy and develop their culture and language

and to practice their religion, in community with other members of the group.'
- 'Accordingly, the Committee observes that these rights must be protected as such and should not be confused with other personal rights conferred on one and all under the Covenant.'[14]

Similarly, the 1992 Declaration became the subject of an authoritative Commentary to explain its purpose: that the protection of minorities 'is intended to ensure that integration does not become unwanted assimilation or undermine the group identity of persons living on the territory of the State'. Consequently, minority protection is based on four requirements: 'protection of the existence; non-exclusion; non-discrimination; and non-assimilation of the groups concerned'. To ensure this, tolerance is not enough and requires 'a positive attitude towards cultural pluralism on the part of the State and the larger society' so that identity is promoted through 'the maintenance, reproduction and further development of their culture'.[15] In specific terms, the right of minorities under Article 2.3 of the Declaration, to participate effectively in decisions concerning themselves has to be made operational in terms of their involvement 'from the initial stages of decision-making'. This would involve their 'representation in legislative, administrative and advisory bodies'. Proportional representation 'may assist in the representation of minorities'.[16]

The UN Commission on Human Rights, through Resolution 2005/79, appointed an Independent Expert on minority issues, with the responsibility to promote the implementation of the 1992 Declaration. The expert identified 'four broad areas of concern relating to minorities around the world': (a) protection of physical integrity and prevention of genocide; (b) protection and promotion of cultural and social identity; (c) 'ensuring effective non-discrimination and equality, including ending structural or systemic discrimination'; (d) 'ensuring effective participation of minorities in public life, especially with regard to decisions that affect them'. Some observations of the independent expert in her first Report are noteworthy:

> 61. The independent expert is deeply concerned by the proliferation of counter-terrorism measures that violate the rights of minority communities and create a climate that emboldens abusive individuals. Some communities, including ethnic and religious minorities, are disproportionately affected by counter-terrorism measures, including

the use of emergency powers in relation to normal judicial processes. These communities are under more stress, their livelihoods are more threatened and the value of their integration is more brazenly questioned in the post-September 11 security environment. The independent expert stresses that counter-terrorism measures should be implemented only in full consideration of minority rights . . .

62. These three broad objectives (on which the independent expert will focus her work) are (a) increasing the focus on minority communities in the context of poverty alleviation and development; (b) to increase the understanding of minority issues in the context of ensuring stable societies; (c) to mainstream the consideration of minority issues within the work of the United Nations and important multilateral forums . . .

84. Anti-discrimination, while a key element, is not sufficient in itself to guarantee fully minority rights. Minority rights go beyond anti-discrimination to address issues of those who may seek to preserve and promote their distinct identity. The opportunity to participate fully and effectively in all aspects of society, while preserving group identity, is essential to true equality and may require positive steps on the part of governments. Minority rights are not about giving some communities more than others. Rather, they are about recognising that, owing to their minority status and distinct identity, some groups are disadvantaged and are at times targeted, and that these communities need special protection and empowerment. All States should seek to realize the goal of equality in diversity, in law and in fact.[17]

Minority Rights in India

The law and the practice in the Indian context, has a longish history. The freedom movement developed in space and time, and took cognisance of the imperatives of the plural, multi-religious and multi-linguistic nature of the Indian society. It was not unaware of the international perceptions on minority questions and the constitution-making exercise was directly and indirectly influenced by it in some measure.

The discussions in the twenties on constitutional arrangements tended to focus on arithmetical proportions in the distribution of political power in a federal set up. Minority rights, in a conceptual sense, were infrequently mentioned. The first attempt to do so in terms of principles was by Jawaharlal Nehru in his Note on Minorities published in *Young India* on 15 May 1930. It addressed the question in its totality:

> But even when the fight [for freedom] is fiercest and consumes all our energies we must remember that the true solution to our difficulties can only when we have won over and given satisfaction to our minorities . . .

The history of India and of many of the countries of Europe has demonstrated that there can be no stable equilibrium in any country so long as an attempt is made to crush a minority or to force it to conform to the ways of the majority. There is no surer method of arousing the resentment of the minority and keeping it apart from the rest of the nation than to make it feel that it has not got the freedom to stick to its own ways.

Therefore we in India . . . can also lay down as our deliberate policy that there shall be no unfair treatment of any minority. Indeed we should go further and state that it will be the business of the State to give favourable treatment to minority and backward communities . . .

In a free India the political representation can only be on national lines . . . But whatever the method of representation adopted may be, it must be such as to carry the goodwill of the minorities . . .

> It is possible however that, while agreeing to these principles, the minority may doubt the *bona fides* of the majority in giving effect to them. To that the only effective answer can be to translate these principles into action. Unfortunately, the ability to translate them into action can only come with the conquest of power in the State.[18]

These principles were amplified in the Congress Working Committee Resolution of 1 November 1937: 'In all matters affecting the minorities in India, the Congress wishes to proceed by their cooperation and through their goodwill in a common undertaking and for the realisation of a common aim which is the freedom and betterment of all the people of India.'[19] Three years later, in 1940, the Congress President Abul Kalam Azad summed up the position in two prepositions: '(i) Whatever constitution is adopted for India, there must be the fullest guarantee in it for the rights and interests of minorities'; and '(ii) The minorities should judge for themselves what safeguards are necessary for the protection of their rights and interests.

The majority should not decide this. Therefore, the decision in this respect must depend upon the consent of the minorities and not on a majority vote.'[20]

The Constitutional Proposals of the non-party Sapru Committee (1945) dwelt upon the educational rights of minorities. Its Report also suggested that 'the Constitution Act shall provide for the establishment at the Centre and in each of the provinces of an independent Minority Commission'.

When the Constituent Assembly commenced its work, the Chairman of the Sub-Committee on Minority Rights circulated a questionnaire to its members on 27 February 1947:

1. What should be the nature and scope of the safeguards for a minority in the new Constitution?

2. What should be the political safeguards of a minority: (a) in the Centre; (b) in the Provinces?

3. What should be the economic safeguards of a minority: (a) in the Centre; (b) in the Provinces?

4. What should be the religious, educational and cultural safeguards for a minority?

5. What machinery should be set up to ensure that safeguards are effective?

6. How is it proposed that the safeguards should be eliminated, in what time and under what circumstances?

In the meantime, the Advisory Committee on Fundamental Rights submitted its Interim Report that covered, inter alia, the right to religion and cultural and educational rights. The Sub-Committee on Minorities thus focused on representation in legislatures and in services and, on the basis of the replies received, submitted its report to the Advisory Committee on 27 July 1947. Its thrust was on minority (a) representation in legislatures; (b) in the Cabinet; and (c) reservation in government services. It recommended, by a majority of 26 to 3, that 'as a general principle, there should be reservation of seats for different recognised minorities in the various Legislatures' for a period of ten years. It felt there should be no statutory reservation for minorities in the Cabinet and that the matter be left to the convention set out in the Instrument of Instructions to the Governors under the Government of India Act, 1935. It recommended that there should be reservation in services for the Scheduled Castes (by a majority of 16 to 1); for Muslims (by a majority of 9 to 7); for Sikhs (by a majority of 6 to 1); for Anglo-Indians (by a majority of 12 to 3); and for Plains tribes in Assam (by a majority of 12 to 1). Pursuant to it the Advisory Committee on Minorities (with Sardar Patel as its Chairman), in its Report of 8 August 1947 recommended that 'as a general rule seats for different recognised minorities shall be reserved in the various legislatures on the basis of their population' in a system of joint electorates. On representation in services, it suggested the formula of *due share*: 'the claims of all minorities shall be kept in view in making appointments to these services consistent with the consideration of efficiency of administration'. The Report was adopted by the Constituent Assembly in August itself.[21]

The question was reopened in December 1948[22] and Sardar Patel reported to the Constituent Assembly in May 1949 that 'conditions have vastly changed since August 1947 and the Committee are satisfied that the minorities themselves feel that in their own interest, no less than in the interest of the country as a whole, the statutory reservation of seats for religious minorities, should be abolished'. An exception was made for the Scheduled Castes and reservations made for them for a period of ten years. Another 'concession' was the inclusion of certain classes of Sikhs in the category of Scheduled Castes. Moving the amendment to the August 1947 decision of the Constituent Assembly, Patel said 'nothing is better for the minorities than to trust the good sense and the sense of fairness of the majority, and place confidence in them'. Nehru called it 'an act of faith for all of us, above all for the majority community because they will have to show after this that they can behave to others in a generous, fair and just way'.[23]

A remark by a member of the Constituent Assembly shed light on the impulse for the change of approach. The birth of Pakistan, said Ajit Prasad Jain on 22 November 1949, 'smoothened our work of constitution-making'; in particular 'the question of minorities, which had been our headache and which had thwarted all our efforts for the solution of the national problems, has ceased to be a live issue'.[24]

Constitutional Protection

The Constitution proclaimed on 26 November 1949 a lawyer's document in which a vision and a programme of social engineering is balanced with social realities and imperatives of statecraft. Its vision is comprehensively reflected in the Preamble wherein the People seek for themselves Justice, social, economic and political; Liberty of thought, expression, belief, faith and worship; Equality of status and opportunity; and Fraternity. These principles were given the shape of legal rights in Part III dealing with Fundamental Rights. Specific to religious minorities are Articles 14 (equality before law), Article 15 (prohibition of discrimination on grounds of religion, race, caste, sex or place of birth), Article 16 (equality of opportunity in matters of public employment), Article 21 (protection of life and personal liberty), Article 25 (freedom of conscience and free profession, practice and propagation of religion), Article 26 (freedom to manage religious affairs—subject to public order, morality and health), Article 29 (protection of interests of minorities in regard to language, script and culture), Article 30 (right of minorities to establish and administer educational institutions) and Article 32 (right to seek constitutional remedies). The weaker sections of the minorities also stand to benefit from Article 46 (promotion of educational and economic interests of Scheduled Castes, Scheduled Tribes and other weaker sections). Article 350A enjoins 'the State and every local authority within the State to provide adequate facilities for instruction in the mother-tongue at the primary stage of education to children belonging to linguistic minority groups'. Article 371A (a)(i) stipulates that no act of Parliament in respect of the religious or social practices of the Nagas shall apply to the State of Nagaland unless the Legislative Assembly of Nagaland by a resolution so decides.

How has this framework been implemented? To what extent have the rights been realized? A formal communication (from the Government of India) to the Human Rights Committee of the United Nations in 1996 summed up the Indian position:

3.   India's general approach to the duties and obligations of States under the Covenant is that each State party must strive to recognize and give effect to the various rights and duties embodied in the Covenant in the best possible manner open to it having regard to the geographical situation of the country, its size, the population, its social structure and the political environment so that each and every section of the society, irrespective of ethnic origin, colour, sex or religious belief, may be enabled to enjoy their human rights. India also perceives it as a duty of the State to promote awareness of rights

among its people and provide adequate and effective machinery to ensure observance and enforcement of such rights. Given its extensive territorial domain, the vastness of its population and the complex social structure, in a country like India cases of violation of rights, whether attributable to the agencies of the State or to private individuals or groups, may sometimes occur despite best efforts. It is incumbent upon the State to provide appropriate machinery for the detection, investigation and punishment of such violations and to ensure that the machinery is readily accessible for the redress of the wrong. India fully recognizes, consistent with what is stated in the preamble to the Covenant, that every individual has a duty to other individuals and to the community in the matter of observance of the rights recognized therein and perceives it as its duty to take preventive measures to ensure that the community as a whole is not deprived of enjoyment of its rights at the hands of individuals or groups of individuals, particularly in the context of increasing acts of terrorism and other disruptive activities. India firmly believes that in the matter of implementation of the provisions of the Covenant, what is of paramount importance is the country's overall performance and its resolve to translate into reality the enjoyment of rights by its people, to be viewed from the Constitution and the laws as well as the effectiveness of the machinery it provides for enforcement of the rights . . .

5. The observance, promotion and protection of human rights is a complex task in a country of India's ethnic, religious, linguistic and economic diversity. India's commitment to the observance, promotion and protection of human rights, however, predates accession to the International Covenant on Civil and Political Rights and indeed permeates the political and social philosophy and foundation of independent India. In essence, India's approach to the observance, promotion and protection of human rights has been characterized by a holistic, multi-pronged effort. Primarily, this effort has revolved around the following constituent elements: (a) creation and strengthening of an institutional framework; (b) an effective network of mutually reinforcing safeguards both within and outside the institutional framework, buttressed by a policy of regular review and strengthening of safeguards; (c) a policy of transparency, responsiveness and dialogue with domestic and

international non-governmental organizations, adherence to major international human rights instruments and cooperation with the United Nations human rights machinery; (d) a holistic approach attempting to tackle poverty and underdevelopment, which in the case of many rights, e.g. the right of a child to be protected against exploitation, right to life, etc., can be a significant impediment in the effective and meaningful exercise of human rights by all citizens in equal measure; (e) integral to this approach has been a policy of affirmative action for the upliftment and promotion of socially and economically vulnerable sections of society; (f) an attempt to generate awareness through dissemination of the relevant covenants and, more significantly, through promotion of literacy and education; and (g) creation of an environment conducive to the exercise of human rights by all citizens, in all parts of India, in equal measure, including through creation of a stable and secure law and order environment.

On the specific question of Article 27 of CCPR, the Indian report stated: 'The Constitution recognizes religious and linguistic minorities and guarantees the right to practice and conserve one's religion, language and culture. Minorities can also establish their own educational institutions.'

Since the consideration of the last report, the Government of India has set up the National Commission for Minorities under the National Commission for Minorities Act, 1992 with the view to protecting the constitutional and legal rights of the minorities. The Minorities Commission evaluates the progress of the development of minorities under the Union and in the States.

Apart from looking into specific complaints regarding violation of individual rights, it also monitors the working of the safeguards provided under the Constitution and other laws and makes recommendations for the effective implementation of the same. It also conducts studies, research and analyses of the issues relating to socio-economic and educational development of minorities and makes appropriate suggestions to the central/ state governments. In performing its functions, the Commission is vested with the powers of a civil court trying a suit which enables it to summon and enforce the attendance of any person, requiring the discovery or production of any document, receiving evidence on affidavits, requisitioning copies of any public record and any other prescribed matter. To safeguard the interests of linguistic minorities a special officer is appointed to investigate all matters relating to the constitutional rights of the minorities.

The Minorities Commission is required to submit annual reports to the government. These reports are tabled before both Houses of Parliament along with a memorandum by the centre/state respectively and the reasons for non-acceptance, if any, of any of such recommendations. The special officers for linguistic minorities are also required to submit reports and such reports are to be laid before each House of Parliament.[25]

The report is candid. It outlines the legal and institutional structures, accepts the limitations of performance, and does not minimise the enormity of the task ahead. How is this to be addressed in actual practice?

The problem of the realization of rights, wrote Harold Laski, 'is best approached by discussing particular rights'. Furthermore,

> The demand for the realisation of rights only secures a hearing when the absence of those rights is felt as injustice. The demand may be postponed; it may suffer temporary defeat; but any demand that is genuinely related to the basic impulses of men must, sooner or later, be given response.[26]

This holds good for the religious minorities in India whose grievances in the past five decades have related principally to the non-realization of rights in adequate measure in four areas: physical safety (Articles 14 and 21); economic opportunity (Articles 15 and 16); practice of religion and safeguarding of places of worship (Articles 25–26); and realization of cultural and educational rights (Articles 29–30). The performance of the State in regard to these has varied; it has been noted by Gay McDougall an eminent American jurist that 'the confidence reposed by the minorities in the guardianship of fundamental rights by the Supreme Court has, *by and large*, been vindicated' [emphasis added].[27]

Despite this, the minorities suffer in varying measure from 'poverty, discrimination, and powerlessness, objective circumstances that have translated into subjective awareness of economic exploitation, status deprivation, and political repression'.[28] The principal responsibility seems to rest with the political and administrative establishment of the state and central governments and on an unstated major premise that may have caused deviations from stated policy. The story is told in data gleaned from riot enquiry commission findings, Census reports, National Sample Surveys (NSS), academic and civil society studies, pronouncements of political parties and leaders as well as the judgements and obiter dicta of the superior judiciary.[29] Nehru's 'act of faith' and Patel's 'sense of fairness of the majority' thus need to be assessed objectively.

An exercise in amnesia in regard to minorities, as well as 'collective myth-making' particularly in relation to Christians and Muslims, characterises the approach of the political class, except at the time of elections when exaggerated promises are made but rarely implemented. Even the annual reports of the National Commission for Minorities are not tabled in Parliament with any regularity nor is the condition of minorities debated.[30] A UN seminar on minority rights in South Asia concluded that the process of nation-building in states of South Asia resulted in 'the marginalization of the minorities in all countries. Invariably, exclusion became the organising principle of national polities'.[31] A corrective is thus essential.

One approach may be 'to move the debate from the general to the specific and direct effort at producing results in a specified time frame' in an effort to make the minorities 'stake holders in the new India that is emerging'.[32] Furthermore, and in view of the twist that has been given in the domestic discourse to the meaning and implications of 'secularism' as part of the assault on minorities in the name of 'cultural nationalism', there is need to rework the concept 'to fit the demands of substantive equality' that is essential to secure minority rights.[33] Such an effort could be assisted by exploring the new conceptual framework available internationally, for ideas of relevance to India.

Religious minorities constitute 18.42 per cent of the population of India and total 189.43 million. Every sixth citizen thus has a minority affiliation in India's plural social fabric. The all-round development of minorities, and their full participation in decision-making, is thus an effective component of good governance. It is a national imperative.

3

Minorities and the Modern State*

I

When I assumed my present responsibility twelve months ago, I was advised by a knowledgeable, well-intentioned friend to endeavour to abolish the distinction between the majority and the minority. His advice compelled me to think, and, in a flight of fancy, a number of questions came to mind:

- Are the terms 'majority' and 'minority' arithmetical ones depicting a ground reality or reflective of a state of mind, or both?
- Is there a magic wand to homogenize the majority and the minority into an undistinguishable whole?
- What would be the shape of the erstwhile minority or majority in the end product?
- What characteristics, attributes and values will be gained or lost in the process of this transmogrification?
- Would the subject matter of the exercise, the minority and the majority, volunteer to undergo this change? If not, what modalities of persuasion would be available, and legally and morally permissible, to accomplish it?
- Is the exercise intrinsically desirable? What would be the consequences of a failed effort?

I found the introspection unnerving. I unburdened my thoughts on another friend who asked me to look instead at patterns of nature where

---

* India-European Commission Seminar on Minorities in India, 16 March 2007.

the operative theme is diversity. In this context, social diversity emerged in a different perspective; it also reshaped the question. It then became evident that homogeneity is essentially a limiting concept, that diversity in society as in nature is a fact of life, and that the central challenge is not diversity but the management of diversity.

This diversity is a reality in the world of the 21st century. Its quantum varies from society to society, state to state.

We live in a world of nation-states shaped by historical forces of the recent or distant past. These states, and their individual societies, are themselves being transformed by newer impulses. Judgements about their social dynamics therefore need to reflect this evolving situation.

II

Today's seminar is timely and reflective of changing perceptions. For much too long, the classical doctrine of sovereignty and its concept of domestic jurisdiction prescribed the limits of what could be discussed. These conceptual boundaries were guarded with the same zeal as national frontiers. Interestingly enough, they were first breached in relation to minorities and took a definitive shape in the treaties that were signed at the end of World War I. Guarantees for minority rights were incorporated in international law through a series of landmark judgements of the Permanent Court of International Justice. These have been diligently built upon in national and international jurisprudence, in international covenants and in the charters of right incorporated in the constitutions of individual States.

The constitutional and legal framework is one aspect of the matter; social behaviour and State practice is another. The gap between the two exists in most situations. Awareness of this gap is an essential first step in correcting it. How is this done in a different situation? How have different states gone about it? An exchange of ideas and information is thus a useful input in comprehending different dimensions of the question of minorities.

Historically speaking, and in regard to minorities, States have chosen from a menu of options: elimination, assimilation, tolerance, protection, promotion. The approach of individual States to each of these sheds much light on their philosophy of governance.

The European Union and India share many characteristics and perceptions:

- Both are characterized by ethnic, linguistic and religious diversity.
- Both are plural societies and democratic polities.
- Both have secular State structures and are devoid of state religions.
- Both have charters of rights written into the basic constitutional documents.
- Both have religious and linguistic minorities, give specific guarantees for minority rights and have institutional mechanisms for ensuring them.
- Both reject the notion that eliminating them can solve the problem of minorities.

With regard to assimilation and tolerance, there has been a good deal of debate. Tolerance is a noble virtue but insufficient because, while it permits a practice or a profession and prohibits discrimination against it, it does not necessarily endorse it and thus places it in the category of the 'other', with all its attendant implications. The argument for assimilation, on the other hand, is premised on the unstated assumption that the identity (linguistic, cultural and religious) of the minority group is eventually to be absorbed in the larger whole, or dominant culture, through a process of consistent integration since the greater good of the larger number lies in such integration. Democratic theory, and the argument of majority rule in decision-making, is used to good purpose to drive home the point.

Both these approaches overlook the minority perspective. Its theoretical foundations, therefore, need to be enunciated carefully. This was done many decades earlier in two judgments of the Permanent Court of International Justice. The first of these defined a community not in terms of numbers but in terms of shared religious, racial and linguistic traditions, traditions that the group wishes to preserve and perpetuate through ritual, education and socialization of the young. The existence of such a community, ruled the Court, is not dependent upon recognition by law.

In a second case, the Court said the objective of minority rights was twofold: to secure for minority groups the possibility of living peaceably alongside the rest of the population and cooperating amicably with them while at the same time preserving the characteristics which distinguish them from the majority and satisfying the ensuing special needs. It held that these two characteristics are indeed closely interlocked, for there would be no true equality between a majority and a minority if the latter were deprived of its own institutions and were consequently compelled to renounce that which constitutes the very essence of its being a minority. The Court therefore held that:

> Equality in law precludes discrimination of any kind, whereas equality in fact may involve the necessity of different treatments in order to attain a result which establishes an equilibrium between different situations. It is easy to imagine cases in which, equality of treatment of the majority and the minority, whose situations and requirements are different, would result in inequality.

This approach underlies the effort by a great many modern States to develop a framework of minority rights on the twin concepts of 'protection' and 'promotion'. India and the European Union would fall in this category.

III

The Indian approach to minority rights was exhaustively debated during the Freedom Movement and in the Constituent Assembly. All segments of the Indian population have been part of the Indian landscape for millennia; none are in the category of recent migrants. The makers of the Constitution accepted as a living reality the diversity of India in religious and linguistic terms. They also accepted the plural ethos. The question of identity, and of multiple identities, did not pose a problem. Protection and promotion are thus writ large in different sections of the Constitution.

Consequently, and in terms of the legal framework, religious and linguistic minorities avail of all the rights of citizens and, in addition, benefit from the guarantees given for the protection and promotion of cultural and educational rights. The framework is comprehensive and was motivated by considerations of cultural pluralism and by the need to protect minority groups and to take affirmative action for the deprived sections of society.

A word about the dimensions of the minority question in India is relevant. Religious minorities constitute 18.4 per cent of the population of India—189 million in absolute numbers. Thus, every sixth Indian has a minority affiliation. As for the linguistic diversity, a look at an Indian currency note is sufficient to comprehend its scale since the value is written in seventeen different scripts!

A number of questions surface when we move from legal structure to actual practice:

- How has the system worked in practice over six decades?
- What have been the impediments to the realization of minority rights?
- What response has emanated from the state when defaults are identified?
- How far has the society helped or hampered the realization of these rights?

An assessment on each of these counts is easier if the questions are deconstructed and subjected to a fourfold analysis to cover matters of (a) identity; (b) security; (c) share in fruits of national development and (d) role in decision-making.

The identity question has been comprehensively treated in the section on fundamental rights of the Constitution and in the judgments of superior courts. The right to freedom of religion, as also of the free profession, practice and propagation of religion, is a fundamental right and has been repeatedly upheld by the highest court. Also guaranteed is the freedom to manage religious affairs. Furthermore, Articles 29 and 30 adequately protect cultural and educational rights of religious and linguistic minorities. Comprehensive case law has given a practical shape to the realization of these rights.

There have been attempts in some quarters to circumscribe or abridge one aspect of the freedom of religion—the right to propagate. Some state legislatures have taken steps to do so through procedural constraints. The debate on this question, reflective of a wider debate on what constitutes Indianness, is yet to be settled.

The security question has many dimensions and remains at the core of the political discourse of the minorities and sections of civil society. One aspect relates to the responsibility of the State to ensure security for all citizens; another aspect concerns the civil society and its responsibility to promote tolerance and social harmony at all levels and in a practical manner. There have been failures on both counts; a glaring instance is what happened in the state of Gujarat in 2002. Conscious of the shortfalls, the draft of a new Bill on communal violence is before the Parliament.

Given the complexity of the Indian scene, it is realistic to expect that the security of minorities would remain on the agenda for some time. The role of the citizen, and of the civil society, would be to demand greater commitment and more consistent performance by the State at the central and state levels.

The equity question has been on the agenda of the State since inception. The operative principles are equality of status and opportunity and social, economic and political justice. Equality before the law, equality of opportunity in matters of public employment and prohibition of discrimination on grounds of religion, race, caste, sex or place of birth are inscribed as fundamental rights and have been built upon by the legal system.

Despite these safeguards, all segments of population have not benefited equally. These include the weaker classes, and many amongst the minorities. Glaring examples of these are highlighted in the recently published Sachar Report, 2006, on India's biggest minority, the Muslims. The official response is a commitment to address and rectify. Civil society's task is to ensure that this is also done so as to assess its speed and extent.

The question of role in decision-making, as citizens and as affected citizens, is viewed in the context of the functioning of a democratic polity. It throws up elected representatives at local, regional and federal levels. Democratic theory assumes that these representatives reflect the wishes and requirements of their constituents. Do they also reflect group wishes or requirements and, if so, how adequately? It has been argued, with some justice, that absence of minority representation at critical levels of the decision-making apparatus results in group interest being neglected. Recent studies of the Indian scene tend to lend credence to this point of view.

IV

Where then do we stand? Is there is a sense of complacency and smugness? The critical Indian, from the viewpoint of the values of the Freedom Movement and of the Constitution, considers the glass half full:

- The plural, democratic and secular framework has, over six decades, catered adequately to requirements of identity.
- Its performance on the security front would have been better if extraneous considerations had not distorted the enforcement of existing laws relating to public safety.
- The record is unsatisfactory in terms of equity and participation in decision-making.

The net result is twofold: (a) fruits of development are not reaching segments of the citizen body and (b) these segments are not sufficiently empowered to reach out and secure these benefits. Given the size of the minorities, this cannot but have an adverse impact on the overall progress of the country. The sectional problem thus becomes a national one.

The Indian scene has not been static. The doctrine of rights has evolved in recent years. A conscious effort is underway to give content to concepts of equality and justice. The area of focus has expanded beyond identity questions to encapsulate social and economic rights. The awareness of group rights, however, remains somewhat hazy and so does the commitment to honour them in their totality. To the proponents of minority rights, therefore, the challenge for the immediate future is

- to raise awareness of minority rights as an inseparable part of human rights, and to seek a commitment to honour them in the same measure.
- to develop strategies of affirmative action to cater to questions of equity and participation and seek to draw upon best practices available elsewhere.

Another dimension of the changing situation is the institutional structure that has been put in place for safeguarding rights. This includes the National Commissions for Human Rights, Minorities, Women, Scheduled Castes, Backward Classes, and Scheduled Tribes. All have steadily developed their investigative and corrective mechanisms. Each, in its own way, confronts institutional and practical obstacles emanating from official apathy and public prejudice. All record instances of success, and of failure. None can say that the task is done.

Having said enough about the Indian scene, let me turn very briefly to two themes of this seminar on which a good deal of discussions would take place in the panels. I refer to questions of 'integration' and 'mainstream'. The debate here, as in the European Union, generates more heat than substance. This Indian's approach is to tread carefully and diffidently. Integration is a function of inclusion; the best recipe for it is integration in prosperity. By the same logic, exclusion of any kind hampers the process.

As for the mainstream, the conceptual and practical challenge is to define it in the context of pluralism and reconcile it to the imperatives of identity. It is an area of receding frontiers. An eclectic approach is preferable to a philosophical one since the former has the virtue of greater flexibility.

4

Majority and Minorities in Secular India

Sensitivity and Responsibility*

This Annual Conference, organized by the National Commission for Minorities, has now become a useful platform for exchange of views between the National Commission, the State Minorities Commissions, and other stakeholders from all over the country. It gives the participants an opportunity to deliberate on the modalities of redressing grievances and of corrective action by central and state government agencies.

This Conference is timely and so is its theme. There is an enhanced awareness, both of the problems of minorities and of the imperative need to address them through affirmative action by the state. Alongside, regrettably, communal tensions appear to have re-emerged in different parts of the country. The conclusion is inescapable that our communal fabric is under pressure.

According to the 2001 census, recognized religious minorities comprise 18.4 per cent of our population, which translates into approximately 185 million people. This number today could be around 220 million. If we include others who are claiming inclusion in this category, it could be said in general terms that every fifth Indian citizen belongs to a religious minority. Their progress and well-being is a prerequisite for us to realize our destiny of becoming a modern, prosperous and developed state.

Given the theme of this conference, allow me to raise a few conceptual questions that come to mind:

- Are the terms 'majority' and 'minority' arithmetical ones depicting a ground reality, or reflective of a state of mind or both?

---

* Annual Conference of State Minority Commissions, New Delhi, 12 March 2013.

29

- Is there a magic wand to homogenize the two into an undistinguishable whole? What would be the shape of the erstwhile minority or majority in the end product?
- What characteristics, attributes, values will be gained or lost in the process of this transmogrification?
- Would the subject matter of the exercise, the minority and the majority, volunteer to undergo this change? If not, what modalities of persuasion would be available, and legally and morally permissible, to accomplish it?
- Is the exercise intrinsically desirable? What would be the consequences of a failed effort?

I confess the questions leave me confounded. A better approach would be to look at patterns of nature where the operative theme is diversity. Thus viewed, social diversity emerges in a different perspective; it also reshapes the question. It then became evident that homogeneity is essentially a limiting concept, that diversity in society as in nature is a reality, and that the central challenge is not diversity but the management of diversity.

This diversity is recognized in the world of the 21st century. Its quantum varies from society to society, state to state, system to system. In our own country, it has been accepted down the ages as a fact of life and is reflected in the plural nature of our society. Independent India's Constitution endowed it with a secular polity and a democratic state structure.

It is the Constitution that gives rights to all citizens and specific rights to minorities. The question of sensitivity and responsibility therefore is equally applicable to all citizens, is to be judged in terms of the provisions of the Constitution only and cannot be assigned or sought selectively.

The Constitution is premised on the ideals of justice, liberty, equality and fraternity and promises them to all citizens. The basic principle is equality before the law and equal protection of the laws.

Away from generalizations in formal and legal terms, an assessment of the ground reality pertaining to minorities needs to cover four areas: (a) identity, (b) security, (c) share in the fruits of development and (d) role in decision-making.

Given the complexity of our societal landscape and its variables, the articulation of grievances by different religious minorities has varied in content and intensity. While some are sporadic, others seem to be endemic.

The identity question has been settled through the enforcement of fundamental rights inscribed in the Constitution. Attempts however are made from time to time to circumscribe the ambit of Article 25 relating to freedom of religion, including the right to propagate.

The security question remains at the core of the political discourse of the minorities and sections of civil society. The requirement of social peace and fraternity demands greater commitment and more persistent performance by governments at central and state levels.

The equity question is a perennial one. The operative principles are equality of status and opportunity and social, economic and political justice. We know that equality before the law, equality of opportunity in matters of public employment and prohibition of discrimination on grounds of religion, race, caste sex or place of birth are fundamental rights but despite these safeguards, many amongst the minorities have not benefited equally or in adequate measure. This is evident from the recently-finalized 12th Five Year Plan's observation in relation to the country's largest minority that 'an important concern vis-à-vis the Muslim Community is the perception of discrimination and alienation'. It goes on to say that:

> While India has experienced accelerated growth and development in recent years, not all religious and social groups have shared equally the benefits of the growth process. Among these, the Muslims, the largest minority in the country, are lagging behind on all human development indices.

The dimensions of the problem were quantified in the Sachar Committee Report of November 2006 and in the Ranganath Mishra Report of May 2007. Pursuant to these, a number of schemes for scholarships and for development of minority-concentration districts were included in the 11th Plan. Their implementation was uneven; the scholarships benefited a good number but reports about the identified districts are less emphatic. Access to credit remains a recurring grievance.

Civil society groups have drawn attention to the need for awareness and community engagement at the local level. As one report put it, 'there is complete disconnect between minority welfare infrastructure and Muslim civil society, and poor effort by government to create awareness of schemes and reach out to beneficiary groups/Muslim civil society. Absence of development-oriented leadership and poor Muslim representation in decision-making bodies at state, district and local levels makes the situation worse. As a result, there is little focused demand making by Muslim groups for better working of schemes and programmes.'

Some correctives are now underway. The role of the state and local administrations remains critical. The 12th Plan schemes, more focused and benefiting from the experience gained, should reach the target areas in greater depth and intensity.

The question of role in decision-making, as citizens and as affected citizens, is to be viewed in the context of the functioning of a democratic polity. It throws up elected representatives at local, regional and national levels. Democratic theory assumes that these representatives reflect the wishes and requirements of their constituents. Do they also reflect group wishes or requirements and, if so, how adequately?

It has been argued, with some justice, that absence of minority representation at critical levels of the decision-making apparatus results in group interest being neglected. Some studies, including the Report of the Expert Group on Diversity Index, tend to lend credence to this point of view.

And so, we come back to the question of sensitivity and responsibility. Both are critical to the discharge of civic responsibilities; both must be inclusive rather than exclusive; both must bear in mind that national progress would be retarded and slanted if every fifth citizen is left out of it.

I conclude with the hope that the question posed for this conference would be deliberated upon in all its manifestations and that the collective wisdom of this gathering would contribute to the national effort of seeking to benefit all segments of our society. We are, after all, the world's largest model of how diversity is accommodated in a functioning democracy.

5

International Human Rights Day*

I

International Human Rights Day is one of those dates in the calendar that is remembered by all who care about humanity and wish to propel it away from brutality and towards humaneness in greater measure.

For this reason, I am happy to be here today to join others to celebrate the occasion.

The concept of human rights is of ancient vintage. Until quite recently, however, it was selective rather than universal. Here lies the uniqueness of the date, December 10, that we have gathered to commemorate and celebrate.

It was on this day in 1948 that the General Assembly of the United Nations adopted the Universal Declaration of Human Rights which recognized 'the inherent dignity and the equal and inalienable rights of all members of the human family' and declared it to be 'the foundation of freedom, justice and peace in the world' for 'all human beings' and 'a common standard of achievement for all peoples and nations'.

Subsequent documents adopted by the international community amplified the principles enunciated in the Universal Declaration and cover basic civil, political, economic, social and cultural rights that all human beings should enjoy and that all societies should respect and protect.

Three characteristics of these rights need to be highlighted: (a) they are 'natural' and accrue to us by the virtue of being humans; (b) they are 'universal' and pertain to all human beings irrespective of nationality, place of residence, sex, national or ethnic origin, colour, religion, language or any

---

* 10 December 2015, New Delhi.

other status; and (c) they are inalienable and cannot be taken away except in specific situations and according to due process.[1]

Pursuant to these basic principles enshrined in the Universal Declaration, a number of covenants and declarations have been subscribed to by most, though not all, members of the international community. Their stated objective is to reinforce the commitment of Member States as 'being an intrinsic element of their obligations of sovereignty.' This principle emanates from the very nature of humans as social beings living in societies in which justice becomes the first virtue endowed with inviolability.

The most recent manifestation of this is the United Nations Human Rights Council (UNHRC) set up by the UN General Assembly in March 2006 to strengthen the promotion and protection of human rights around the globe and for addressing situations of human rights violation and making recommendations on them. Its operational mechanisms include the Universal Periodic Review to assess the human rights situations in all Member States and special procedures to examine, advise and publicly report on thematic issues or human rights situations in specific countries.

Thus, the responsibility of national governments to uphold and implement international human rights standards is not in doubt. And yet, as T.S. Eliot wrote,

> Between the idea
> And the reality
> Between the motion
> And the act
> Falls the Shadow

The effort to bridge this gap continues. The question has been considered in the International Law Commission's work on the Responsibility of States for Internationally Wrongful Acts and in conjunction with implementation of the International Covenant on Economic, Social and Cultural Rights.

Over the past two decades a consensus has emerged that with respect to human rights, States have a threefold responsibility: to respect, to protect and to fulfil their obligations. This has been expounded upon by the Office of the UN High Commissioner for Human Rights:

- The obligation to respect means that States must refrain from interfering with or curtailing the enjoyment of human rights.

- The obligation to protect requires States to protect individuals and groups against human rights abuses.
- The obligation to fulfil means that States must take positive action to facilitate the enjoyment of basic human rights.

The extent to which these principles and the international mechanisms based on them can and do go, as also the question of their universal applicability without exceptions, is the subject of vigorous debate and much controversy on international forums premised as these are on the Westphalian principle and where the effort, genuine as well as motivated, to reconcile law and morality is unlikely to be fruitful in the foreseeable future.

While persisting in the effort to attain the desirable, it is somewhat easier to focus on the doable. I refer here to the human rights commitment and performance of our own country.

II

The framers of our own Constitution were aware of the Universal Declaration of Human Rights. The fundamental rights enshrined in the Constitution cover most of the rights that had been articulated in the Universal Declaration. Article 14 establishes the Right to Equality creating the basis of non-discrimination, a cornerstone for the application of human rights.

Over the years our courts have dwelt on the notion of fundamental rights in the Constitution and have expanded their scope and nature. It can thus be argued with justice that many of the rights articulated in the Universal Declaration have now been subsumed under the expanded meaning of the fundamental rights. Article 21 in particular has seen intervention by courts to expand the meaning and scope as something more dynamic than the meaning attached to life and liberty. Right to life now includes right to human dignity and quality of life.

Similarly, the Directive Principles of State Policy in Part IV of the Constitution go beyond the International Covenant on Economic, Social and Cultural Rights.

A mechanism, in the shape of the Protection of the of Human Rights Act, 1993, and the constitution of the NHRC, the State Human Rights Commissions and Human Rights courts, has been put in place for the enforcement of these rights. Certain other legislations which may be referred to in the context of human rights, including Protection of Civil Rights Act, 1955, and Rules, 1977, as well as legislation providing for care and protection of especially vulnerable groups.

Thus, the institutional structure for the attainment and enforcement of human rights is firmly in place. Our quest, today therefore, needs to focus on:

- The extent to which the desired objectives have been attained,
- The practical impediments to their achievement,
- The efficacy of the governmental efforts to overcome them and
- Civil society's role and its assessment of the human rights situation in the country.

A perusal of reports from Government and non-Government Organizations, both domestic and international, provides an overview of the human rights monitoring and safeguard mechanisms in India.

The Annual report of our NHRC for 2011–2012 (the most recent one available) indicates the typology of human rights violations: (1) Custodial deaths; (2) Police high-handedness, firing, encounters; (3) Illegal detention, torture or firing by military, paramilitary forces and police; (4) Violation of rights of Scheduled Castes and Scheduled Tribes; (5) Atrocities on women and children; (6) Bonded labour and child labour; (7) Right to Health; (8) Cases of suo moto cognizance taken by NHRC.

The Annual Report of the Ministry of Home Affairs for 2014–2015 states that in this period the NHRC's investigation division dealt with 5439 cases of custodial death, including 3707 cases of death in judicial custody, 326 cases of deaths in police custody and another 1406 fact-finding cases. The number of cases of custodial death in 2011–2012 stood at 1302.

The Universal Periodic Review on India for 2012–2016 by the Special Rapporteur in the Office of the UN High Commissioner for Human Rights carries a number of observations that need to be noted:

- A significant role has been played by the Supreme Court in interpreting the Constitution with a view to achieving justifiability of economic, social and cultural rights. The functioning of the judiciary, however, was hampered by a backlog and significant delay in administering cases of human rights violations due to lack of capacity, manpower and resources.

- While welcoming the continuing work of the NHRC, and the establishment of National Commission for the Protection of Child Rights, it expressed concern that the investigation of human right abuses continues to be conducted by the police who, in many cases, were also the alleged perpetrators. It urged the government to consider enacting special legislation to protect human rights defenders.

- Expression of deep concern that 'despite the Constitutional guarantee of non-discrimination, as well as the criminal law provisions punishing acts of discrimination, widespread and, often, socially accepted discrimination, harassment and violence persisted against members of disadvantaged and marginalized groups, including women, Scheduled Castes and Tribes, urban poor, informal sector workers and religious minorities.'

- Expression of concern that the Prevention of Torture Bill, 2010, introduced in the Indian Parliament following India's ratification of Convention against Torture, was much diluted. Even this was eventually not approved by the Parliament.

- India was one of the few countries retaining the death penalty and in 2010 had voted against UN General Assembly resolution 65/206 on the 'Moratorium on the use of the death penalty'.[2]

The Global Citizenship country report card,[3] which covers human rights indicators, as well as transparency and good governance, in its latest report on India, calls India a 'climber' ranked 5th among its list of twelve pilot countries, behind Germany, Brazil, Peru and United States. It noted that India had ratified five of the six international Human Rights Convention and also ranked India high on account of the performance in right to self-determination indicator due to large-scale participation and conduct of a free and fair elections in 2014. It, however, ranked India poorly on the non-discrimination index, particularly due to the continuing criminalization of homosexuality.*

The Human Rights Watch World Report for 2015 criticized India for continuing with state censorship and imposition of certain restrictions

---

* Since decriminalized.

on non-governmental organizations (NGOs).[4] It noted that caste-based discrimination, neglect of marginalized communities and violence against women continued. It expressed concern on what it called 'the lack of accountability of security forces' and recommended urgent police reforms to increase capacity and accountability. It also expressed concern at the continuation of the Armed Forces (Special Powers) Act, 1958, in several parts of India.

It applauded the January 2014 judgment of the Supreme Court commuting the death sentence of fifteen prisoners and establishing guidelines to safeguard the rights of prisoners on death row but expressed concern at India's continuing use of the death penalty. The report commended India for continuing to accept refugees from Tibet, Myanmar and Afghanistan while noting that India had not ratified the UN Refugee conventions.

The Amnesty International Report 2014/15[5] noted that despite 'progressive legal reforms in court rulings the state authorities had failed to prevent crimes against Indian citizens, including children, women, Dalits and Adivasis'. It expressed concern over the human right abuses by armed insurgent/terrorist groups, which killed and injured civilians and destroyed property. It regretted India's failure to pass a strong anti-torture bill, noting that torture and other ill treatment continued to be used in state detention.

III

Many of the shortcomings mentioned in these reports have also figured in periodic reports of some national NGOs, in the media and in Parliament. It is evident, therefore, that there is at times a gap between what the official agencies project and what is perceived to be the situation on the ground. One reason for this is wider public awareness of human rights norms; another is the extent and speed with which defaults or alleged violations are brought to public notice.

Many new issues have become part of the human rights agenda and will remain crucial in the coming decades. The conflict over natural resources, the issue of gender equality and the increasing incidence of gender violence and of caste, communal, ethnic and sub-national conflicts among communities and environmental implications of some developmental projects are some examples. Human rights abuses by non-state actors, such as violent insurgent groups, terrorists and extremists, both from the left and right, has also emerged as a major challenge.

Faced with these candid assessments, how should we, as a society, react to them? One possible reaction is to dismiss them as devoid of veracity or denounce them as the work of hostile elements, even consider their work as 'detrimental to national interest'. The other is to respond to them in a mature fashion.

In a vibrant and robust democracy like ours, there is no shame in acknowledging the faults and the lacunae that exist in the policies and institutions pertaining to human rights. Our point of reference should be the Constitution of India and the principles, rights and duties enunciated therein. On this basis, we are duty bound, legally and morally, to address these challenges through firm and unbiased corrective actions by the state, civil society and other stakeholders. It is, and should be viewed as, a societal duty.

It is here that education in human rights culture becomes critically important in educational institutions. Citizens and civil society institutions must therefore take a lead in helping us meet the moral challenges of our times.

We as a nation have to awaken our collective conscience. We also need to strive for global standards.

SECTION TWO

INDIAN POLITY, IDENTITY, DIVERSITY AND CITIZENSHIP

6

Nehru's Vision for India as a Major Power*

I

'We are potentially a great nation and a big power.'
— Nehru, speech in Constituent Assembly, 8 March 1948

'Our position in the world ultimately depends on the unity and strength of the country, on how far we proceed in the solution of our economic and other problems and how much we can raise the depressed masses of India.'
— Nehru, 15 August 1949

'Whatever the activity—and this applies specially to the field of foreign policy—India must function according to the ways and methods of her own thinking, if she has to have any weight'.
— Nehru, 17 March 1950

A recent biographer of Nehru has concluded that he 'was central to the making of modern India, with its strength and weaknesses, its successes and failure'. Another has sought 'to rescue Nehru from the mythologies' created around him and his work.[1] Together they highlight the fact that four decades after his death, Jawaharlal Nehru and his work continue to be relevant to modern India. This in itself is a tribute to his centrality.

This paper is on one aspect of the foreign policy approach of Nehru. How did he view the role of India on the global stage? It is more about

---

* *Contemporary India*, Vol. 3, No. 4 (October–December 2004, pp. 47–58)

the vision than about the actualization of that vision. This is in no way intended to ignore, or minimise, the inherent linkage between the two.

II

Much of the literature on international relations theory uses the terms 'major power' and 'great power' interchangeably. Both relate to the concept of power. The genesis of power in society, and its legitimacy, has been the principal concern of political philosophy down the ages. A community of such societies in the shape of *States*, each enjoying authority and autonomy in its decision-making and endeavouring to attain its primary and secondary goals, necessitates a concept of 'order' so that disharmony is eliminated or at least regulated. The modern State system, emerging in Europe in the 17th century, developed the concept of order in an international society consisting of members having greater or lesser potential to contribute to its functioning. The *hierarchy* that came into existence produced the notion of 'great power', defined by Leopold Von Ranke as an 'ability to maintain itself against all others even when they are united' and, by implication, recognized as such by other members of the international community. This recognition also conferred on 'great powers' certain special responsibilities such as: (i) preserving the general balance of power; (ii) seeking to avoid or control crises in their relations with one another and (iii) seeking to limit or contain wars among themselves. The privileges flowing out of this statute, says Hedley Bull, are: (a) unilateral utilization of their local preponderance; (b) agreeing to respect one another's spheres of influence and (c) joint action, as is implied by the idea of a great power concert or condominium.[2]

In our own times, a framework for the role of great powers was spelt out by US President Franklin Roosevelt in 1942 while considering, along with his allies, the shape of the post-war world. Harry Hopkins recorded it for posterity: 'Roosevelt had spoken to Molotov of a system allowing only the great powers, Great Britain, the United States, the Soviet Union and possibly China, to have arms. These "policemen" would work together to preserve peace.' The idea was 'to preserve peace through a coalition of victors upholding shared values'.[3] This arrangement finds reflection in Articles 23(1), 27(1) and 108 of the Charter of the United Nations relating to the responsibilities of the permanent members of the Security Council.

The meaning of the concept of 'major or great power' has changed over time. In contemporary literature Samuel Kim has produced a comprehensive definition of great power status in the context of China:

A state that easily ranks among the top five in the primary global structures—economic, military, knowledge and normative—and that enjoys relatively low sensitivity, vulnerability and security interdependence because of massive resources and skill differentials and relative economic self-sufficiency. A great power is a strong state with the ability to mobilize the country's human and material resources in the service of its worldview and policy objectives.[4]

Baldev Raj Nayar and T.V. Paul have suggested that comprehensive national power leading to the claim of great power status should have ten ingredients consisting of four hard and six soft ones, with the first consisting of military, economic, technology/knowledge and demographic factors; and the second of norms, a leadership role in international institutions, culture, state capacity, strategic/diplomacy and national leadership.[5] In each of these, the transition has to be made from claimed status to its acceptance by the international community.

III

Independent India arrived on the global scene in 1947. It had, without being free of the British bondage, attended the San Francisco Conference in 1945 and was an original member of the United Nations. Jawaharlal Nehru, as the principal spokesman of the Congress in the decades before Independence, and a Member of External Affairs in the Interim Government, was fully aware of this background in local and global terms.

Nehru's vision of India as a player on the world stage can be assessed, firstly, in terms of declaratory principles and secondly, in the conduct of policy in relation to specific situations and crises as they surfaced in the 1947–1963 period. The latter would assist in the identification of the distinctly Indian traits of policy and practice that Nehru wished to impart to the conduct of foreign affairs.

The enunciation of his basic approach is to be found in a number of statements over a period of time. Before taking office as the head of the Interim Government, Nehru emphasized that need for policy to be compatible with national interest.[6] In his first broadcast to the nation on 7 September 1946, Nehru spelt out the objectives of foreign policy:

> We hope to develop close and direct contacts with other nations and to cooperate with them in the furtherance of world peace and freedom . . . We believe that peace and freedom are indivisible and the denial of freedom anywhere must endanger freedom elsewhere and lead to conflict and war. We are particularly interested in the emancipation of colonial and dependent countries and peoples, and in the recognition in theory and practice of equal opportunities for all races . . .
>
> We propose, as far as possible to keep away from the power politics of groups, aligned against one another, which have led in the past to world wars and which may again lead to disaster on an even vaster scale.

The focus, therefore, was on the maintenance of freedom of policy, the promotion of international peace, the emancipation of colonial and dependent territories and the promotion of racial equality. Later that month he wrote to the Soviet Foreign Minister Molotov expressing his desire for friendly relations with the Soviet Union, sought assistance in food grains and explored the possibility of Soviet military experts visiting India.[7] He returned to the theme of an independent foreign policy vision in his inaugural address to the *Asian Relations Conference* in New Delhi in February 1947:

> We propose to stand on our feet and to cooperate with all others who are prepared to cooperate with us. We do not intend to be the plaything of others.

Two years later he spelt out the concept with greater clarity:

> What does independence consist of? It consists of fundamentally and basically foreign relations. That is the test of independence. All else is local autonomy. Once foreign relations go out of your hands into the charge of somebody else, to that extent and in that measure you are not independent.[8]

The crafting of foreign policy was not undertaken in a vacuum. Nehru was the leader of the country and of the government and addressed a comprehensive agenda. A remark in 1954 summed up the work undertaken: 'Almost all our activities are aimed at laying the foundations of a new India.' The first of these activities related to the consolidation of national unity in a territorial sense and took the shape of the integration of princely states. This work, undertaken with tremendous energy by Sardar Patel, produced quick and satisfactory results. Its success led to irritation in Britain, and some alarm in the United States:

> The vigour and the methods which have characterized India's execution of its policy of consolidating the princely states, and its inflexible attitude with regard to Kashmir, may indicate national traits which in time if not controlled, could make India Japan's successor in Asiatic imperialism.[9]

Beyond political unity, Nehru also spoke, as a first essential, of the 'unity of the mind and the heart, which precludes the narrow urges that make for disunity and which breaks down the barriers raised in the name of religion or those between State and State or, for that matter, any other barrier'.[10]

The occasion of his visit to the United States in 1949 provided opportunities to elucidate the basic themes:

> The objectives of our foreign policy are the preservation of world peace and enlargement of human freedom . . . We are neither blind to reality nor do we propose to acquiesce in any challenge to man's freedom from whatever quarter it may come. Where freedom is menaced or justice threatened or where aggression takes place, we cannot be and shall not be neutral. What we plead for and endeavour to practice in our own imperfect way is a binding faith in peace and an unfailing endeavour of thought and action to ensure it.[11]

> The great leader of my country, Mahatma Gandhi, under whose inspiration and sheltering care I grew up, always laid stress on moral values and warned us never to subordinate means to ends . . . India came into the family of nations with no prejudices and enmities, ready to welcome and be welcomed. Inevitably she had to consider her foreign policy in terms of enlightened self-interest but at the same time she brought to it a touch of her idealism. Thus she had tried to combine idealism with national interest.[12]

These pronouncements had limited impact on official US perceptions and both sides were disappointed with the results of the visit.[13]

Another subject of importance on the national agenda was the framing of the Constitution, completed in November 1949. Article 51 (in Part IV, on Directive Principles of State Policy) relates to foreign policy and enjoins upon the state to promote: (a) international peace and security; (b) maintain just and honourable relations between nations; (c) foster respect for international law and treaty obligations in the dealings of organized peoples with one another and (d) encourage settlement of international disputes by arbitration.

Yet another imperative was all-round development, and the need for security assistance and technology for it from available external sources. Nehru at one stage toyed with an idea: 'Why not align with the United States *somewhat* [italics in original]and build up our economic and military power?'[14] The idea was abandoned. India too, he felt, had a relevance for the US:

> India has much to give, not in gold or silver or even in exportable commodities, but by virtue of her position. It is well recognised today all over the world that the future of Asia will be powerfully determined by the future of India. India becomes more and more the pivot of Asia.[15]

The thrust of Nehru's effort was on capacity building—in industry, in science and technology, and above all in human resources. The emphasis on self-sufficiency in the capacity to defend India was part of the effort to develop a capability for freedom of action. This idea was articulated as early as 25 August 1945:

> So long as the world is constituted as it is, every country will have to devise and use the latest scientific methods for its protection. I have no doubt India will develop it scientific researches and hope Indian scientists will use the atomic force for constructive purposes. But if India is threatened, it will inevitably try to defend itself by all means at its disposal. I hope India in common with other countries will prevent it being used.[16]

The possibility of the use of nuclear power for the defence of India was reiterated in the Constituent Assembly in 1948:

> Indeed, I think we must develop it [atomic energy] for peaceful purposes. Of course, if we are compelled as a nation to use it for other purposes,

possibly no pious sentiments of any of us will stop the nation from using it that way.[17]

The implementation of these ideals and principles, and the satisfaction of essential national requirements, required both a methodology and an instrumentality. It is relevant to note that given the negotiated transfer of power, Nehru worked within the inherited framework. He accepted that to some extent policy would be 'a continuation of British foreign policy, to some extent a reaction against it'.[18] He had greater freedom of action with regard to the instrumentality and consequently developed a three-pronged approach: non-alignment, the temper of peace and friendship with all nations. Each had a rationale, a pragmatic one, but in a world slipping into the Cold War mores of power blocs, this amounted to heresy and was even characterized as 'immoral' in some quarters.

This pragmatism in approach was articulated in a speech in Parliament:

Finally, a foreign policy is not just a declaration of fine principles; nor is it a directive to tell the world how to behave. It is conditioned and controlled by a country's own strength. If the policy does not take the capacity of the country into account, it cannot be followed up. If a country talks bigger than it is, it brings little credit to itself . . . It is obvious that India neither has military nor financial strength. Furthermore, we have no desire to—and we cannot—impose our will on others. We are, however, anxious to prevent catastrophes and, where possible, to help in the general progress of humanity . . . Instead of calling it a third force or a third bloc, it can be called a third area, an area which—let us put it negatively, does not want war, works for peace in a positive way and believes in cooperation.[19]

This approach of non-alignment in a world that was aligned into power blocs of great powers 'was not so much a code of conduct as a technique to be tested by results'. Equidistance from power blocs was perceived to be of benefit to India. It also meant non-alignment with other countries so as to retain freedom of decision and action. Nehru was averse to considering the non-aligned countries as a bloc, except in terms of the general principles of a common approach. There was also a distaste for the crude manner in which 'the Great Powers behaved to each other', and an assumption that they would show some understanding of India's position.[20]

IV

Foreign policy is in effect a set of policies, each directed to a situation or a country, mostly within the wider framework of an overall approach and aimed at securing the national interest as perceived by the government of the day. How then, in Nehru's case, were these perceptions made applicable? The challenge is to de-segregate the cases in which the traditional major power approach was adopted from the ones in which the new, Nehruvian, approach was applied. For purposes of analysis, these cases can be divided into four groups: (a) countries on the periphery of India, principally Pakistan and China; (b) colonial possessions on the Indian mainland; (c) de-colonization in Africa and (d) a few major international crises of the 1950s, for instance, Korea, Suez and Hungary. It is also instructive to identify, in each category, the primary and secondary impulse of action.

In the case of Pakistan and given the situation that developed in the immediate aftermath of Independence, there was little option but to adopt a 'decisive politico-military posture'.[21] Pakistan's aggression in Jammu & Kashmir, its inclusion in Western bloc military alliances, and the support extended to her by the Western powers on the Kashmir question, became the determinants of New Delhi's Pakistan policy. This also resulted in contortions of the Kashmir policy. At another level, however, Nehru noted in 1953 that 'Probably, at no other time during the last five or six years, has the public of Pakistan been more friendly, or to put it better in a negative way, less unfriendly to India than now. There is a genuine desire both in the public and among the leadership for some way to be found to settle the issues between India and Pakistan, which have created so much trouble and ill-will'.[22]

The crisis in Nepal in 1950 created domestic pressures for an activist posture. Despite this, and the shared cultural and religious identities as well as close affinities with the Nepal Congress, Nehru resisted pressures for 'adventurist tactics' and instead worked successfully for the return and restoration of the king.[23]

The China policy of Nehru, motivated by a utopian belief in the common destiny of Asia and based on misperceptions and miscalculations, was a failure and had damaging implications for the regional and global standing of India and to the policy of non-alignment. There is, on the other hand, a case for examining the impact of inherited British perception on aspects of China policy; one of these related to the boundary question:

'Our maps show that the McMahon Line is our boundary and that is our boundary—map or no map.'[24]

After the departure of the British, French and Portuguese colonial passions remained on the Indian mainland. These were considered 'a continuous source of irritation'.[25] There was also an apprehension that the North Atlantic Treaty Organization (NATO) umbrella may be extended to them.[26] It was nevertheless 'better to proceed cautiously, step by step, whether in Goa or in Pondicherry'.[27] Earlier the French Settlements in India was unacceptable.[28] Eventually, an amicable solution was negotiated in 1954. In the case of Goa, negotiations were attempted but without success. A plebiscite was ruled out. In 1958 the US government was informed that India was even willing to accept a solution involving 'close association with India, with possible internal autonomy'.[29] The reluctance to use force was evident but when nothing happened for another two years, 'the lesser evil' was chosen in December 1961 and Goa was liberated.

The conflict in Korea focused attention on India's role: 'There is no other country that could do it or that would have been acceptable to both the parties.'[30]

Two case studies of prime importance in regard to Nehru's approach to international crises pertain to Suez and Hungary. On Suez, Nehru was critical of the US decision to withdraw financial assistance for the Aswan Dam. He also thought that Nasser's move to nationalise the Suez Canal, and the statements associated with it, was provocative. India therefore informed all governments that it would make no commitment of support to either side and, instead, watch developments.[31] Nehru sought to play a helpful, non-partisan role in the negotiations that preceded the war, but when the attack on Egypt took place, he was unequivocal in condemning it: 'I cannot imagine a worse case of aggression . . . The whole future of relations between Europe and Asia hangs in the balance', he said in his letter to the US Secretary of State.[32]

The crisis in Hungary commenced before the fire had been extinguished in Egypt. Nehru's initial hesitation to take a clear position resulted in criticism at home and abroad. The advice given to him was unambiguous: 'The time has come for us to give further thought to the Hungarian situation with a view to deciding our attitude in the light of the principles we have been advocating.'[33] He tended to accept this and told his Ambassador in Moscow accordingly: 'I have no doubt that the action of the Soviet Union is deplorable.'[34] Two days later he wrote to Eisenhower that there was nothing to choose between Suez and Hungary. 'I entirely agree with you that armed intervention of any country in another is highly objectionable and that people in any country must be free to choose their own government without interference from others.'[35] A public expression of this perception finally came in the shape of a joint communiqué issued on 14 November after a meeting in New Delhi of the Prime Ministers of India, Burma, Ceylon and Indonesia calling for a speedy withdrawal of Soviet troops from Hungary and leaving the choice of forming of government to the people themselves. This evolution in Indian position took place despite some crude Soviet pressure.[36]

V

Simple conclusions about policies pursued over a period of seventeen years can only be simplistic and must be eschewed. A complex judgement on Jawaharlal Nehru is unavoidable: he visualized India's destiny to be that of a major power by virtue of her past, her existing assets and her potential. Aware of the difference between the potential and its realization, he set about the arduous task of capacity building—human, industrial, technological. The objectives of foreign policy were world peace and enlargement of freedom as also the specifics spelt out in Article 51 of the Constitution. He developed a methodology that would assist this process, an approach focused on the consolidation of the Indian State in its period of infancy, on the avoidance of war, on furtherance of cooperation with all countries to India's benefit and above all on retention of policy choice in an age when power bloc politics tended to predetermine them. He sought to accommodate this approach to the imperatives of power politics that were thrust upon him; these imperatives determined the mix of the different ingredients in specific situations. The end product was a visionary who also possessed the requisite traits of realpolitik and who undoubtedly knew that politics is not an exact science, and that in the business of statecraft neither principles nor recollections take precedence over considerations of national interest, whatever be its limitations.

7

Identity and Citizenship

An Indian Perspective*

I

A few years ago, when I was in the vicinity of Oxford in a group dabbling in the unfathomable mysteries of the Iraq quagmire, Dr Nizami provided a welcome distraction by inviting me to see the site, and the plans, for the new building of the Centre. He also mentioned the debate on the proposed architectural design and of the view in some quarters that it would change the inherited landscape of a hallowed community.

The change, as I understood it, implied an assertion of identity. It is now conceded, I am told, that the new structure did no aesthetic or spiritual damage to the skyline of Oxford. Perhaps, the injection of diversity has enriched it.

Speculating on the 'if's of history, Edward Gibbon had visualized a course of events that might have resulted in the teaching of the interpretations of the Qur'an at Oxford. He could not foresee a happier, intellectually more rewarding, happening that the concluding decades of the 20th century would bring forth. Among its manifestations is the establishment of this Centre.

This is a tribute to Oxford's capacity to accommodate the unusual.

II

Encouraged by this accommodative approach, I wish today to share some thoughts on the twin concepts of identity and citizenship and the manner of their impact on the building blocks of modern States.

---

* Address at the Oxford Centre for Islamic Studies, 1 November 2013.

Needless to say, it is an Indian perspective and draws in good measure on the Indian experience. It may be of relevance to some of the objectives of this Centre since India counts amongst its citizens the third largest Muslim population in the world and the largest Muslim minority anywhere.

It is a truism that the human being is a social creature and societies consist of individuals who come together for a set of common purposes for whose achievement they agree to abide by a set of rules and, to that extent and for those purposes, give their tacit or explicit consent to the abridgment of individual free will or action. They, in other words, do not get subsumed totally in a larger whole and retain their individual identity. This identity, as pointed out by William James and sustained by more recent social-psychological research, is a compound of the material, social and spiritual self. Furthermore, and when acting together in smaller groups, they develop group identities, and these too are retained. Thus, in every society we have identities at three or four levels, namely individual, group, regional and national. We can also, in this age of globalization, add an international dimension to it. The challenge in all societies, therefore, is to accommodate these layered identities in a framework that is harmonious and optimally conducive to social purpose.

Much has been written about identity, its theoretical framework and practical manifestations. An eminent sociologist has defined it as 'the process of construction of meaning on the basis of a cultural attribute, or a related set of cultural attributes, that is given priority over other sources of meaning. For a given individual, or a collective of actors, there may be a plurality of identities.'[1] The question is to determine how this identification is expressed in everyday life of individuals who members of such specific groups are.

Conceptually and legally, citizenship of a modern State provides this framework and encapsulates the totality of rights and duties emanating from the membership of the citizen body, inclusive of the right of representation and the right to hold office under the State. By the same logic, a certain tension is built into the relationship, even if the society happens to be relatively homogenous, in itself a rarity in modern times. Rabindranath Tagore described his family background as a 'confluence of three cultures, Hindu, Mohammedan and British'.[2] Away from India but in our own neighbourhood, Abdolkarim Soroush depicted the Iranian Muslim as 'the carrier of three cultures at once' having national, religious and Western origins.[3]

Thus, instead of a narrow concept of a singular identity implied by the classical concept of citizenship, the need is to recognise and accommodate the existence of a plurality of social identities. The contours of this were explored earlier by Thomas Marshall, and more recently by Will Kymlicka, Manuel Castells, Charles Taylor, Gurpreet Mahajan and others. Put simply, it has been argued that identity encapsulates the notion of authenticity, the demand for recognition, the idea of difference and the principle of equal dignity.[4]

What then has been the Indian approach to, and experience of, the concepts of identity and of citizenship in a modern state? What is the accommodative framework for identities in modern India?

A distinctive feature of Indian society is its heterogeneity. The historian Ramachandra Guha depicts our recent history as 'a series of conflict maps' involving caste, language, religion and class and opines that conflicts relating to these 'operate both singly and in tandem'.[5] Each of these also brings forth an identity of varying intensity; together, they constitute what the opening line of the Preamble of our Constitution depicts as 'We, the People of India'.

In other words, the superstructure of a democratic polity and a secular state structure put in place after Independence on 15 August 1947 is anchored in the existential reality of a plural society. It is reflective of India's cultural past. Our culture is synthetic in character and, as a historian of another generation put it, 'embraces in its orbit beliefs, customs, rites, institutions, arts, religions and philosophies belonging to different strata of societies in varying stages of development. It eternally seeks to find a unity for the heterogeneous elements which make up its totality'.[6] It is a veritable human laboratory where the crossbreeding of ideas, beliefs and cultural traditions has been in progress for a few thousand years. The national movement recognized this cultural plurality and sought to base a national identity on it. The size and diversity of the Indian landscape make it essential. A population of 1.27 billion comprising of over 4,635 communities, 78 per cent of whom are not only linguistic and cultural but social categories. Religious minorities constitute 19.4 per cent of the population; of these, Muslims account for 13.4 per cent amounting in absolute terms to around 160 million. The human diversities are both hierarchical and spatial. 'The de jure WE, the sovereign people is in reality a fragmented "we", divided by yawning gaps that remain to be bridged.'[7] Around 22 per cent of our people live below the official poverty line and the health and education indicators for the population as a whole, despite recent correctives, leave much to be desired.

The contestation over citizenship surfaced early and was evident in the debates of the Constituent Assembly. The notion of citizenship was historically alien to Indian experience since throughout our long history (barring a few exceptions in the earliest period) the operative framework was that of ruler and subject. There was, of course, no dearth of prescriptions about the duties of rulers towards their subjects and about the dispensation of justice but none of these went beyond Kautilya's pious dictum that 'a king who observes his duty of protecting his people justly and according to the law will go to heaven, whereas one who does not protect them or inflict unjust punishment will not'.[8]

The constitution-makers, therefore, had to address three dimensions of the question relating to status, rights and identity: to determine who is to be a citizen, what rights are to be bestowed on the citizen and the manner in which the multiplicity of claimed identities is to be accommodated. This involved addressing three aspects of the question: legal, political and psychological. The outcome was the notion of national-civic rather than national-ethnic, emphasizing that the individual was the basic unit of citizenship whose inclusion in the polity was on terms of equality with every other citizen. At the same time and taking societal realities into account, the concept of group-differentiated citizenship was grafted to assure the minorities and other identity-based groups that

> the application of difference-blind principles of equality will not be allowed to operate in a way that is unmindful of their special needs, and that these needs arising out of cultural difference or minority status will receive due attention in policy, and that the polity will be truly inclusive in its embrace.[9]

The crafting of the Constitution was diligent and its contents reflective of the high ideals that motivated its authors. The Preamble moved Sir Earnest Barker to reproduce it at the beginning of his last book because, as he put it, it seemed 'to state in a brief and pithy form the argument of much of the book and it may accordingly serve as a keynote'.[10] The Constitution's chapter on fundamental rights addresses inter alia the protection of identities, and accommodation of diversities. These identities could be regional, religious, linguistic, tribal, caste-based and gender-based.

The right to equality and equal protection of the laws and prohibition of discrimination on grounds only of religion, race, caste, sex or place of birth is guaranteed. Affirmative action is mandated by law in favour of those historically discriminated against on grounds of caste or tribal origin as well as all those who are identified as socially and educationally backward. Also guaranteed is freedom of conscience and the right freely to profess, practice and propagate religion. Yet another section safeguards the right to have and conserve language, script or culture and the right of religious or linguistic minorities to establish and administer educational institutions of their choice. The purpose of these, taken together, is to bestow recognition, acknowledge the difference and thereby confer dignity that is an essential concomitant of equality.

An inherent problem nevertheless was evident to the constitution-makers, or at least to some of them. This was expressed candidly, almost prophetically, by Ambedkar in words that need to be cited in full:

> On the 26th of January 1950, we are going to enter into a life of contradictions. In politics we will have equality and in social and economic life we will have inequality. In politics we will be recognizing the principle of one man one vote and one vote one value. In our social and economic life, we shall, by reason of our social and economic structure, continue to deny the principle of one man one value. How long shall we continue to live this life of contradictions? How long shall we continue to deny equality in our social and economic life? If we continue to deny it for long, we will do so only by putting our political democracy in peril. We must remove this contradiction at the earliest possible moment or else those who suffer from inequality will blow up the structure of political democracy which this Assembly has so laboriously built up.[11]

Thus, the objective of securing civic, political, economic, social and cultural rights as essential ingredients of citizenship was clearly delineated and the challenge squarely posed to the beneficiaries of the new dispensation. The dire prognosis of the last sentence, however, has not come to pass! The very complexity of the landscape impedes linear and drastic happenings. One serious student of Indian polity has noted that 'the Indian model of development is characterised by the politicisation of a fragmented social structure, through a wide dispersal and permeation of political forms, values and ideologies'.[12] As a result and in a segmented society and unequal economy, the quest for substantive equality and justice remains a work in progress. Nevertheless, the slowing down of the egalitarian social revolution that was envisaged by the Constitution-makers and the implicit social contract inherent in it, does give rise to wider concerns about its implications.[13]

Two questions arise out of this and need to be explored. Firstly, what has been the impact of this on the perception of identity? Secondly, how has the challenge been addressed?

Identity assertion in any society has three sets of impulses: civic equality, liberty and opportunity. Identity groups are a by-product of the right of freedom of association. They can be cultural, voluntary, ascriptive and religious. They are neither good nor bad in themselves but do present challenges to democratic justice.[14] This is true for India also. The functioning of democratic institutions and the deepening of the democratic process, along with the efforts to implement constitutional mandates for affirmative action, induced higher levels of political mobilization. These manifested themselves, most visibly, in demand groups each with its own identity. A multiplication of identities seeking social status and economic well-being through the route of politics thus emerged as a logical consequence.

It has been has argued that 'casteism in politics is no more and no less than politicisation of caste which, in turn, leads to a transformation of the caste system'.[15] The same holds for religious and tribal minorities. In an evolving quasi-federal state structure, yet another imperative emanates from the requirements of regional or state identity. 'The new politics of caste has also reinforced old, upper caste solidarities. Brahmins, Kshatriya, Brahmarshi Sabhas have reemerged and the logic of electoral politics has forced the forces of social justice to strike strategic alliances with them.'[16] These, together, have induced political actors to develop narrower foci on their electoral management methodologies; these have been reinforced by the shortcomings of the first-past-the-post electoral system and the ability of a high percentage of candidates to win on a plurality rather than the majority of votes cast in an election.

III

A society so diverse inevitably faced the challenge of integration. It was twofold, physical and emotional. The former, involving the merger of 554 large and miniscule princely states with those parts of the former British

India that became the Indian Republic, was attended to with commendable speed and was almost completed by the end of 1949. Emotional integration, on the other hand, was a more complex process. As early as 1902, Tagore had cautioned that unity cannot be brought about by enacting a law and in 1949 Sardar Patel, the architect of integration of states, had laid emphasis on the process taking 'healthy roots' and bringing forth 'a wider outlook and a broader vision'.[17] The challenges posed by it were aptly summed up by a political scientist:

> In the semantics of functional politics the term national integration means, and ought to mean, cohesion and not fusion, unity and not uniformity, reconciliation and not merger, accommodation and not annihilation, synthesis and not dissolution, solidarity and not regimentation of the several discrete segments of the people constituting the larger political community . . . Obviously, then, Integration is not a process of conversion of diversities into a uniformity but a congruence of diversities leading to a unity in which both the varieties and similarities are maintained.[18]

Thus, the Indian approach steers clear of notions of assimilation and adaptation, philosophically and in practice. Instead, the management of diversity to ensure (in Nehru's words) the integration of minds and hearts is accepted as an ongoing national priority. Some have described it as the 'salad bowl' approach, with each ingredient identifiable and yet together bringing forth an appetizing product.

The question of minority rights as a marker of identity, and their accommodation within the ambit of citizenship rights, remains a live one. It is not so much on the principle of minority rights (which is unambiguously recognized in the Constitution) as to the extent of their realization in actual practice. A government-commissioned report on diversity index some years back concluded that 'unequal economic opportunities lead to unequal outcomes which in turn lead to unequal access to political power. This creates a vicious circle since unequal power structure determines the nature and functioning of the institutions and their policies'.[19] This and other official reports delineate areas that need to be visited more purposefully.

How far can this to be taken? A Constitutional Amendment in 1977, adding a section on the fundamental duties of citizens as part of the Directive Principles of State Policy, carries a clause stipulating promotion of harmony and spirit of brotherhood '*transcending religious, linguistic and*

regional or sectional diversities' [emphasis added]. It is at this point that the
rights of identity and the duties of citizenship intersect. The identification
of this point, with any degree of precision, is another matter. The litmus
test, eventually, must be the maintenance of social cohesiveness through
a sense of citizenship premised on equality of status and opportunity so
essential for the maintenance of democracy. The need for sustaining and
reinvigorating this sentiment is thus essential.

IV

The Constitution of India was promulgated in 1950. The past six decades
have witnessed immense changes in social and political perceptions in
societies the world over. Theories and practices of 'assimilation', 'one
national mould' and the 'melting pot' have been discredited and generally
abandoned; instead, evolving perceptions and practical compulsions led
individual societies to accept diversity and cultural pluralism. In many
places, on the other hand, a process of reversal induced by xenophobia,
Islamophobia and migrant-related anxieties, is also under way. The
concept of multiculturalism, pioneered to address accommodation of
diversity within the framework of democracy, is being openly or tacitly
challenged. An ardent advocate of multiculturalism concedes that 'not all
attempts to adopt new models of multicultural citizenship have taken root
or succeeded in achieving their intended effects' because 'multiculturalism
works best if relations between the state and minorities are seen as an issue
of social policy, not as an issue of state security'.[20]

There is an Indian segment to the debate on multiculturalism. It has
been argued that 'while a multicultural polity was designed, the principles
of multiculturalism were not systematically enunciated'. It is asserted
that multiculturalism goes beyond tolerance and probes areas of cultural
discrimination that may exist even after legal equality has been established;
it therefore

> needs to explore ways by which the sense of alienation and disadvantage
> that comes with being a minority is visibly diminished, but in a way that
> does not replace the power of the homogenising state with that of the
> community. It should therefore aspire towards a form of citizenship that is
> marked neither by a universalism generated by complete homogenisation,
> nor by particularism of self-identical and closed communities.[21]

These debates and practices vindicate in good measure the vision and foresight displayed by the founding fathers of the Republic of India. The vindication is greater when considered in the context of the size and diversity of India and the stresses and strains it has withstood in this period. And yet, we cannot rest on our laurels since impulses tilting towards 'assimilationist' and homogenizing approaches do exist, suggestive of imagined otherness and seeking uniformity at the expense of diversity. Indian pluralism, as a careful observer puts it, 'continues to be hard won'.[22] Hence the persisting need of reinforcing and improving present practices and the principles underlying them. Such an endeavour would continue to be fruitful as long as 'the glue of solidarity' around the civic ideal remains sufficiently cohesive, reinforced by the existential reality of market unity and the imperative of national security. There is no reason to be sceptical about the stability of the tripod.

8

Cohesion, Fragility and the
Challenge of Our Times*

I

This institution is of ancient vintage. Its founder found time, and inclination, to combine his colonial pursuits with serious scholarly inclinations and to inscribe an expansive objective in its Memorandum of Articles delineating its area of work. 'The bounds of its investigations', it said, 'would be the geographical limits of Asia and within these limits its enquiries will be extended to whatever is performed by MAN or produced by NATURE.'

Three years later, in 1787, he spelt out his personal objective in a letter to Lord Althorp: 'It is my ambition to know India better than any other European ever knew it.'[1]

Colonial rule ended in August 1947. The institution created by Sir William Jones, and some others like it remained relevant and continue to do good work of investigating and understanding the work of man and of nature. If the primary objective of the colonial rulers was to understand India to control and rule it more effectively and exploit it more thoroughly, the task bestowed on us today as the citizen-body of the Republic is to assess and comprehend the direction of change achieved, or is desirable, to fulfil the ideals set out in the Preamble of the Constitution.

The political and administrative integration of post-independence India was at times an exercise in 'blood and iron' and achieved in 1947–1948.

---

* Indira Gandhi Memorial Lecture by Shri M. Hamid Ansari, Honourable Vice President of India at the Asiatic Society, Kolkata on 3 October 2016.

The achievement, and its limitation, was commented upon authoritatively by its principal architect, Sardar Vallabhbhai Patel:

> Almost overnight we have introduced in these (Princely) States the super-structure of modern system of government. The inspiration and stimulus has come from above rather than from below and unless the transplanted growth takes a healthy root in the soil, there will be a danger of collapse and chaos.

This was amplified by V.P. Menon who played a critical role in the endeavour:

> We had demolished the artificial barriers between the States inter se and the rest of India and had indeed laid the foundations for an integrated administrative and financial structure. But the real integration had to take place in the minds of the people. This could not be accomplished overnight. It would take some time for the people of erstwhile States to outgrow their regional loyalties and to develop a wider outlook and a broader vision.[2]

This integration of minds extended beyond the formerly princely states and covered the rest of the country also. The reason for this was the presence of human diversities that are both hierarchical and spatial; hence the necessity of building the political structure keeping in mind the need to accommodate linguistic, religious and caste sentiments that together account for the 4,635 communities 78 per cent of whom are not only linguistic and cultural but social categories including religious minorities amounting to 19.4 per cent of the population; of these, Muslims account for 13.4 per cent amounting in absolute terms to around 180 million.

Much has happened in the past seven decades. A complex Indian reality has emerged. There is much to celebrate, much to ponder over. Sociologists have argued that the requirement is of 'a broad societal rather than a just political perspective'[3] Some years ago the late George Verghese had noted the emerging trends of opinion, observed that 'a culture of silence has yielded to protest', and suggested that 'we need instrumentalities of communication, education, institutions and policies to help negotiate the country's myriad diversities in the years ahead'.[4]

Two eminent scholars of socio-economic development in modern India have noted that 'the societal reach of economic progress in India has been remarkably limited', adding that the agenda for political, economic and social democracy remains unfinished because of continued disparity between the lives of the privileged and the rest and because of persistent ineptitude and unaccountability in the way the economy and society are organized.[5]

Given the dimensions of the challenge, the relevance of the course of action suggested by Bhimrao Ambedkar to his followers many years before independence needs to be recalled: 'My final words of advice to you are educate, agitate and organize, have faith in yourself, and never lose hope.'[6]

It has been opined that the modern state is a fictive entity that also maintains a stubborn reality.[7] This necessitates the effort to make it acceptable and trustworthy to its citizens through a state structure and practices that provide physical and emotional security by making it sufficiently accommodative. It leads us to interrogate the evident. The quest could, as with Ananya Vajpeyi, begin with the search for self in modern India and in going beyond a series of binaries like modernity/ tradition, secular/religious, Hindu/Muslim, the social/the transcendental, egalitarianism/inequality, modern political society/pre-modern cultural communities.[8]

Each of these compels us to question the obvious and the manifest. Thus, the de jure 'WE, the sovereign people' in the first line of the Preamble is in reality a fragmented 'we', divided by yawning gaps that remain to be bridged.

This exercise was conducted in the Constituent Assembly and is reflected in its totality in the Preamble to the Constitution. It sought to attain Justice (social, economic and political); Liberty (of thought, expression, belief, faith and worship); Equality (of status and of opportunity) and promotion of Fraternity (assuring the dignity of the individual and the unity and integrity of the Nation).

The Constitution was adopted by the Constituent Assembly on 26 November 1949 and formally came into force on 26 January 1950. Almost three years later, Dr Ambedkar, who chaired the drafting Committee gave a speech on 'Conditions Precedent for the Successful Working of Democracy' wherein he defined democracy 'as a form and method of government whereby revolutionary changes in the economic and social life of the people are brought about without bloodshed'. He went on to list the essential ingredients of a working democracy: (a) absence of glaring inequalities; (b) presence of an opposition; (c) equality in law and administration; (d) observance of constitutional morality; (e) avoidance of tyranny of majority over minority; (f) a functioning of moral order in society and (g) public conscience.[9]

Given the overall sense of debates in the Constituent Assembly, it is safe to assume that this text reflected the general approach of those who drafted the document. At the same time, one does not have to be a sceptic to conclude that the last two in Ambedkar's list of requirements might be in short supply today, as also the avoidance of Mahatma Gandhi's Seven Social Sins* inscribed on a tablet near his Samadhi at Raj Ghat in New Delhi!

These fissures raise questions. 'Democratic mobilization, while it has produced an intense struggle for power, has not delivered millions of citizens from abject dictates of poverty.'[10]

Our quest today is to assess the balance between factors of cohesion and fragility in the polity and in the process to gauge the achievements and shortcomings on each of these counts—particularly on institutions, integration, empowerment and identity—and gauge their impact on social cohesion in whose absence inclusive development would be impeded, even distorted. We would overlook at our own peril Ambedkar's caution about 'a life of contradictions'.[11]

For this purpose, social cohesion may be defined as the capacity of a society to ensure the welfare of all its members, minimizing disparities and avoiding polarization; its absence, on the other hand, contributes to fragility.

II

Justice, it has been rightly said, is the first virtue of social institutions and in a just society the rights secured by justice are not subject to political bargaining or to the calculus of social interests.[12] It is therefore a matter of satisfaction to us as citizens that the bill of rights in our Constitution is comprehensive and includes a judicial mechanism for the enforcement of these rights.

---

* The seven sins were: wealth without work; pleasure without conscience; knowledge without character; business without morality; science without humanity; religion without sacrifice; politics without principle.

Notwithstanding the formal position, however, the challenge of securing justice is a complex process and has been dwelt upon by Amartya Sen:

> The question to ask, then, is this: if the justice of what happens in a society depends on a combination of institutional features and actual behavioural characteristics, along with other influences that determine the social realizations, then is it possible to identify 'just' institutions for a society without making them contingent on actual behaviour? . . .
>
> Indeed, we have good reasons for recognising that the pursuit of justice is partly a matter of the gradual formation of behaviour patterns—there is no immediate jump from the acceptance of some principles of justice and a total redesign of everyone's actual behaviour in line with that political concept of justice.[13]

The discussion thus leads us to assess the efficacy of institutions beginning with the ones relating to representative government. Universal adult franchise has given us an effective tool that has been exercised with great effect for over six decades at state and national levels and has been supplemented powerfully by the 73rd and 74th Amendments of 1992. We also hold that the first-past-the-post (FPTP) system has served us adequately. The Supreme Court in 1994 had characterized it as possessing 'the merit of preponderance of decisiveness over representativeness'.[14]

Despite this, the FPTP continues to be the subject of considerable discussion. It has been argued that 'it has not been able to uphold majoritarianism in a multiparty system since the winning candidate wins only about 20–30% of the votes'.[15] In fact, in the 2014 general election only 117 of the 539 winning candidates secured 5 per cent or more of the votes cast. This, in the context of the overall national voting percentage of 66.4 per cent makes evident the actual representativeness of the elected representative. One study shows that it was 31 per cent in 2014.[16] This is accentuated by the unequal presence of weaker sections, especially women and minorities, in the power structure as reflected in elected bodies. In the 2014 general election, women constituted 11 per cent of the total elected Lok Sabha members and while some religious minorities are well represented, the representation of others is noticeable deficient.

A related question pertains to the financing of elections. It is corroding the system. A remedy may lie in state funding that will curb corruption by wealthy parties and support resource crunched parties; opinion on implementing it, however, is divided and this is reflected in the Law Commission Report.

Today, we are confronted by a paradox. While the registered voter participation in elections has steadily increased, the actual functioning of the legislatures has steadily decreased. The Lok Sabha, in the period 1952–1974 uniformly registered more than 100 sittings each year; the corresponding figure in the 2000–2015 period has never exceeded 85 and has in some years gone as low as 46. (The Rajya Sabha sittings in earlier years were at times fewer but now the two Houses adjourn on the same dates.) As a consequence, scrutiny of proposed legislation is in many cases perfunctory;[17] also, less time is available for seeking the accountability of the executive through procedural devices like questions, debates and discussion.

The picture in state legislatures is worse with some state assemblies being convened, in a pro forma exercise, for less than ten days every year.

Thus, while the public participation in the electoral exercise has noticeably improved, public satisfaction from the functioning of elected bodies is breeding cynicism with the democratic process itself. The imperative for a corrective is evident to reinforce public confidence in the ability of the system to deliver, as intended.

III

Representative governance functions at levels other than national. The Constitution was crafted in the context of its times. Its predecessor, the stillborn Government of India Act, 1935, visualized a transition from a unitary to 'a centralized federal system' with provision for 'accession' by the princely states. The text produced by Constituent Assembly depicted the Republic as 'a union of states', aptly described by Ambedkar as 'both unitary as well as federal according to the requirement of time and circumstances'. It was understood to be 'a live document in a society rapidly changing and almost frenetically political'.[18]

Over succeeding decades, and contingent on issues and the balance of political forces, the debate over the operational modalities of the centre–state relations has developed. An early advocate of decentralization was C. Rajagopalachari 'who thought that the solution to centrifugal forces was to concede greater autonomy to the states'. The same line of argument was adopted by Tamil Nadu's Rajmannar Commission in its 1971 Report of the Centre-State Relations Inquiry Committee.[19] Some years later, the Sarkaria Committee noted that 'while the Union–State relations were intended to be worked on the basis of co-operative federalism and consensus in all areas of common interest, they have not been so worked and the forums envisaged by the Constitution for that purpose have not been established'.[20]

Emanating from different quarters and premised on the actual experience of political parties that came to power in state elections, a generalized approach was suggested that 'for proper and ideal Centre–State relations, there should be more powers for the States. To be more appropriate and precise, there should be autonomy for the States and federalism at the Centre'.[21]

In recent years, and whenever a party in opposition to the ruling establishment in the centre was in power in the state(s), somewhat similar views were articulated in Bihar, Gujarat, Kerala, Karnataka, Tamil Nadu, Uttar Pradesh and West Bengal. More specific demands for devolution of powers and for 'autonomy' have also been made in Jammu & Kashmir and in Nagaland.

The debate on co-operative federalism was rekindled after the last general election. A meeting of the Inter State Council, envisaged under Article 263, was held on 16 July this year after a gap of a decade. Several strident comments on centre–state relation relations and for 'a radical rearrangements of the Union-State relationship' were articulated. The prime minister, on his part, said his government's 'main aim has been to promote federalism, be it cooperative or competitive'.

The Inter State Council, however, is not a permanent body and is not viewed by many as satisfying the demand for 'a truly federalist structure of governance . . . (since) the liberalised economy requires that the Centre expand the co-operation with the states on issues relating to land, natural resources and investment. It is time to enhance, and not reduce, states' powers'.[22]

This demand for devolution of powers is, however, selective and there is a marked propensity in most states to deny or delay financial empowerment of local bodies under the 73rd and 74th Amendments.

Can we do better?

As Niraja Gopal Jayal, the political scientist, has noted,

The trajectories of federalism and democracy in India have thus frequently intersected, with more federalism containing the potential for greater democratisation. In neither case, however, is there cause for complacency, for both projects have yet to realise their fullest potential.[23]

One observer of the national scene has argued that 'the metaphors with which we like to think of the federal arrangement are outdated', that 'the idea of centre and periphery creates the sense of the marginality of the outer, instead of the diversity of the whole' and that 'the current politics can create an empty or indifferent Centre, enacting a form of federalism where the whole is less than the sum of the parts'.[24]

In technical parlance, the Indian Union is an 'asymmetrical federation' and instances of it exist in the text of the Constitution itself.[25] This suggests the need for a wider, reinvigorated, perspective on the shape of the Union of India. Such an exercise would challenge the maturity and creative capacity of the polity and should be welcomed.[26]

IV

Liberty, equality and fraternity form, as Ambedkar put it, a trinity and divorcing one from the other is to defeat the very purpose of democracy. Liberty necessitates accommodation and acceptance of the 'other'; this generates fraternity. The critical link in this chain is provided by equality—substantive and not merely formal.

It was assessed a few years ago that poverty rates in the country have declined substantially going from 54.9 per cent of people in poverty in 1973–1974 to 27.5 per cent in 2004–2005 as measured by the NSS. This has improved further in the past decade. Despite it, three challenges remain:

- Historical fault lines along gender, caste and religious boundaries remain persistent.
- Global forces have widened the disparities between big cities and villages and between more advanced states and those mired in economic doldrums.
- Despite some noteworthy achievements, public institutions in most parts of the country have failed in delivering basic services.[27]

Thus, the ingredients that would help promote equality remain undelivered in many cases and unevenly distributed in others. It is these impulses that have shifted the political discourse from mere growth-centric to vociferous demands for affirmative action and militant protest politics. Urban middle class activism, often taking the form of violence, is being increasingly witnessed; Maoism is an extreme manifestation of it. Both are tending to exercise a new hegemony over civil society; both are also inviting a strong response from the state apparatus which is alleged by its proponents as 'endemic, extra-judicial and unaccounted violence'.[28] One consequence of it is reflected in allegations of constraints on freedom of expression; another in dilution of efforts at promoting fraternity by constricting the accepted norms of pluralism in our society.

'Where does India's democratic project stand today?' is the question posed recently by an eminent political scientist. He opines that having successfully overcome the challenges posed by questions of procedural and social legitimacy, the crisis of 'moral legitimacy is perhaps the severest test yet' and has rekindled the impulse on the one side for 'a strong leader' to fix problems and on the other for 'a stronger participatory impulse that demands more information, accountability and transparency from the rulers . . . where people act as watch dogs and vote-wielders . . . so that public policy is shaped by popular participation' since only thus 'will the overall life of the vulnerable and marginalised get better'.[29]

Others in the same vein have argued that

> any form of direct democracy complements representative democracy and does not replace it. Introducing them therefore does not require an overhaul of our existing democratic set-up, but an addition to it. Committing ourselves 60 years ago to a representative democracy with universal adult suffrage was a progressive step. The time has come to further recommit ourselves to a deeper and more participatory and decentralised democracy—a democracy with greater congruence between people's interests and public policy.[30]

Do we then, as citizens of the Republic, stand at a crossroad undecided on how to proceed?

We have to acknowledge that the representation system in Indian democracy has fissures that need attendance, that claims of inclusiveness are only partially valid, that the objective of bestowing equality of opportunity to all citizens remains a promise particularly to the weakest segment, that demands and pressures generated by non-fulfilment of commitments emanating from the Constitution are propelling the State apparatus to resort at times to violent suppression accompanied by curtailment of some fundamental freedoms, that the inherent plurality of Indian society can be endangered by suggestions of uniformity, and that sufficient effort remains to be made to promote tolerance and acceptance as essential civic virtue essential for achievement of fraternity.

Immobility is not an option; nor is certitude bordering on smugness or panic on an impending doom. A saner course may be to be receptive to the complexities of the Indian reality and its contradictions, respond to it in all its diversity and refrain from a priori solutions not embedded in ground realities. This is our creed and has been reiterated to be so by leaders of governments, past and present.

The question of its fuller implementation remains in the realm of public debate. This, to me, is the imperative challenge of our times.

9

Religion, Religiosity and World Order*

I

I deem it a great privilege to be invited to deliver the Prem Bhatia Memorial Lecture and I thank the Trustees for it. Today's is the 23rd Lecture and this testifies to the esteem and respect accorded to this eminent editor and public personality of an earlier generation that has all but gone in the pages of history.

I met the late Mr Prem Bhatia once only. He was invited by President Sanjiva Reddy to accompany him on his official visit to Kenya in 1983 where Mr Bhatia had been our high commissioner in the late 1960s. It was a late morning flight; in the aircraft I was seated next to him, and both were imbibing something appropriate for that time of the day. In the course of the conversation that veered to the communal situation, he asked me what it was to be a Muslim in India. When I got over the surprise of the question and told him something about my own views, I posed a counter question to him. I said that every incident of serious communal trouble in post-1947 years was followed by a formal enquiry but, to the best of my knowledge, the full reports of these commissions of enquiry were rarely if ever published. He felt it was a valid observation, said he had not thought about it and that he would take it up when he next met the Home Minister.

I am recalling this chance encounter and the conversation to highlight the continuing, albeit heightened, relevance of faith-related disruptions in domestic and international discourses. Much of it, I submit, is a function of politics and geopolitics and is not, on empirical evidence, suggestive of heightened piety.

---

* Prem Bhatia Memorial Lecture, 11 August 2018.

Some conceptual clarity by way of definitions would enable us to proceed in this quest. I understand by 'religion' any system of faith subscribed to by human beings involving reverence for a superior being, usually but not necessarily transcendental, and a set of ethical norms of behaviour emanating from it. Karen Armstrong has written that 'human beings are spiritual animals'. In a lecture in Ramakrishna Mission in 1952, Dr Radhakrishnan said that the object of religion 'should be to bring people together, make them love each other and raise standards of living'. Much earlier Swami Vivekananda had at the 1893 World Congress of Religions proclaimed the Hindu belief in universal tolerance and truth of all religions; the central point of all religions, he said, is 'to evolve a God out of man'.

This takes us to the role of religion in society as a social phenomenon and leads to questions about the nature of society, its components and its professed norms of social conduct. The historical record of human societies also shows that religion has been used to motivate, denigrate or divert attention from real issues. A distinction therefore is to be made on the one hand between religious sentiments and practices in terms of individuals and, on the other, in behaviour patterns as collectives and members of societal groups. The first is sui generis, reflective of normal human nature, while the second takes shape in terms of the perceived socio-political or ideological objectives and undeniably carries, in some measure, the civilizational imprint of that society. In the case of India, for instance, both are expressed in the principle and characteristic of 'secular' in the Preamble and in Articles 15, 16, 25, 26, 27, 28, 29 and 30 of the Constitution. By the same logic it would be different in what the sociologist Sammy Smooha has called 'an ethnic democracy'.[1]

'Religiosity' on the other hand, is defined in the thesaurus as a state of extreme religious ardour. It denotes exaggerated embodiment, involvement or zeal for certain aspects of religious activity and enforcing it through social or governmental pressure. The term 'zeal' itself has its origin in 'zealot' defined as a person uncompromising in pursuit of religious or political ideals and in the 1st century CE signified a group who regarded themselves as soldiers of God and sought to establish a world Jewish theocracy. Thus, while peaceful propagation of religion and voluntary conversion would be within the pale of law, resort to force, threat, fraud or illicit inducement would be beyond it. Instances of each of these can be located in recent and not so recent history and seem to abound in our own times. It is therefore important to ensure that the impulse and methodology in each case is carefully identified.

Writing in 2011 a scholar observed that 'the past two decades appear to have been marked by a return or revival of religion on the international scene' and drew attention to 'the growing activism and visibility of private religious or ecclesiastical organizations with the rise of religious fundamentalism and the related attempt to impose a chosen reading of basic scriptures on the conduct of public affairs'. He cited one instance of this in 'the American way of proselytism' (mega-church model) and wrote that it has 'spread worldwide promising God's help for earthly wealth and health and making ample use of the media, commercial slogans and private funds'.[2]

In another study, a set of scholars have observed that while 'before the nineteenth century, religion motivated virtually all terrorist activity; in 1968, it motivated none of the world's existing eleven terrorist groups. The difference was secularization, which gave rise to terrorist groups motivated not only by nationalist and political ideologies but also by a host of unpredictable and unknown factors'. Since 1968, they added, 'Religious terrorism has risen and become more global (and) is responsible for the largest proportion of terrorist attacks with known perpetrators from 1998 to 2004.'[3]

This has been true, based on time and location, of persons and organizations propagating their beliefs with explicit or tacit societal or governmental support, and using overt force or covert pressure of faith. The common element in each case, their lowest common multiple, is zeal for the cause and resort to available means to further it, including what has been called 'the politics of the death wish'. The most lethal example of it, in the use of cyber technology, is what came to be known successively as ISI, ISIS (Islamic State of Iraq and Syria) and the Islamic Caliphate.[4]

'World Order' is suggestive of a quest by political entities in the world in different places and ages for moulding divergent historical experience and values into a commonly accepted behaviour pattern. To scholars like Headley Bull, world order means 'those patterns of disposition of human activity that sustain the elementary or primary goals of social life among mankind as a whole' and 'does not exist except as an aspiration';[5] to others, it has varied with time and distribution of political power and is reflective of what Henry Kissinger has called 'practical accommodation to reality, not a unique moral insight'.[6] Such accommodation is impacted on by perceptions and realities of great power ambitions as also of strident nationalisms. Modern history has witnessed manifestations of each of these.

An early and eminently practical instance of the approach of statecraft to faith is to be found in Edward Gibbons' observation that 'the various modes of worship, which prevailed in the Roman world were all considered by the people as equally true, by the philosopher as equally false and by the magistrate as equally useful. And thus toleration produced not only mutual indulgence but even religious concord'.[7]

In succeeding centuries, many rulers in many places displayed lesser wisdom and history records innumerable instances of the use of religion by the State to reinforce and extend its authority, as also of the use of State power by religious establishments to impose their doctrines and rules on others. In turn, as Ibn Khaldun observed, 'the vanquished can always be observed to assimilate themselves to the victor'. A later variant of this surfaced in Rousseau's idea of 'civic religion'; it was described in *The Social Contract* as

> a kind of theocracy in which there ought to be no pontiff but the Prince, no other priests than the magistrates. Then to die for one's country is to suffer martyrdom, to violate the laws is to be impious, and to subject a guilty man to public execration is to devote him to the wrath of the gods.

This was translated into practice by Robespierre during the French Revolution and has been refined in our own times by authoritarian regimes of the Right and the Left, some with their own visions of militant cultural nationalism.

A term in contemporary discourse is 'Fundamentalism'. It surfaced in the early decades of the twentieth century in debates in American protestant circles. In 1990 the American Academy of Arts and Sciences initiated a project to examine its dimensions and defined the concept as 'a tendency or habit of mind in religious communities as a strategy or sets of strategies by which beleaguered believers attempt to preserve their distinctive identity as a people or group' felt to be at risk and attempting to fortify itself by resorting to 'selective retrieval of doctrines, beliefs and practices from a sacred past'. In this sense, contemporary fundamentalism is at once both derivative and vitally original since the political and social order thus sought to be re-created 'is oriented to the future rather than the past'.[8] And while fundamentalists are not entirely unlike other religious or ideologist activists, (but) they also face an additional challenge of having to justify ideological shifts, and programmatic changes accompanying them, to members who base their loyalty in part upon the assumption of both consistency and immutability in the fundamental doctrines and goals of the movement.[9]

On the other hand, it has been argued that

the prevailing association between fundamentalism and violence, particularly terrorism, should not be regarded as self-evidently true. It is, instead, often an act of labeling for the purpose of condemnation with little regard for the beliefs to which the label is attached.[10]

Terrorism itself is a complex phenomenon and is yet to be defined despite years of tussle in the United Nations. A study published last year by the Center for Strategic and International Studies, Washington D.C., highlighted some of the difficulties in existing analyses: (a) there is no agreed definition of terrorism; (b) no reporting on state terrorism; (c) failure to distinguish between insurgency and terrorism; (d) frequent depiction of enemies as terrorists for political purposes and (e) focus on ideology and religion rather than on the full range of causes of terrorism.[11]

This note of caution is also necessary to ensure that expressions of grievance premised on valid socio-political or economic reasons are not necessarily typecast as 'religion-inspired' with a view to denigrate them more, because some acts of violence, irrespective of their lethality, are depicted as 'terrorism' selectively.[12]

Before delving into specifics, some questions about perceptions and practices of fundamentalists or zealots come to mind:

- Is religiosity or religious zeal integral to faith per se? Is it desirable and conducive to it?
- What impulses in a society propel individuals to resort to selective retrieval of principles and practices: religious, socio-political or politico-religious?
- What have been its results and implications?
- How did it impact the world order of the day?

A look at the global religious scene is relevant. The Washington D.C. based Pew Research Center data indicates the following facts on the major religions of the world today. According to it, Christianity accounts for 31.2 per cent of the world's population, followed by Islam at 24.1 per cent, Hinduism at 15.1 per cent and Buddhism at 6.9 per cent, Jews at 0.2 per cent and other religions (including Sikhism at 0.8 per cent). In numbers, Christians are 2.3 billion, Muslims 1.8 billion, Hindus 1.1 billion; Buddhists are 500 million, Sikhs 25 million and Jews 14 million. Atheists or agnostics are said to number 1.1 billion and adherents of traditional Chinese religion 394 million.

So, it is in relation to the followers of these faiths that contemporary trends of religiosity or religious zeal have to be traced.

II

Since both religion and politics relate to societies, 'The relationship between the two becomes highly complex given the coexistence of religious and secular normative orders, the differentiation of the religious and political spheres and the international interpenetration of diverse traditions.' Sociologists also draw a distinction between 'absolute' politics and routine politics and define the former as 'the state of affairs where no boundaries are set to political will and everything social is seen as transformable by politics'. In routine politics, however, it is possible to distinguish between (a) politically relevant religious action; (b) religiously conditioned political action; (c) religiously relevant political action and (d) politically conditioned religious action.[13] Thus in terms of motivation of action, religion can provide a source of normative guide for political action: 'Millennialism is perhaps the most dramatic instance of the religious motivation of revolutionary action, and one of the oldest forms of absolute politics. Millennial beliefs motivate political action by upholding utopia, ideal order to be realized by revolutionary action.'[14]

A cursory look at human history does suggest the validity of this fourfold categorization and the felt need to cloak human motives in supra-human considerations. Evidence of this is to be found in stated objectives of political leaders, battlefield commanders and the motivating slogans for soldiers in the field. Good instances are the remarks of Generals Allenby and Henri Gourand about the end of the Crusades as they entered Jerusalem on 18 December 1918, the 'crusade against terrorism' expression used by

President Bush in 2003, and in the frequent use of the expression 'Jihad' for motivational purposes by Muslim extremist groups in different places. The same holds for motivating cries for mob action. Religion or religious symbolism have also been used deliberately to mislead, denigrate or divert attention and even to pre-judge or prejudice the assessment of an event.

Terminology matters. Some may be familiar with the debate in early decades of the 20th century about the impact of Christian fundamentalism in American society. A survey conducted in 1992 showed that nine per cent of adult Americans identified themselves as 'fundamentalist'[15] and a report in the *New York Times* on 28 May 2018 indicates that in California, one in five adults are evangelists. Other scholars have argued that fundamentalism is part of the rear-guard action with which small town America and commercial capitalism fight their losing battle against nationalized culture and industrial economy of mass organizations. It is distinguished in recent times by political militancy focused in an earlier period on the Roman Catholics and the Jews and more recently on Muslims, environmentalists, homosexuals and political groups like the communists. In its external manifestation, different societies in the developing world have had difficulties with evangelical activities of US-based church groups.

Some scholars have opined that President Truman's decision on 14 May 1948 to extend a de facto recognition to the newly formed State of Israel did have an element of 'religiously relevant political action' premised on evangelical Christianity; others have attributed it to American voter supportive of Zionism. Some light on this was shed by a report by Davis Kirkpatrick and Elisabeth Dias in the *New York Times* of 19 May 2018 quoting US Ambassador to Israel's remark that 'evangelical Christians support Israel with much more fervour and devotion than many in the Jewish community'.

Islamic fundamentalism, perceived today as a generic term, in fact covers three separate movements namely revivalism, reformism and radicalism. The first was induced in the 16th and 17th centuries by the European commercial and political expansion; these were accompanied by missionary activities that had limited success in the face of what Curzon called 'the impregnable rock wall of Islam'. Movements of Islamic revival in different Muslim societies in Asia and Africa were also a reaction against contraction of internal and external trade brought about by the mercantile activities of European nations. It induced an internal dialogue without reference to other systems of thought. Islamic reformism, on the other hand, was a modern movement in the wake of European supremacy, expansion and consolidation. It focused on political and social reforms induced by European ideas but riveted on revivalist and Salafi principles.[16]

Islamic radicalism or Islamism however is a 20th century phenomenon principally in the Arab societies of West Asia and North Africa in which the Islamic theory of State, on consent being the basis of political legitimacy, was invoked in the context of the autocratic nation state and of the failure of nationalism. An impetus was provided by the cataclysmic political happenings like Palestine in 1948, the war of 1967, the Intifada of 1987, the Soviet intervention in Afghanistan in 1979, the Algerian army's reversal of election results in December 1991, and US-led allied invasion of Iraq in 1991 and 2003. These propelled resort in each case to armed resistance as a religious duty and brought forth a British ambassador's remark in 2004 that President George W. Bush was 'Al Qaida's best recruiting sergeant'. They did not result in a unified movement; instead, diverse and polymorphous movements developed in individual societies to respond to the perceived local challenges broadly contextualized with a reference to the Muslim condition globally.[17] In each case, it drew selectively upon the foundational texts and their contemporary interpretations. Its early manifestation in Nasser's Egypt in the period of the Cold War was not viewed as a threat by the United States since the Islamists were 'opposed to left-wing nationalist regimes that the Americans themselves despised and wanted to see removed'.[18]

Separately, the Iranian Revolution of 1979 generated its own impulses. 'For its leaders', an eminent Israeli scholar has observed, 'the "Islamic Revolution" was a vision of an ideal Islamic order, not only in Iran itself but as a model for other Islamic communities to imitate' and to 'provide a fundamental cure, based on Islamic doctrine and revolutionary politics, for the ideological, social and economic malaise that has plagued Iranian society in modern times'. The Islamic imperative was thus 'both individual and collective'.[19] Given the nature of the convulsion and the geopolitical centrality of Iran, developments there had regional and global implications and were viewed as such. One result of it was the eight-year-long Iraq–Iran war in which many powers, regional and extra-regional, were complicit on the side of Iraq.

Perceptions underwent change with time and political priorities. After the experience of post-Soviet Afghanistan and by mid-1990s, the critical

questions were posed differently in a conference in Tel Aviv University in
March 1996:

> Is Islamism driven by religious fervor, social protest, or nationalist
> xenophobia? Is the rise of Islamism a threat to stability, tolerance
> and order? Or is it the first step towards reform, participation and
> democratization? Does repression of Islamists radicalize them or tame
> them? Are Islamists in power guided by their ideals or their interests?
> Should the governments of the West base their policy on human rights
> or *realpolitik*?[20]

After the invasion of Iraq in 2003 and its aftermath in the West Asian
region, Islamism took the shape of militant activity against its domestic
opponents (autocratic regimes) and their external support system (Western
powers led by the United States). The Arab Spring of 2011 did not emanate
from Islamist movements[21] but did result in success for the Islamists in
some lands; the Arab counter-revolution was the response in others. As
a result, 'Islamism has returned to the debate and the definition of Islam
is fiercely contested between [the] religious/state establishment, middle
class commercial Islam and militant insurrectionary Islam.'[22] The latter
manifested itself in Al Qaeda Central, Al Qaeda in the Arabian Peninsula,
Al Qaeda in Iraq, Al Qaeda in the Islamic Maghreb and finally in the ISIS.
They all 'offered a route to a past that never existed' and resorted to the use
of indiscriminate violence to achieve it. The ISIS also developed a social
base in poorer segments of society and sustained it by promoting anti-Shia
and anti-Iranian passions based on real or perceived victimization.[23]

Elsewhere in the world, developments in West Asia and the emergence
of Muslim individuals and organizations which use religious motivation
for violence to attain political goals and have trans-national dimensions
have been witnessed in some countries of Southeast Asia, South Asia and
in some central and west African countries. A similar impulse surfaced in
the case of Chechnya and Dagestan in the Russian Federation and among
Uyghurs in China. The presence of volunteer fighters from some of these
countries, as also from the European Union, in Iraq and Syria suggest
newer dimensions to the motivational factor. The journalist Jason Burke
has called them 'inspired warriors' who with or without assistance from
organized groups and acting alone or in small networks commit violent
acts in the name of God in their home countries.[24]

A good example of excessive religious zeal to promote an engineered narrative of history and aspiration is Pakistan where the promotion of violent extremism has made Jihad 'a pliable instrument in the hands of a few who are more politically motivated than ethically grounded'.[25] It has resulted in making the state and society dysfunctional in good measure.

After decades of support and funding for versions of religious conservatism and activism the world over, some Arab governments registered alarm at its impact on their own populations and have sought to undo Salafi and 'Jihadist' thinking by promotion selectively of versions of 'Moderate Islam'. A somewhat similar effort is underway in Indonesia through the 2017 Ansor Declaration on Humanitarian Islam.

In the case of India, a different set of impulses induced revivalist thinking. Many followers of the Hindu faith were influenced by strains of thought of the sages of the 19th-century renaissance movements, leading to an attempt to conflate ideas of Hindu cultural nationalism with mainstream nationalism. This was succinctly expressed by Sri Aurobindo in his famous Uttarpara speech of 30 May 1909: 'I say no longer that nationalism is a creed, a religion, a faith; I say that it is the Sanatan Dharma which for us is nationalism. The Hindu nation was born with Sanatan Dharma, with it moves and with it grows.'

Rabindranath Tagore on the other hand called nationalism 'a great menace' and 'one of the most powerful anesthetics that man has invented'; he expressed himself emphatically against 'the idolatry of nation'.[26]

An eminent commentator has recently observed that 'politics is religion in India, and religion is politics'.[27] There is some truth in this dictum. Socio-religious rituals do tend to overflow into everyday politics. The focus of the recent effort here has not been about preaching of faith per se but in its conflation with a religiopolitcal ideology. It emerged in the shape of Hindutva as a concept of cultural revitalization and political mobilization. Hindutva, wrote Savarkar, 'is not a word but a history. Hinduism is only a derivative, a fraction, of Hindutva. Hindutva embraces all the departments of thought and activity, of the whole being of our Hindu race'.[28] Savarkar's effort was to define the two main coordinates of the Indian nation, its territoriality and its culture, and to demonstrate their congruence.

The ingredients of the concept, spelt out with greater specificity by Golwalkar, depicted India as *matrbhumi* (motherland), *dharmabhumi* (land of dharma), *karmabhumi* (land of duty), *punyabhumi* (land of virtuous deeds), *devabhumi* (a land of gods) and *moksabhumi* (*land of liberation*).

Iran, interestingly, is depicted as 'nothing but the base of Aryabhumi'.[29] Golwalkar also expressed himself candidly on authoritarian centralism:

> The most important and effective step will be to bury for good all talk of a federal structure, to sweep away the existence of all autonomous and semi-autonomous states within Bharat [India] and proclaim: 'One Country, One State, One Legislature, One Executive' with no trace of fragmentational (*sic*), regional, sectarian, linguistic, or other type of pride being given scope for playing havoc with our integrated harmony! Let the Constitution be redrafted, so as to establish this Unitary form of Government.[30]

This ideological formulation however does not seem to gel with the more recent political pronouncements on cooperative federalism; does this signal a change of objective or a deferred agenda?

The approach of ethnic specificity, in the words of sociologists D.L. Sheth and Ashis Nandy, 'seeks to subjugate and homogenize the ethnic pluralities by establishing the hegemony of an imagined cultural mainstream'.[31] These principles, depicting Indian nationalism in terms of the faith of the religious majority, have serious negative political implications for sections of the citizen-body and are in violation of the principles of the Constitution. The distinction, an observer has noted, 'was meant to exclude all except Hindus, though Sikhs, Jains and Buddhists would also qualify. It was Muslims, Christians, Jews and Parsis who would be excluded'.[32] It has led to the generation of politically relevant social violence in different guises by some adherents of this approach, has been reported in sections of the media and studied by many observers including the journalist Dhirendra Jha.[33] A recent publication, *Dismantling India: A 4 Year Report* presents this in graphic detail.[34]

These manifestations of Hindutva combined with frequent ineptitude in governance and departures from the Rule of Law, have led to expressions of unease among minorities. Observers have noted 'chain reactions of fear (that) have largely accounted for counter-fundamentalism (and) have spurred reactions by Muslims, Sikhs, Christians and Buddhists'.[35] Some of them have resorted to sporadic, and others to organized, violence bringing in its wake harsh responses from the State machinery.

In a different but related context and based on analysis of basic doctrinal texts, it has been argued that 'an exclusionary nationalism actually hinders rather than enhances, national power' and 'hampers economic development'.[36]

Beyond the shores of India, Buddhist fundamentalism in the shape of ethno-religious nationalism has assumed violent dimensions in Thailand, Sri Lanka and Myanmar. In each case, it is directed against religious minorities—Hindu, Muslim or Christian. Available literature suggests some form of state or quasi-state encouragement or complicity in most case. Earlier examples of religion-supported terrorism are the Irish Republican Army in Northern Ireland and the Jewish-Zionist group Irgun which opposed British rule in Palestine before 1948.[37]

It is thus evident that zeal or extreme ardour invoked by religious motivations, or attributed to them, has today come to occupy an unprecedented centrality in human affairs in a global community of sovereign States at different levels of development and having divergent interests and varying capacities to pursue them. This at times has resulted in xenophobia and fear of the 'other', leading to demonization or the deliberate use of fear for political purposes, ignoring in the process the real sources of alienation in individual societies. The phobia or irrational fear thus generated has been disruptive of social harmony in individual societies.

III

Do we then confront a contradiction between the propensity to be religious as a human trait and the requirement of a global order as an unavoidable necessity for the world we live in? To resolve it, we need to probe deeper into the imperatives of both.

Apart from philosophical discussions on belief, disbelief or lack of belief, Karen Armstrong's observation that 'human beings cannot endure emptiness and desolation (and that) they will fill the vacuum by creating new focus of meaning' in future millennia does seem to hold true.[38] The challenge then is to restrain expressions of religiosity or zeal within the framework of Sarvepelli Radhakrishnan's remark cited at the beginning of this talk, that is, 'to bring people together, make them love each other and raise standards of living.' This requires a level of understanding, tolerance, acceptance and accommodation that does not seem to prevail in our present-day experience. If forthcoming, would it have space for religious zeal in the accepted sense? Would not persuasion based on accommodation be the preferred approach?

The world order today is premised on the Charter of the United Nations and the compendium of Covenants, Conventions, Declarations and Resolutions proclaimed or adopted by different bodies of the UN system since their inception; these include inter alia peaceful settlement of disputes, non-interference in domestic affairs and commitment to the totality of human rights. The emerging challenges emanating from pandemics and climate change add to these. Together, they constitute what could be called a broad consensus on normative standards for the member states. This framework remains fragile since the sovereignty impulse in member states propels them to violate or sidestep their commitments to it with impunity and comply only when they must. These commitments are within the ambit of the state system and leave little or no space for non-state actors and for the addressing of their grievances.

A few questions arise here. Why does an individual or a group think beyond the framework of law and of the available mechanism for correctives? Why and how is the individual radicalized? Is religious zeal an inevitable consequence of it? Can an easier approach of acceptance and empowerment bring forth better results? Do all radicals end up as terrorists? Is all violence terroristic? Can the social dimensions of radicalism be addressed meaningfully to identify underlying and indirect sources of conflict and correctives explored and undertaken? Can member states be persuaded to adhere meaningfully to their commitments under the UN Charter? This would perhaps be more effective and productive than generalized condemnatory pronouncements.

The phenomenon of global terrorism needs to be viewed in this context. By its transnational nature in organization and impact, it is a threat to global order. Its articulation and expression in the language of religiosity empowers it. This has propelled the world community to address the menace, resulting in as many as 34 UN Security Council Resolutions in the 1999 to 2017 period. These are unambiguously condemnatory of terrorism, consider it a threat to international peace and security, and emphasize that 'terrorism and violent extremism conducive to terrorism should not be associated with any religion, nationality or civilization'. The SCO meeting in June added that terrorism extremism and separatism are the 'three evils' bedevilling the world view of the participants. And yet, neither national nor global efforts aimed at preventing, containing and reversing these acts (emanating proximately or remotely from violent expressions of religious zeal) are altogether successful because they do not seem to address its primary impulses or 'root causes' and instead depict such suggestions as diversionary or evasive.

A corrective in thinking is thus imperative since we seem to be on the horns of a dilemma. Can two *desirables*, 'religion' and 'global order', negate or contain an *undesirable*, namely, 'religiosity'? If not, an epoch of chaos can be predicted at the expense of human well-being in the world we live in. And yet, it is not beyond our capacity to think through this self-inflicted misery and anticipate outcomes in terms of the future that, as Philip Bobbitt had observed, 'is unlikely to be very much like the past' and in which 'three earlier certainties about national security—that it is national (not international), that it is public (not private) and that it seeks victory (not stalemate) are about to be turned upside down by the new age of indeterminacy into which we are plunging'.[39]

Would this induce us to proclaim a new triad that religion is not politics, that religiosity is not religion, and that global order is to be premised on global interests and not on exclusively national ones? Are we prepared, conceptually and organizationally, to undertake it even if it involves as it must going beyond the traditional paradigm of faith and of national interest? Or could the alternative be a modern-day version of Milton's Pandemonium, the High Capital of Satan and his Peers, built by little demons?

I suspect Prem Bhatia saheb may not disagree and might even devote an editorial to it.

10

Indira Gandhi

A Vision for Global Justice and Social Democracy*

I

Personal reminisces tend to be subjective, more so in relation to iconic personalities. They nevertheless remain a segment of living memory and contribute to the totality of impressions emanating from contemporaries.

In the early 1980s I was heading the protocol department of the Ministry of External Affairs in New Delhi and in that capacity had occasion to come in contact with Prime Minister Indira Gandhi fairly regularly from February 1980 till her assassination on 31 October 1984. I also shared with some others the heart-rending task of her funeral arrangements. I was not privy to the secrets of statecraft but nevertheless had a ringside view of some happenings pertaining to her conduct of foreign affairs and interaction with foreign dignitaries.

In one sense, she was a protocol person's delight. Her knowledge of procedures and diplomatic etiquette was amazing and so was her eye for detail; for the same reason, faults were invariably detected and frowned upon. She could be gracious as well as unforgiving; she was 'a tough politician' as she described herself in an interview with Oriana Fallaci.

Indira Gandhi's pragmatism and flexibility in the conduct of foreign policy was much in evidence. Her approach, as she put it, was 'to strengthen friendships, to change indifference into friendship, and to lessen the hostility where it exists'. Asked about her diplomatic style by a foreign dignitary, she said: 'I look for the minimum area of agreement and build

---

* First published in the Indira Gandhi Centenary Volume, 2017.

upon it.' She recognized power as a crucial determinant in international relations and over time used it to India's advantage.

Most observers of the Indian scene consider her handling of the Bangladesh crisis masterly. A good deal of archival material is now available from Indian and foreign sources to substantiate this judgment. Given the view taken in Washington of the developing situation, she opted for the Treaty of Peace, Friendship and Cooperation with the Soviet Union. Its purpose, as she put it, was to 'discourage adventurism' from quarters that have 'a pathological hostility towards India'. It contributed to difficulties with the United States; these nevertheless remained within the framework of mutual imperatives and years later were summed up in Henry Kissinger's remark that 'relations returned quite rapidly to their previous state of frustrated incomprehension within a framework of compatible objectives'.

The Soviet intervention in Afghanistan in December 1979 tested India's commitment to its principles. The statement in General Assembly on 12 January 1980 broadly supportive of the intervention, caused surprise and dismay in non-aligned circles. Indira Gandhi was quick to notice it and sought to develop a more nuanced response to the crisis. Foreign Minister Gromyko, who came to Delhi on 13 February was told quite bluntly that she could not accept the Soviet justification for the action. Later in the year an unsuccessful effort to persuade the Soviet leadership to accept a suggestion for partial withdrawal and the installation of a non-aligned government in Kabul, forced New Delhi to make public through a Parliament statement the divergence of views. Faced with this clash of perceptions, India opted to isolate the Afghan factor from the totality of the Indo-Soviet framework of wide-ranging cooperation.

Almost two years later in Moscow in October 1982, Brezhnev asked her: 'Show me a way out of Afghanistan.' Her reply was laconic: 'The way out is the same as the way in.'

Indira Gandhi used her Chairmanship of the Non-Aligned Movement to highlight India's perceptions. She noted

> The paradox of our times: that while weapons become increasingly sophisticated, minds remain imprisoned in ideas of simpler times. Technically, the colonial age has ended. But the wish to dominate persists. Neo-colonialism comes wrapped in all types of packages—in technology and communications, commerce and culture. It takes boldness and integrity to resist.[1]

Non-alignment, she added, 'is not vague, not negative, not neutral . . . It aims
to keep away from military alliances. It embodies the courage and strength
of self reliance. Alignment denotes dependence'. Non-alignment means
'equality among nations and democratization of international relations,
economic and political. It wants global cooperation for development on
the basis of mutual benefit'.[2] She amplified this on another occasion: 'We
have neither natural allies nor natural adversaries. We have tried not to be
openly critical (of anyone) or use a strident type of voice.'[3]

The two themes that characterized her role as Non-Aligned Movement
Chairperson were to press for a restructuring of the world economic order
and to make a plea for nuclear disarmament.

II

The leadership of a country with abject poverty in its huge population
compelled Indira Gandhi to face the challenges emanating from it. The
general approach of the Indian freedom movement and the legacy of
ideas inherited from her father propelled her from childhood towards a
philosophy of social justice.

She understood the relationship of food self-sufficiency and national
sovereignty and, in the words of the eminent agricultural scientist M.S.
Swaminathan, 'was convinced that an independent foreign policy could be
built only on a foundation of food security based on home-grown food',[4]
and that the foundation laid by her in the 1960s made it possible many
decades later to make access to food a legal right.

Indira Gandhi considered three streams of thought which depicted the
Indian approach to democracy: liberalism and parliamentary democracy;
socialist thought with emphasis on social democracy, economic planning
and development; and Gandhian philosophy and non-violent revolution.

The events of June 1975 and its aftermath cast a shadow on her
commitment to liberalism and democracy. It was described by an eminent
authority as a 'constitutional watershed'. Faced with mounting criticism,
she brought about the corrective of March 1977.

Her approach to social justice was spelt out while inaugurating a
seminar in New Delhi in October 1980. 'Our freedom movement', she said,
'was a fight not merely against foreign rule, but against our own inherited
injustices . . . Today our task is to achieve the objectives adumbrated in our
Constitution (for which) we need a climate of proper interaction among

the people and the government to nurture and promote our declared social goals.'

She went on to add that

a major ideological battle has been raging in our country between those who swear only by the Fundamental Rights chapter of our Constitution and those who hold that legislation should strive to fulfill the hopes held out in the Directive Principles chapter. I should like to add that the common man's faith in democracy in our country depends in large measure upon the manner and speed with which we can solve his economic problems. To him, the Constitution should be a charter for change rather than a bulwark of the *status quo*.

A few years later, in 1984, she observed in an international gathering of judges that 'India is nowhere near the level of social justice at which we aim' and went on to mention, pointedly, the remarks of Justice Oliver Wendell Holmes about the 'inarticulate major premise' of those who occupy the judicial seat. She dwelt on the 'need for a great movement for judicial reforms initiated by the legal community itself on how to make justice expeditious and inexpensive' and on the need to balance rights and duties.

Almost three decades after her death, the leadership of the United Progressive Alliance depicted 'Growth with social justice' as the essence of Indira Gandhi's concept of social democracy that has four essential pillars: be responsive and responsible and representative of social diversities; unachievable without economic growth that empowers the disadvantaged, deprived, and discriminated against; pays attention to environmental protections and regeneration of natural resources; and provides for a nation state as an instrument of change and as a protector of national sovereignty. The challenge of translating this into practice remains formidable; it was spelt out in Manmohan Singh's remark that 'the vision of social democracy can only be translated into practical possibilities by institutions of governance at the level where the state interacts with the citizen'.

It is here that a yawning gap continues to exist between our penchant for passing legislation and our inability to implement them to the requisite degree. A change in the philosophy of governance, however subtle, could have been another constraint. There may therefore be merit in Professor of International Relations at Princeton, Atul Kohli's observation that 'over time the state in India has shifted from a reluctant pro-capitalist state with a socialist ideology, to an enthusiastic pro-capitalist state with a neo-liberal ideology. This shift has significant implications for the politics of redistribution in India'.[5]

III

The theme of social justice, emanating from the Preamble and the text of the Constitution, is a constant in Indian political discourse and has been dwelt upon by all public figures. Closer scrutiny, therefore, needs to focus on its socio-political backdrop and the efficacy of the policies proposed to address it.

A first step is to delineate a typology of injustice and ascertain the extent to which it is remediable. This necessitates practical reasoning and the presence of institutions through which it is pursued. A standard answer is democracy which, as Amartya Sen put it, 'has to be judged not just by the institutions that formally exist but by the extent to which different voices from diverse sections of the people can actually be heard'.[6]

Democracy has two dimensions, political and social. The first implies universal suffrage and protection of universally recognized individual and group rights and their actual realization without abridgement on specious grounds of expediency; the second implies equality, emanating from a sense of justice and fairness in terms of vulnerability, discrimination and marginalization. There also has to be a structural distinction between individual and collective rights. Meaningful democracy therefore implies more substantive participation by the citizens individually and in terms of groups in matters relating to their civic, economic and cultural rights at all levels of society. It is this participatory citizenship that lies at the core of social democracy. By the same token, cleavages in the process detract from the fulfilment of its purposes.

Given the diversity of Indian society, these cleavages are to be traced vertically and horizontally. New manifestations of social conflict have emerged; the power of caste has not diminished; together, these hamper the capacity of the State to deliver equality to the excluded groups without whom an inclusive social democracy becomes meaningless. That this has yet to happen meaningfully, despite governmental interventions and judicial verdicts, is evident from data in the public domain.

Indira Gandhi's vision remains a beacon of light on the horizon, attainable but yet to be reached.

* * *

Remarks at Function on 13 May 2017

A centenary volume is in the nature of an offering; it is perhaps the best way of paying homage to a historic personality and in understanding the significance of her or his life and work and its relevance to a new and younger generation inadequately acquainted with the world of yesterday.

Indira Gandhi ji was such a personality. She lived in a period of turmoil and change in the country, in the neighbourhood and in the world. Destiny bestowed on her the role of being a principal actor.

She was revered, admired, even disliked. Controversy did not deter her; on the contrary, it strengthened her resolve to persist in her quest for ideals dear to her. She succeeded in good measure, faltered in places, left her imprint and earned her place in history. The contributions to the volume before us testify to it.

References

Indira Gandhi's Speeches, 26 August 1971 (Interview to Romesh Chandra); 29 October 1971 (Indian Democracy); 31 October 1980 (Dynamics of Social Justice); 4 March 1984 (Social Justice).

Inder Malhotra, *A Personal and Political Biography* (1989).

Katherine Frank, *Indira—the Life of Indira Nehru Gandhi* (2001).

M. Rasgortra, *A Life in Diplomacy* (2016).

Surjit Mansingh, *India's Search for Power: Indira Gandhi's Foreign Policy 1966–1982* (New Delhi, 1984).

Sunil Khilnani and Manmohan Malhotra, *An Indian Social Democracy: Integrating Markets, Democracy and Social Justice* (New Delhi, 2013).

11

Two Obligatory Isms

Why Pluralism and Secularism
Are Essential for Our Democracy*

I

It is a privilege to be invited to this most prestigious of law schools in the country, more so for someone not formally lettered in the discipline of law. I thank the Director and the faculty for this honour.

The nebulous universe of law and legal procedures is well known to this audience and there is precariously little that I can say of relevance to them. And, for reasons of prudence and much else, I dare not repeat here either Mr Bumble's remark that 'the law is an ass' or the suggestion of a Shakespearean character who outrageously proposed in *Henry VI* to 'kill all lawyers'. Instead, my effort today will be to explore the practical implications that some constitutional principles, legal dicta and judicial pronouncements have for the lives of citizens.

An interest in political philosophy has been a lifelong pursuit. I recall John Locke's dictum that 'wherever law ends, tyranny begins'. Also in my mind is John Rawl's assertion that 'justice is the first virtue of social institutions' and that in 'a just society the liberties of equal citizenship are taken as settled and the rights secured by justice and are not subject to political bargaining or to the calculus of social interest'.[1] To Rawls, the first task of political philosophy is its practical role to see, whether despite appearances on deeply disputed questions, some philosophical or moral

---

* Address to the National Law School Convocation, Bengaluru, 6 August 2017.

grounds can be located to further social cooperation on a footing of mutual respect among citizens.[2]

The Constitution of India and its Preamble are an embodiment of the ideals and principles that I hold dear.

II

The People of India gave themselves a Republic that is Sovereign, Socialist, Secular and Democratic and a constitutional system with its focus on Justice, Liberty, Equality and Fraternity. These have been embodied in a set of institutions and laws, conventions and practices.

Our founding fathers took cognizance of an existential reality. Ours is a plural society and a culture imbued with considerable doses of syncretism. Our population of 1.3 billion comprises over 4,635 communities, 78 per cent of whom are not only linguistic and cultural but social categories. Religious minorities constitute 19.4 per cent of the total. The human diversities are both hierarchical and spatial.

It is this plurality that the Constitution endowed with a democratic polity and a secular State structure. Pluralism as a moral value seeks to 'transpose social plurality to the level of politics, and to suggest arrangements which articulate plurality with a single political order in which all duly constituted groups and all individuals are actors on an equal footing, reflected in the uniformity of legal capacity. Pluralism in this modern sense presupposes citizenship'.[3]

Citizenship as the basic unit is conceptualized as 'national-civic rather than national-ethnic' 'even as national identity remained a rather fragile construct, a complex and increasingly fraught 'national-civic-plural-ethnic' combinations'.[4] In the same vein, 'Indianness' came to be defined not as a singular or exhaustive identity but as embodying the idea of layered 'Indianness', an accretion of identities.[5]

Modern democracy offers the prospect of the most inclusive politics of human history. By the same logic, there is a thrust for exclusion that is a by-product of the need for cohesion in democratic societies; hence the resultant need for dealing with exclusion 'creatively' through sharing identity space by 'negotiating a commonly acceptable political identity between the different personal and group identities which want to/have to live in the polity'.[6] Democracy 'has to be judged not just by the institutions that formally exist but by the extent to which different voices from diverse sections of the people can actually be heard.' Its 'raison d'être is the recognition of the other'.[7]

III

Secularism as a concept and as a political instrumentality has been debated extensively.[8] A definitive pronouncement pertaining to it for purposes of statecraft in India was made by the Supreme Court in the Bommai case and bears reiteration:

> Secularism has both positive and negative contents. The Constitution struck a balance between temporal parts confining it to the person professing a particular religious faith or belief and allows him to practice profess and propagate his religion, subject to public order, morality and health. The positive part of secularism has been entrusted to the State to regulate by law or by an executive order. The State is prohibited to patronise any particular religion as State religion and is enjoined to observe neutrality. The State strikes a balance to ensure an atmosphere of full faith and confidence among its people to realise full growth of personality and to make him a rational being on secular lines, to improve individual excellence, regional growth, progress and national integrity . . . Religious tolerance and fraternity are basic features and postulates of the Constitution as a scheme for national integration and sectional or religious unity. Programmes or principles evolved by political parties based on religion amount to recognizing religion as a part of the political governance which the Constitution expressly prohibits. It violates the basic features of the Constitution. Positive secularism negates such a policy and any action in furtherance thereof would be violative of the basic features of the Constitution.[9]

Despite its clarity, various attempts, judicial and political, have been made to dilute its import and to read new meaning into it. Credible critics have opined that the 11 December 1995 judgment of the Supreme Court Bench[10] 'are highly derogatory of the principle of secular democracy' and that a larger Bench should reconsider them 'and undo the great harm caused by them'.[11] This remains to be done; 'instead, a regression of consciousness (has) set in' and 'the slide is now sought to be accelerated and is threatening to wipe out even the gains of the national movement summed up in *sarvadharma sambhav*.[12]

It has been observed, with much justice, that 'the relationship between identity and inequality lies at the heart of secularism and democracy in India'.[13] The challenge today then is to reiterate and rejuvenate secularism's basic principles: equality, freedom of religion and tolerance, and to emphasize that equality has to be substantive; that freedom of religion be re-infused with its collectivist dimensions; and that toleration should be reflective of the realities of Indian society and lead to acceptance.[14]

IV

The experience of almost seven decades sheds light on the extent of our success, and of our limitations, on the actualizations of these values and objectives. The optimistic narrative is of deepening; the grim narrative of decline or crisis.[15]

Three questions thus come to mind:

- How has the inherent plurality of our polity reflected itself in the functioning of Indian democracy?
- How has democracy contributed to the various dimensions of Indian pluralism?
- How consistent are we in our adherence to secularism?

Our democratic polity is pluralist because it recognizes and endorses this plurality in (a) its federal structure; (b) linguistic and religious rights to minorities and (c) a set of individual rights. The first has sought to contain, with varying degrees of success, regional pressures; the second has ensured space for religious and linguistic minorities and the third protects freedom of opinion and the right to dissent.

A question is often raised about national integration: conceptually and practically, integration is not synonymous with assimilation or homogenization. Some years ago, political scientist Rasheeduddin Khan had amplified the nuances:

> In the semantics of functional politics the term national integration means, and ought to mean, cohesion and not fusion, unity and not uniformity, reconciliation and not merger, accommodation and not annihilation,

synthesis and not dissolution, solidarity and not regimentation of the
several discrete segments of the people constituting the larger political
community . . . Obviously, then, Integration is not a process of conversion
of diversities into a uniformity but a congruence of diversities leading to a
unity in which both the varieties and similarities are maintained.[16]

How and to what extent has this worked in the case of Indian democracy
with its ground reality of exclusions arising from stratification, heterogeneity
and hierarchy that often 'operate conjointly and create intersectionality'?[17]

Given the pervasive inequalities and social diversities, the choice of
a system committed to political inclusiveness was itself 'a leap of faith'.
The Constitution instituted universal adult suffrage and a system of
representation on the first-past-the-post (Westminster) model. An
underlying premise was the rule of law that is reflective of the desire of
people 'to make power accountable, governance just, and state ethical'.[18]

Much earlier, Gandhiji had predicted that democracy would be
safeguarded if people 'have a keen sense of independence, self-respect
and their oneness and should insist upon choosing as their representatives
only persons as are good and true'. This, when read alongside Ambedkar's
apprehension that the absence of equality and fraternity could bring forth
'a life of contradictions' if the ideal of 'one person, one vote, one value' was
not achieved, framed the challenge posed by democracy.

Any assessment of the functioning of our democracy has to be both
procedural and substantive. On a procedural count, the system has
developed roots with the regularity of elections, the efficacy of the electoral
machinery, an ever-increasing percentage of voter participation in the
electoral process and the formal functioning of legislatures thus elected.
The record gives cause for much satisfaction.

The score is less emphatic on the substantive aspects. Five of these
bear closer scrutiny: (a) the gap between 'equality before the law' and
'equal protection of the law'; (b) the representativeness of the elected
representative; (c) the functioning of legislatures; (d) gender and diversity
imbalance; and (e) secularism in practice.

- **Equality before the law and equal protection of the law:** 'The effort
to pursue equality has been made at two levels. At one level was the
constitutional effort to change the very structure of social relations:
practicing caste and untouchability was made illegal and allowing

religious considerations to influence state activity was not permitted. At the second level the effort was to bring about economic equality, although in this endeavour the right to property and class inequality was not seriously curbed . . . Thus the reference to economic equality in the Constitution, in the courts or from political platforms remained basically rhetorical.'[19]

- **Representativeness of the elected representative:** In the 2014 general election, 61 per cent of the elected MPs obtained less than 50 per cent of the votes polled. This can be attributed in some measure to the first-past-the-post system in a fragmented polity and multiplicity of parties and contestants.[20] The fact nevertheless remains that representation obtained on non-majority basis does impact on the overall approach in which the politics of identity prevails over the common interest.[21]

- **Functioning of legislatures, accountability and responsiveness:** The primary tasks of legislators are legislation, seeking accountability of the executive, articulation of grievances and discussion of matters of public concern. The three often overlap; all require sufficient time being made available. It is the latter that is now a matter of concern. The number of sittings of the Lok Sabha and the Rajya Sabha which stood at 137 and 100 respectively in 1953 declined to 49 and 52 in 2016. The paucity of time thus created results in shrinkage of space made available to each of these with resultant impact on quality and productivity and a corresponding lessening of executive's accountability. According to one assessment some years ago, 'Over 40 percent of the Bills were passed in Lok Sabha with less than one hour of debate. The situation is marginally better in the Rajya Sabha.'[22] Substantive debates on public policy issues are few and far in between. More recently, the efficacy of the Standing Committee mechanism has been dented by resort to tactics of evasion by critical witnesses. A study on '*Indian Parliament as an Instrument of Accountability*' concluded that the institution is 'increasingly becoming ineffective in providing surveillance of the executive branch of the government.[23] The picture with regard to the functioning of the State Assemblies is generally much worse. Thus, while public participation in the electoral exercise has noticeably improved, public satisfaction with the functioning of the elected bodies is breeding cynicism with the democratic process itself. It has also been argued that 'the time has come to further commit ourselves to a deeper and more participatory and decentralized democracy—a democracy with greater congruence between people's interests and public policy'.[24]

- **Gender and diversity imbalance:** Women MPs constituted 12.15 per cent of the total in 2014. This compares unfavourably globally as well as within South Asian Association for Regional Cooperation (SAARC) and is reflective of pervasive neo-patriarchal attitudes. The Women's Reservation Bill of 2010 was passed by the Rajya Sabha, but was not taken up in Lok Sabha, and lapsed when Parliament was dissolved before the 2014 general elections. It has not been resurrected. Much the same (for other reasons of perception and prejudice) holds for Minority representation. Muslims constitute 14.23 per cent of the population of India. The total strength of the two Houses of Parliament is 790; the number of Muslim MPs stood at forty-nine in 1980, ranged between thirty and thirty-five in the 1999 to 2009 period, but declined to twenty-three in 2014. An Expert Committee report to the government some years ago had urged the need for a Diversity Index to identify 'inequality traps' which hold back the marginalized and work in favour of the dominant groups in society and result in unequal access to political power that in turn determines the nature and functioning of institutions and policies.[25]

- **Secularism in actual practice:** Experience shows that secularism has become a site for political and legal contestation. The difficulty lies in delineating, for purposes of public policy and practice, the line that separates them from religion. For this, religion per se, and each individual religion figuring in the discourse, has to be defined in terms of its stated tenets. The 'way of life' argument, used in philosophical texts and some judicial pronouncements, does not help the process of identifying common principles of equity in a multi-religious society in which the religious majority is not synonymous with totality of the citizen body. Since a wall of separation is not possible under Indian conditions, the challenge is to develop and implement a formula for equidistance and minimum involvement. For this purpose, principles of faith need to be segregated from contours of culture since a conflation of the two obfuscates the boundaries of both and creates space to equivocalness.[26] Furthermore, such an argument could be availed of by other faiths in the land since all claim a cultural sphere and a historical justification for it.

In life as in law, terminological inexactitude has its implications. In electoral terms, 'majority' is numerical majority as reflected in a particular exercise (e.g., an election), does not have permanence and is generally time-specific; the same holds for 'minority'. Both find reflection in value judgments. In sociopolitical terminology (e.g., demographic data) 'majority' and 'minority' are terms indicative of settled situations. These too bring forth value judgments. The question then is whether in regard to 'citizenship' under our Constitution, with its explicit injunctions on rights and duties, any value judgments should emerge from expressions like 'majority' and 'minority' and the associated adjectives like 'majoritarian' and 'majorityism' and 'minoritarian' and 'minorityism'? The record shows that these have divisive implications and detract from the Preamble's quest for 'Fraternity'.

Within the same ambit, but distinct from it, is the constitutional principle of equality of status and opportunity, amplified through Articles 14, 15 and 16. This equality has to be substantive rather than merely formal and has to be given shape through requisite measures of affirmative action needed in each case so that the journey on the path to development has a common starting point. This would be an effective way of giving shape to Prime Minister Narendra Modi's policy of *Sabka Saath Sabka Vikas*.

It is here that the role of the judicial arm of the state comes into play and, as an acknowledged authority on the Constitution, Granville Austin put it, 'Unless the Court strives in every possible way to assure that the Constitution, the law, applies fairly to all citizens, the Court cannot be said to have fulfilled its custodial responsibility.'[27]

V

How then do we go about creating conditions and space for a more comprehensive realization of the twin objectives of pluralism and secularism and weaving it into the fabric of a comprehensive actualization of the democratic objectives set forth in the Constitution?

The answer would seem to lie, firstly, in the negation of impediments to the accommodation of diversity institutionally and amongst citizens; and, secondly, in the rejuvenation of the institutions and practices through which pluralism and secularism cease to be sites for politico-legal contestation in the functioning of Indian democracy. The two approaches are to be parallel, not sequential. Both necessitate avoidance of sophistry in discourse or induction of personal inclinations in State practice. A more diligent promotion of fraternity, and of our composite culture, in terms of

Article 51A (e) and (f) is clearly required. It needs to be done in practice by leaders and followers.

A commonplace suggestion is advocacy of tolerance. Tolerance is a virtue. It is freedom from bigotry. It is also a pragmatic formula for the functioning of society without conflict between different religions, political ideologies, nationalities, ethnic groups, or other us-versus-them divisions.

Yet tolerance alone is not a strong enough foundation for building an inclusive and pluralistic society. It must be coupled with understanding and acceptance. We must, said Swami Vivekananda, 'not only tolerate other religions, but positively embrace them, as truth is the basis of all religions'.

Acceptance goes a step beyond tolerance. Moving from tolerance to acceptance is a journey that starts within ourselves, within our own understanding and compassion for people who are different to us, and from our recognition and acceptance of the 'other' that is the raison d'être of democracy. The challenge is to look beyond the stereotypes and preconceptions that prevent us from accepting others. This makes continuous dialogue unavoidable. It has to become an essential national virtue to promote harmony transcending sectional diversities. The urgency of giving this a practical shape at national, state and local levels through various suggestions in the public domain is highlighted by enhanced apprehensions of insecurity amongst segments of our citizen body, particularly Dalits, Muslims and Christians.

The alternative, however unpalatable, also has to be visualized. There is evidence to suggest that we are a polity at war with itself in which the process of emotional integration has faltered and is in dire need of reinvigoration. On one plane is the question of our commitment to rule of law that seems to be under serious threat arising out of the noticeable decline in the efficacy of the institutions of the State, lapses into arbitrary decision-making and even 'ochlocracy' or mob rule, and the resultant public disillusionment. On another hand are questions of fragility and cohesion emanating from impulses that have shifted the political discourse from mere growth centric to vociferous demands for affirmative action and militant protest politics. 'A culture of silence has yielded to protests.'[28] The vocal distress in the farm sector in different states, the persistence of Naxalite insurgencies, the re-emergence of language related identity questions, the seeming indifference to excesses pertaining to weaker sections of society, and the as yet unsettled claims of local nationalisms can no longer be ignored or brushed under the carpet. The political immobility in relation to Jammu & Kashmir is disconcerting. Alongside are questions about the functioning of what has been called our 'asymmetrical federation' and 'the felt need for a wider, reinvigorated, perspective on the shape of the Union of India' to overcome the crisis of 'moral legitimacy' in its different manifestations.[29]

VI

I have in the foregoing dwelt on two 'isms', two value systems, and the imperative need to invest them with greater commitment in word and deed so that the principles of the Constitution and the structure emanating from it are energized. Allow me now to refer to a third 'ism' that is foundational for the modern State, is not of recent origin, but much in vogue in an exaggerated manifestation. I refer here to nationalism.

Scholars have dwelt on the evolution of the idea. The historical precondition of Indian identity was one element of it; so was regional and anti-colonial patriotism. By the 1920s a form of pluralistic nationalism had answered the question of how to integrate within it the divergent aspirations of identities based on regional vernacular cultures and religious communities.[30] A few years earlier, Rabindranath Tagore had expressed his views on the 'idolatry of Nation'.[31]

For many decades after Independence, a pluralist view of nationalism and Indianness reflective of the widest possible circle of inclusiveness and a 'salad bowl' approach, characterized our thinking. More recently an alternate viewpoint of 'purifying exclusivism' has tended to intrude into and take over the political and cultural landscape. One manifestation of it is 'an increasingly fragile national ego' that threatens to rule out any dissent however innocent.[32] Hyper-nationalism and the closing of the mind is also 'a manifestation of insecurity about one's place in the world'.[33]

While ensuring external and domestic security is an essential duty of the State, there seems to be a trend towards sanctification of military might overlooking George Washington's caution to his countrymen over two centuries earlier about 'overgrown military establishments which, under any form of government, are inauspicious to liberty'.[34]

Citizenship does imply national obligations. It necessitates adherence to and affection for the nation in all its rich diversity. This is what nationalism means, and should mean, in a global community of nations. The Israeli scholar Yael Tamir has dwelt on this at some length. Liberal nationalism, she opines, 'requires a state of mind characterized by tolerance and respect of diversity for members of one's own group and for others'; hence it is 'polycentric by definition' and 'celebrates the particularity of culture with the universality of human rights, the social and cultural embeddedness of individuals together with their personal autonomy'. On the other hand, 'The version of nationalism that places cultural commitments at its core is usually perceived as the most conservative and illiberal form of nationalism. It promotes intolerance and arrogant patriotism.'[35]

What are, or could be, the implications of the latter for pluralism and secularism? It is evident that both would be abridged since both require for their sustenance a climate of opinion and a State practice that eschews intolerance, distances itself from extremist and illiberal nationalism, subscribes in word and deed to the Constitution and its Preamble, and ensures that citizenship irrespective of caste, creed or ideological affiliation is the sole determinant of Indianness.

In our plural secular democracy, therefore, the 'other' is to be none other than the 'self'. Any derogation from it would be detrimental to its core values.

12

Democracy and the Perils of Bending Reality*

I

The theme, *Journalism as the Fourth Pillar of Democracy*, induces conceptual speculation. Architecturally speaking, human endeavour generally is to create structures in consonance with the laws of gravity—stable, balanced and self-sustaining. Structural engineering permits it to be uni-pillar, bi-pillar, tri-pillar or multi-pillar depending on functional requirements, aesthetics, individual preferences and prejudices. Each of these plays a role in determining shape and size; equally relevant is the subsoil and its strength to support the structure.

The structure we are discussing today is democracy and the relevance of journalism to it. Speaking on parliamentary democracy in Pune in December 1952, Dr Ambedkar added his own definition of it after citing the standard definitions by Abraham Lincoln and Walter Bagehot. Democracy, he said, is 'a form and a method of government whereby revolutionary changes in the economic and social life of the people are brought about without bloodshed.' He went on to list seven conditions for its successful functioning: (a) no glaring inequalities in society; (b) a strong opposition; (c) no tyranny of the majority over the minority; (d) equality in law and administration; (e) observance of constitutional morality; (f) functioning of moral order in society; (g) public conscience.[1]

In democratic theory the individual citizen is sovereign and practises democracy through open discussion. In actual practice, however, the citizen does not have the knowledge to make judgments on all matters in

---

* Keynote address delivered at the Fourth Pillar India Journalism Week on 14 December 2018 at IIC New Delhi.

the public domain and be 'an active and intelligent participant'. Access to information, therefore, is critical and this is where fact-finding individuals and agencies are required. What holds good for the individual is most of the time equally true of groups. Many years ago, Walter Lippman had observed that 'the force of public opinion is partisan, spasmodic, simple-minded and external' and that even 'when power, however absolute and unaccountable, reigns without provoking a crisis, public opinion does not challenge it. Somebody must challenge arbitrary power first. The public can only come to his assistance'.[2]

That 'somebody' is often a well-researched report in the media.

If journalism's primary role is to inform and educate, it needs human and technological wherewithal to do it and has the right to do so without unreasonable constraint. In other words, the functioning norms and modalities of journalism are necessarily impacted upon by the atmospherics in which it functions.

A journalist of another generation had given a description, in contrasting expressions, on the role of the press in different societies:

> The role of the press in a democracy is different from that in a totalitarian state. Democracy is government by law; a totalitarian state is government by authority; in the former decisions are arrived at by discussion, and in the latter by dictation; in the former the press acts as a check on authority, in the latter it is the hand maid of authority; in the former the press makes the people to think, in the latter to obey without question; in the former the press is necessarily to be free, as without free press there is no free discussion, in the latter the press supports authority.[3]

This provides the rationale for journalism in a democracy. A simple description of its functions is to inform, educate, guide and entertain. Each of these is a valid and essential function, more so in modern societies whose size and numbers need means of communication other than direct face-to-face ones. This is sustained by law. The Supreme Court has held that

> the fundamental freedom under Article 19(1)(a) can be reasonably restricted only for the purposes mentioned in Article 19(2) and the restriction must be justified on the anvil of necessity and not the quirks of convenience or expediency. Open criticism of Government policies and operations is not a ground for restricting expression. We must practice

tolerance to the views of others. Intolerance is as much dangerous to democracy as to the person himself.[4]

The legacy of our freedom movement includes a distinguished record of the role of the Indian press. Gandhiji was probably the first editor to have started a newspaper for the express purpose of breaking the law governing the publication of newspapers. This mood was well reflected in the Urdu couplet:

Khanjar na nikalo na talwar nikalo
Jab top muqabil ho to akhbar nikalo

(Resort to neither dagger nor sword
When confronted by cannons, bring out a newspaper)

The consequences of this in non-democratic setups can be troublesome. Some in this audience may recall that the Intelligence Bureau of the British Indian government kept a close watch on politically provocative poems. Some years ago a researcher in the National Archives published a selection of these.

It was therefore not surprising that independent India set up a Press Commission in 1952 whose first recommendation was to safeguard the freedom of the press and help the press maintain its independence and adopt practices and procedures to this end. Its report in 1959 was given legislative shape by the Press Council Act, 1965. The underlying logic was Gandhiji's caution that 'an uncontrolled pen serves but to destroy' and Nehru's observation that 'if there is no responsibility and no obligation attached to it, freedom gradually withers away'.

A second Press Commission was set up in 1978. Its report in 1982 put the focus on development and opined that a responsible press could also be a free press and vice versa. It recommended that the newspaper business should be separated from industries and commercial interests; that there should be a Board of Trustees between editors and proprietors of the newspaper; that there should be a fixed proportion of news and advertisement in small, medium and big newspapers and the Government should prepare a stable Advertisement Policy.

While the Press Council's charter aims to preserve the freedom of the press and maintain and improve the standards of press in India, it has no authority as a quasi-judicial body to impose punishments or enforce its directions for professional or ethical violations. Its objectives nevertheless remain laudable. Thus the 2010 guidelines state

> The media today does not remain satisfied as the Fourth Estate, it has assumed the foremost importance in society and governance. Such is the influence of media that it can make or unmake any individual, institution or any thought. So all pervasive and all-powerful is today its impact on the society. With so much power and strength, the media cannot lose sight of its privileges, duties and obligations.

II

What is the ground reality? Is this being done, and to what extent?

The socio-economic changes of recent decades have highlighted a facet of the Fourth Estate that was less adequately appreciated earlier. The media now has an identifiable business and commercial persona and has been integrated in the market. Today's media organizations are large business entities with thousands of employees and huge financial and other assets. While their primary professional duty is to their readership for keeping them informed and apprised of the news, views and ideas, the commercial logic brings in a new set of stakeholders; I refer to the shareholders of these companies.

These developments have brought into play a new set of considerations that guide the professional decisions of the press. The days of the great editors who had a decisive say in newspaper policy on public issues are perhaps a matter of the past; instead, we have a basket of considerations in which the demands of professional journalism are carefully balanced with the interests of owners and stakeholders of media companies and their cross-media interests.

The interplay of these conflicting demands is evident and subject of public debate. The phenomenal growth in the media industry, and intense competition in it, induces journalists and their supervisors to look as much at the top line and bottom line growth as at headlines and editorial content. An eminent journalist observed some time back, 'Even editors who support the liberalization of the Indian economy have become increasingly concerned over the growing control that advertisers wield over news content' and had expressed the apprehension that the media's 'growing distance from its historic role as the provider of public information threatens to transform communities of citizens into islands of consumers'.[5]

A perusal of the print and electronic media today is suggestive of the tilting balance between news and advertising content and the fading distinction between editorials and advertorials. The emergence of the Internet and 24×7 television as also of social media reporting have put additional pressure on the print media.

The phenomenon is global. Earlier this year a former editor of the *Guardian* newspaper, Alan Rusbridger, wrote a book on the remaking of journalism and concluded that 'journalists no longer have a near monopoly on news and the means of distribution' and that 'journalism has to rethink its methods; reconfigure its relationship with the new kaleidoscope of other voices. It has to be more open about what it does and how it does it'.[6]

At the other end of the spectrum, we have the development of grassroot journalism, subject of an interesting study by Alan Gillmor two years before Twitter was born. He opined that

> tomorrow's news reporting and production will be more of a conversation . . . The lines will blur between producers and consumers, changing the role of both in ways we're only beginning to grasp now. The communication network itself will be a medium for everyone's voice, not just the few who can afford to buy multimillion-dollar printing presses, launch satellites, or win the government's permission to squat on the public's airwaves.[7]

Some aspects of this paradigm shift in the production, transmission, and consumption of media products are worthy of mention.

Technology is value neutral. It is only an instrumentality and not a panacea. The work of defining and implementing a value system and a vision for an organization, a society or polity cannot be substituted by technology.

The collision of journalism and technology is having major consequences for three constituencies: journalists, newsmakers, and the audience. The evidence seems persuasive that something big has happened.

The convergence between news media, entertainment and social media has eroded the demarcation between journalism, public relations, advertising and entertainment. It is a continuum of information in which traditional definitions of news overlap and blur.

This has created new ethical dilemmas that lie at the core of many issues of public debate today and pose questions: who sets the terms of the public debate? Is there enough media space for the marginalized, the disposed and the vulnerable? Have sections of the media developed stereotypes of reportable subjects? Has the media upheld the social and political compact that our people have given to them through our Constitution?

It is not clear where public interest ends and private interest begins; where profit ends and the not-for-profit begins; where government ends and the non-government begins; where one's fist ends and the other's nose begins. There are no easy answers to these questions. The room for introspection remains. This has to take into account the political atmospherics of society.

III

Our democratic State structure dedicated to pursue a development model premised on justice, equality and fraternity is in reality, as Rajni Kothari put it, 'characterized by the politicization of a fragmented social structure through a wide dispersal and permeation of political forms, values and ideologies'. Others have spoken of institutional decay and cancerous growth within them. One observer of the national scene has resorted to a line from the poet Yeats to describe the situation: 'The best lack all conviction while the worst are full of passionate intensity.' Lost in the process is Ambedkar's focus on public conscience and the observance of constitutional morality. There has been some debate of late about this latter term but, as a former judge of the Supreme Court has observed, it comes under three aspects: equality, liberty and dignity.[8]

This general malaise across all sections of society has its media version. The World Press Freedom Index for 2018 based on a set of known parameters including media independence, transparency and violence against media persons has given India a ranking of 138 in a total of 180 countries. It was 136 a year earlier and 105 in 2009. Similarly, the Freedom of Press report of the Freedom House categorizes India as 'party free' with an overall score of 43 (out of 100). The Press Council of India is dismissive of these rankings but does not assign reasons for it.

Violence against journalists remains a matter of serious concern. It has two aspects: firstly, violence by those in segments of the militant public who do not want coverage of misdeeds, the case of Gauri Lankesh, the radical editor who was assassinated in September 2017, being the most condemnable instance of it; and secondly by the authorities in the shape of local security forces who do not want the media to report strong-arm tactics used against public expressions of outrage in specific happenings. Correctives to the latter are few and rarely prompt, as in the Hashimpura killings case[9] of 1986. In most of these, there is usually State complicity in acts of omission or commission. Both transgress what the law permits; both violate the rule of law.

Some writings in the media are candid about a crisis of credibility, internal constraints, curtailment of dissent and an atmosphere of intimidation highlighted by specific instances of violence. Veteran journalist Karan Thapar has also attributed this to lack of economic security: 'If you challenge the government you run the risk of losing your job. Yet for many this is not just their livelihood but the anchor of their (and sometimes their families) existence.'[10] Pronouncements of government personalities are occasionally suggestive of derision of the media. The phenomenon of fake news, 'alternate facts' and trolling has added to it in good measure. O.P. Rawat, a former Chief Election Commissioner has recently commented on the adverse impact 'in a big way' on voter behaviour in elections and the need 'to bring in a robust mechanism for conduct of social media platforms'.[11]

In most cases, the working conditions of journalists are not in consonance of legal requirements, and this has its impact on their work. Some might recall that in hearings before the Parliamentary Standing Committee on Information Technology (whose report was submitted in May 2013) a witness had observed that 'there are two types of journalists, those who are not influenced by ideals and principles of journalism, they are happy; and those want to be really journalists, they are unhappy'.

An instance of the despicable practice of 'paid news' came to public notice a few months ago in the revelation by the website *Cobrapost* on the effort to influence media owners to bend content to political opinion of certain religious propensities. A single-judge high court ex parte injunction given at the behest of one of the named parties was vacated by a larger bench on the ground that the courts cannot stifle debate unless offending content is demonstrated to be malicious or palpably false. The exposure was significant enough for the Washington journal *Foreign Policy* to carry a detailed report on it which observed that it 'reveals the ease with which the Indian press seems to be willing to peddle a political agenda'.

There are others that have wider bearings. I refer to the Editors Guild's statement of 8 August this year titled *An Increasingly Challenging Environment on Freedom of the Press.* It

> condemned the manner in which the right to practice free and independent journalism is seen to be undermined by a combination of forces—some media owners' inability to withstand covert political pressure from the political establishment and frequent instances of blocking or interference in the transmission of television content that is seen to be critical of the government.

It cited specific instances, decried 'all attempts on the part of the government to interfere in the free and independent functioning of journalists, either put under pressure directly, or through the proprietors'. The statement urged media owners 'not to cow down to political pressure', described as 'Orwellian' the interference with TV signals and demanded that corrective action be taken. It decried the tendency 'on the part of the government and the political class to 'use selective denial of journalistic access as a weapon'.

What is the system's response to it? The term 'regulator' is anathema to democratic vocabulary, yet its end result can and is achieved by means indirect or subtle. One aspect of it, often invoked for reasons of convenience and/or 'national interest' is called 'the administrative truth' that on transmission to a believing media becomes 'the media truth' and the two together get transmuted in many instances into 'the judicial truth' psychologically satisfying to a believing public.

In our system, advertisements emanating from government agencies and public sector undertakings (PSUs) are a major source of income for sustenance and both are known to be used for influencing the media. Similarly, the most effective de facto media regulators happen to be the advertisers and sponsors who determine the bulk of the revenue stream of our media industry. Their aims and desired outcomes, however, might not align with public policy goals of the government or markers of public interests and may, instead, stand in opposition to them.

Each of these trends in the changed and changing media world is an instance of bending reality to convenience, to becoming a propaganda model of manufacturing consent and 'news filters' about which Chomsky and Herman have written so powerfully. Does this serve the objectives of democracy, of speaking truth to power, of journalism being the watchdog of democracy, of standing up for the rights and freedoms of citizens?

Vibrant journalism is based on professional ethics and should be the rule in a democracy, rather than the exception it has come to be. Last year an eminent former judge rightly observed that 'the strength of a nation is not gauged by the uniformity of its citizens (but) is revealed when it does not feel threatened by its citizens expressing revolutionary views; when its citizens do not resort to violence against fellow citizens, merely for expressing a contrary view'.[12]

Anything less than this would be an admission of succumbing to pressures, governmental or market or a mix of both however subtle; it would be tantamount to impuissance.

There is perhaps an imperative need for a Third Press Commission to examine the qualitative changes that technology and changing public perceptions have brought forth, to study the impact of cross media holding, the decline of the institution of Editor, the phenomenon of fake news and to find ways to strengthen the media, while ensuring its financial independence alongside its editorial independence.

Allow me to conclude. I have ventured to give expression to thoughts of a concerned citizen about disturbing trends in dire need of correctives. A couplet of the poet Faiz Ahmad Faiz who in his various incarnations was also a journalist is expressive of my approach:

Hum sheikh na leader na sahib na sahafi
Jo khud naheen karte wo hidayat na karainge

(I am neither a sheikh, nor a leader, nor a follower, nor a journalist
I shall not recommend what I myself do not do)

13

The Ethics of Gandhi and the Dead Weight of Statecraft*

A non-historian in a houseful of those who worship at the Temple of Mnemosyne, the Greek goddess of memory, is an oddity. I accepted your invitation without considering its possible consequences and can ascribe it to an occasional propensity to succumb to temptation!

Even though history was not the discipline formally pursued by me, I confess to having dabbled in it from time to time. I recall Ibn Khaldun's dicta that 'the pasture of stupidity is unwholesome for mankind' and that the historian, in his quest for truth, should 'lift the veil' from the condition of the previous generations to 'wash his hands of any blind trust in tradition'.

History and particularly recent history thus remain critically relevant to our daily life, to the perceptions that shape our approach to contemporary questions and to the lessons that we tend to draw from proximate or distant past.

Our subject today is India and the making of modern India. The subcontinent as an entity can be defined geographically in geological terms and as sufficiently ancient in cultural terms. In political terms, however, its contours are recent. The historical process of the latter, as depicted by Tilak and some others of that period, was a nation in the making. Nationhood, therefore, could not be taken for granted and had to be constantly developed and consolidated. This process was undertaken by the freedom movement which defined its diverse identity and plurality and provided a platform for its articulation.

---

* Address to the History Congress panel on 'Mahatma Gandhi and the Making of the Indian Nation', organized by the Indian History Congress at Bhopal on Wednesday, 27 February 2019.

This nation-in-the-making exercise necessarily had many dimensions. It meant freedom from constraints as also the freedom to act in pursuit of certain desired objectives. The struggle to be free to decide our own destiny involved in the first place a moral and ethical judgment about the desirability of freedom. Next to it was the question of methodology: how to achieve this objective and how not to proceed in pursuit of it.

The religio-philosophical legacy of the Indian civilization was an existential reality and had its impact in varying degrees on Indian minds. The initiation and consolidation of the British rule in India also resulted in the emergence of a class of Indians who imbibed modern education and familiarized themselves with many of the principles that were being articulated in the philosophical, political and legal debates in the world beyond our borders. Both these streams of thought influenced those who led our freedom movement; both impacted on the ideas of the Mahatma.

Gandhiji once told an interlocutor that 'most religious men I have met are politicians in disguise; I, however, who wear the guise of a politician am at heart a religious man. My bent is not political but religious'. He said to him religion meant not a particular creed but 'belief in the ordered moral government of the universe and is identical with morality' that has to be embedded in truth.[1]

How did Gandhi express this in practical terms? He looked upon politics as an unavoidable evil involving the control and use of state authority which is essentially coercive. 'If I seem to take part in politics', he said, 'it is only because politics today encircles us like the coil of a snake from which one cannot get out no matter how one tries. I wish to wrestle with the snake . . . I am trying to introduce religion into politics.'[2] By religion he meant not a particular faith but the underlying principles that harmonize all faiths.

The Raj Ghat at New Delhi is visited reverentially by the public, ritually by public figures and out of curiosity by tourists. A little away from the Samadhi is a stone tablet with the inscription: *Seven Social Sins*. These are listed on the tablet:

- Politics without principle
- Pleasure without conscience
- Wealth without work
- Knowledge without character
- Commerce without morality

- Science without humanity
- Worship without sacrifice

Each of these is a statement of principle that can be comprehended, interpreted and implemented, individually and collectively. On my part, I would like to discern a pattern in the last words of each dictum: *principle, conscience, work, character, morality, humanity* and *sacrifice*. A similar pattern, summing up different forms of human activity, is discernable when the first words of the statements are put together.

In the Gandhian approach, therefore, conscience is motivated by considerations of humanity and sacrifice to develop a moral character that holds aloft in its work the banner of a principled approach. The reverse of it would be selfishness inducing an unprincipled, opportunistic approach to work. The latter would produce neither justice nor humaneness. On this approach, the choice would be clear if the human being is a moral creature with a sense of right and wrong in his or her individual and group conduct.

Gandhi's philosophy dealt with the method of regulating, along non-violent lines, group life in its political, economic, national and international aspects. Thus, the Gandhian State was meant to be a non-violent State in which authority would be diffused and would perform its functions with a minimum of coercion.

Here we are confronted by a set of questions:

- Can the principles of public morality be different from those of private morality?
- Can a society have one set of ethical norms for governing the conduct of public institutions and another set of norms for citizens in their individual capacities?
- Is the State required to observe norms of behaviour in its functioning (a) in relation to its citizens; and (b) in inter-State relations?

In the Gandhian approach, the answer is in the negative to the first two questions and in the affirmative for the third. In other words, the theory of morality has to be a unified one rather than occasion-differentiated. Such an approach would be in consonance with Gandhi's philosophy of a code of morality which is universally applicable; it would also embody the essence of the Preamble to our Constitution and the injunctions in Articles 51 and 51A. The alternative, of having different sets of principles for judging an individual's or a society's moral or legal actions, can only promote legal confusion or amoral or immoral judgments that may tide over specific situations but could end up doing longer term damage to a society's ethos.

It will of course be argued, as Lord Gray did in 1828, 'I am a great lover of morality, public and private, but the intercourse of nations cannot be strictly regulated by that rule.'[3] This, however, is a slippery slope and has been used down the ages for State conduct that violated the norms of legality. The global community, in any case, has in recent decades moved some distance towards the development of normative standards, however imperfect, be they in human rights, environmental protection or even brazen use of force.

An instance of the deadweight of statecraft is the debate on the law of sedition—Section 124A of the Indian Penal Code. It was drafted by our colonial masters to suppress expression of opinion not to the liking of the government. Gandhiji accepted the charge and caused consternation with the presiding judge calling him 'a man of high ideals and of noble and even saintly life'. A good number of freedom fighters contested the charge of sedition brilliantly. When it came up for discussion in the Lok Sabha in May 1951 Prime Minister Nehru said 'so far as I am concerned that particular section is highly objectionable and obnoxious and it should have no place both for practical and historical reasons'. Notwithstanding this, it has remained on the statute book till now and has been used frequently enough against those who articulate views not to the liking of the authorities. It was only in July last year that the Law Commission of India initiated a Consultation Paper to ascertain views on 'public friendly amendments' to the law 'so that it is not misused to curb free speech'.

On individual conduct in public affairs, modern India's record can only be described as patchy. There is enough in the public domain to substantiate it. I have only to mention official documents like the Vohra Committee Report of 1993 and the Ethics in Governance Report of the 2nd Administrative Reforms Commission of 2007. No less scathing is the Transparency International India's Report of the same year. Together they bring out the moral crisis in the ranks of public figures involved in statecraft. Nothing has happened since then to belie these perceptions.

Individual conduct apart, what then has been the record of the Indian State in such matters? The Constitution prescribed a set of rights and duties. We dedicated ourselves to the concept of the rule of law and established legislative, executive and judicial institutions to implement these principles. Together they constitute a charter of citizenship that would pass, it was hoped, the test of Gandhian principles. And yet, credible observers have spoken of the rule of law being under serious threat and of 'cancerous developments eating into the fabric of each institution'.[4] This is a far cry from what Professor Upendra Baxi has sought to read in the rule of law as going beyond a mere division of functions in modes of governance; to him, it is the rule of good law and is as such reflective of the struggle of a people 'to make power accountable, governance just, and state ethical'.[5] He adds that the Indian constitutional conception of the rule of law links its four core notions: rights, development, governance and justice.

Our failure on these counts is thus writ large; the saving grace is our dedication to them, even as distant horizons.

Alongside, our commitment to liberal democracy reflective of the ground reality of a plural society is being diluted in favour of an illiberal or ethnic one premised on cultural vigilantism and its attendant consequences. The Preamble enjoins us to secure Fraternity; instead, today we have pervasive intolerance forgetting Gandhi's observation that 'intolerance betrays want of faith in one's own cause'.

The nation-in-the-making exercise has clearly deviated from its Gandhian premises even if ritual homage to Gandhi continues to be offered year after year. One can fervently hope that this nation in the making is not leading us to being a nation of hypocrites.

14

India's Plural Diversity Is under Threat

Some Thoughts on Contemporary Challenges in the Realm of Culture*

Writing is the product of hard work. It requires a sensitivity to register and interpret human experience. This gathering of writers knows only too well the role they and their writings play in shaping public taste and consciousness just as their predecessors did in earlier times. A good work of literature creates a stream of consciousness; a bad one evokes contempt and cynicism. Writers generally work in time and space; those blessed with deeper insight transcend these boundaries.

Writers thus have a social responsibility since their work influences and helps shape public perceptions. The reading public, consciously or otherwise, judges the social purpose, intellectual depth and emotional sincerity of their writings. Their work is and should be reflective of contemporary cultural mores and of national identity.

We thus come to the critical question: What is Indian national identity?

There could be two ways of answering the question: the first would be a priori or deductive, independent of experience or facts; the second would be inductive, based on facts and experience.

The first, on assumed infallibility of tradition, suggests uniformity, homogeneity, oneness; the second, based on ground reality, identifies diversity, heterogeneity, complexity.

It is a truism that all perceptions have to be tested on discernable facts. What then is the factual reality of the Indian social landscape?

---

* Address at the inauguration of the national seminar on 'Nationalism and Culture: A Dialogue' at Punjab Kala Bhavan, Chandigarh, 28 October 2017.

The Anthropological Survey of India indicates that our land has 4,635 communities diverse in biological traits, dress, languages, form of worship, occupation, food habits and kinship patterns. The Linguistic Survey of India indicates that apart from the 22 languages in the Eighth Schedule of the Constitution, there are 100 other languages and thousands of dialects in the country.

As a result, the identity of India is plural and diverse, a consequence of coming together of people with such different social and cultural traits. It is this plurality that constitutes Indian identity expressed in the Constitution through the principles of democracy and secularism. It is not a melting pot because each ingredient retains its identity. It is perhaps a salad bowl. Jawaharlal Nehru said it is a palimpsest on which the imprint of succeeding generations has unrecognizably merged.

For the same reason, Indian culture is not to be conceived as a static phenomenon tracing its identity to a single unchanging source; instead, it is dynamic and interrogates critically and creatively all that is new.

This, friends, then is the reality. Can we homogenize it? Can we initiate a process of assimilation? In a democratic polity, how is any ingredient to be subsumed in another? Can we visualize an India that is non-democratic, non-plural, non-secular?

Why then is an effort underway to subsume diversity in a notional identity? Is its purpose to erase, subjugate or dominate this diversity and replace it with an imagined uniformity based on a version of history that corresponds neither to the authentic record of India's past nor to the rich diversity of her present?

Alternatively, our approach could be accommodative based on the principles of pluralism and secularism with three ingredients:

- Energetic engagement with diversity, educating all sections of the public, particularly students, about the uniqueness of our structure and the benefits flowing from it.
- Going beyond mere tolerance, seeking active understanding across lines of differences and considering community disharmony a threat to national security and dealing with it in the same manner as other such threats.
- Having a continuous inter-community, inter-faith and cross-cultural dialogue, of speaking and listening in a process that reveals both common understanding and real differences.

History thus itself has becomes a site for struggle; it draws within its ambit all those who register and interpret human experience, particularly writers. As citizens they cannot remain oblivious to what happens in the polity. While remaining committed to their chosen art, their social responsibility requires that they use their art to guide the public and lead them out of the poisonous haze of ignorance, superstition and unreasoned prejudice and to ensure that our secular culture and liberal democracy are preserved.

Friends, we live in difficult times. The hitherto accepted norms of Indian culture are being re-packaged, distorted out of shape. The values of liberal nationalism are sought to be substituted by illiberal doctrines and practices that impact adversely on individual freedoms guaranteed by the Constitution of India. All citizens, particularly those who mould public perceptions through their work, need to respond to this challenge.

India has an age-old tradition of religious and philosophical dissent and of bringing forth multiple traditions of authenticity. Indians take pride in being argumentative. Again and again our writers have penned anthems of resistance; many have recalled the words of Faiz Ahmad Faiz's clarion call in the poem *Bol*.

bol ki lab āzād haiñ tere
bol zaban ab tak teri hai

15

Some Thoughts on the Dichotomies of Our Times

The Philosophy of Guru Nanak*

This international conference is focused on the life and teachings of an iconic personality, the founder of a faith who was a model for emulation, a mediator between the divine and human realms who devoted his life to bringing hope to anxious human beings in a period of turmoil and despair.

The simplicity and power of his teachings, endowed with practical common sense rather than high philosophy, is compelling. It is based on the acceptance of one God, present in every object of His creation. Baba Nanak advocated brotherhood of all humans, espoused the cause of the downtrodden and advocated what in modern terminology is called interfaith dialogue.

Faith, as we know, is a powerful motivator in human behaviour. It manifests itself in different ways: as a source of spiritual power that brings forth the noblest in human character; the same adherence to faith however can do the reverse when it emerges as a motivator for lesser objectives. The challenge for humans at every stage of history has been to promote the former and control the latter.

Religious faiths today tend to get involved with contemporary global conditions and in our collective imagination of what our values are and what we deem to be a society that fosters human well-being.

---

* Centre for Research in Rural and Industrial Development, Chandigarh, 7 November 2019.

Zbigniew Brzezinski, an eminent strategic thinker, had observed in his book *Out of Control*[1] that towards the end of the 20th century that it was a century characterized by arrogant assertions of total righteousness and imagined Utopia, resulting in a period of organized insanity and deaths on a massive scale. He had expressed the hope that the 21st century would bring forth a corrective by making humanity overcome the crisis of the spirit.

A quarter of a century later, we have to admit that this expectation was misplaced even if his diagnosis was accurate. If anything, the situation has deteriorated globally. Lost in the process among other things are the teachings of promoting peace, harmony and human happiness that were the essence of Baba Nanak's message.

The challenge today is to revive them and find common threads in the teachings of all faith systems.

How is this to be done?

It is evident that many societies today are victims of two pandemics that impact their behaviour patterns. One is 'religiosity' and the other 'strident nationalism'.

Religiosity is defined as extreme religious ardour denoting exaggerated embodiment, involvement or zeal for certain aspects of religious activity enforced through social or even governmental pressure.

A scrutiny of the historical record would show that the founders of faiths and religious systems themselves did not exhibit religiosity, nor did they place any right or duty above the base moral precepts. Their followers may have done so and diluted or corrupted the teachings.

Nationalism means identifying oneself with a single nation placing it beyond good and evil, right or wrong, suspending individual judgment, and recognizing no other duty than of advancing its perceived interests. It is often confused with patriotism and used interchangeably. Both are words of unstable and explosive content and so need to be handled with care since they differ in meaning and content.

Nationalism in its strident form is inseparable from the desire for power. It is an 'ideological poison' that has no hesitation in transcending and transgressing individual rights. Its record the world over shows that it at times takes the form of hatred as a tonic that inspires vengeance as mass ideology.

Decades earlier, Rabindranath Tagore had called nationalism 'a great menace' and described it as 'one of the most powerful anaesthetics that man has invented'.[2] He had expressed himself against 'the idolatry of the nation'. Albert Einstein considered it 'an infantile disease'.[3]

Patriotism, on the other hand, is defensive both militarily and culturally. It inspires nobler sentiments but must not be allowed to run amuck since in that condition it 'will trample the very values that the country seeks to defend'.[4]

Thus, humanity can be saved only if both pandemics are evaded to overcome the global crisis of the spirit and replaced by human behaviour in the light of our collective experience and people seek moral guidance directed at achieving common good.

We therefore have to begin by proclaiming a new triad that (a) religion is not politics; (b) that religiosity is not religion; and (c) that peace, harmony and happiness can emanate only from adherence to principles of justice in human dealings with each other at the individual and group levels—local, national and international.

Similarly, in a world full of sovereign State entities, espousing strident nationalism cannot but propel them to violence or the threat of violence and result in a fragile framework that would not be in consonance with the global order we are seeking to build on agreed principles of cooperation and for the mutual benefit for humankind.

The conclusion is unavoidable that both religiosity and strident nationalism are undesirable. Alternatives to both are within human reach. We are thus driven to accept the logic of the teaching of all religious personalities who have taught us that the salvation of humanity and of human happiness lies in the promotion of peace and harmony through tolerance, dialogue, accommodation and acceptance.

Tolerance is a virtue but insufficient unless accompanied by acceptance of the 'other'. Without it, accommodation is unachievable and in our plural polity, the 'Other' has to be none other than the 'Self'. Any derogation from it is detrimental to its core values.

For an effective dialogue, we need to appreciate the force of traditional cosmological models and the force of the sense of participation in an order greater than the individual. In such a dialogue the religious practitioners need to share a language of understanding that draws on cultural values both parties agree to name, namely a framework ensured by the modern, secular state and developed within a framework of human rights.

This is the universal message of Baba Nanak that must be reiterated.

16

Sins and Sinners

Where Did It Go Wrong?*

I

Yaad-e-maazi azaab hai yaa Rab
Cheen le mujhse hafiza mera

(The memory of the past is torturous, O God
Take away my memory from me)

The late Fakhruddin Ali Ahmad saheb belonged to and represented another era in the life of modern India. He participated in the freedom movement and occupied high offices in state and central governments, including the highest. It was my privilege to receive him in Abu Dhabi when he paid a State visit to the United Arab Emirates in October 1976.

My generation grew up in that period of the early years of independence and imbibed the values enshrined in the Constitution of India which itself was a product of the freedom struggle and the principles on which it was conducted. In a plural landscape, we sought to shape a secular polity, create a liberal democracy premised on the principles of Justice, Liberty, Equality and Fraternity to preserve the heritage of our composite culture and develop a scientific temper.

In a thought-provoking book a few years ago, the historian Ananya Vajpeyi wrote:

---

* Fakhruddin Ali Ahmed Memorial Lecture on 19 July 2019, Aiwan-e-Ghalib, New Delhi.

What is valuable in the idea of India and what makes India worth preserving is not just its modern political form of a plural, secular, egalitarian democracy, but its legacy of centuries of reflection on the avenues available to the human mind to transcend the suffering inherent in the human condition . . . Free India, India that has won its swaraj, the India hard fought for and envisioned by extraordinary figures like Gandhi and Ambedkar, Tagore and Nehru, was the dream of realizing both the norm of righteousness and the form of a republic. Accounts of its quest for sovereignty I found aplenty. I wanted to track its still elusive search for the self.[1]

More recently, she has bemoaned the most damaging impact in recent years of 'the slow, steady erosion of empathy as a public value, leaving us morally impoverished—lesser human beings and lesser Indians'.[2]

The India of today, I confess, appears to be a very different place in its perception, articulation and practice. Above all, sections of opinion are purposefully involved in disowning the past, re-writing parts of it, distorting it to create new idols and ideas. Old India, it is claimed, is dead, that 40 per cent of voters are now middle class, that their 'aspirations' are understood by the Leader, and that it represents a triumph of chemistry over arithmetic. Less candidly, the ideology of a 'cultural' organization has been injected in segments of public opinion and has been imbibed almost imperceptibly in the name of the 'nation' and 'national security'.

In a recently published book, Niraja Gopal Jayal, a political scientist and scholar of eminence has observed that 'in a short space of four years, India has made a very long journey. It has travelled from its founding vision of civic nationalism to a new political imaginary of cultural nationalism that appears to be firmly embedded in the public realm'.[3]

Why has this happened? Why has a plural society, with a long tradition of accommodation of diversity reflected with some care in its Constitution, decided to abandon it in favour of a unilateral and distorted reading of its own past? Why is it attempting to rewrite the history of its own freedom struggle and the values enshrined in it?

Some careful observers of the Indian scene have attributed the changes underway to populism, authoritarianism, nationalism and majoritarianism.[4] Each of these requires careful scrutiny:

Populism: Two years ago an article in the US magazine *Atlantic* shed light on its contours. It is not an ideology but a strategy to obtain and retain power. It is divisive, thrives on conspiracy, find enemies even when they do not exist, criminalizes all opposition to them and plays up external threats.

In such an approach success is sure, as Mark Twain would have said, through a combination of ignorance and confidence.

Authoritarianism in government denotes the concentration of power in the hands of a leader or small elite to the detriment of well-settled procedures of governance.

Nationalism is often confused with patriotism and used interchangeably. Both, in the words of George Orwell, are 'unstable and explosive content and so need to be handled with care'. They differ in meaning and content, as Orwell pointed out many years ago. Nationalism means identifying oneself with a single nation placing it beyond good and evil and recognizing no other duty than of advancing its interests; patriotism, on the other hand, is devotion to a particular place or way of life without wishing to force it on others.

Thus, patriotism is of its nature defensive both militarily and culturally; and nationalism is inseparable from the desire for power. It is an 'ideological poison' that has no hesitation in transcending and transgressing individual rights.

Decades earlier Rabindranath Tagore had called nationalism 'a great menace', described it as 'one of the most powerful anesthetics that man has invented.' He had expressed himself against 'the idolatry of the nation'.

Majoritarianism in the Indian context implies that a religious majority is entitled to primacy in society and has the right by virtue of it to take basic decisions relating to the whole society. This is very different from an electoral majority emanating from an electoral process whose results are time specific and subject to periodic review in a democratic system. Implicit in this approach is the propensity to sidestep or override the basic principle of equality enshrined in Article 14 of the Constitution. Thus, it is the antithesis of equality and justice and its emerging manifestations have been commented upon in public discourse and in debates in the current session of Parliament.

Some questions arise here:

- Has populism and demagoguery resulted from a lack of performance?
- Why have democratic procedures and commitment to rule of law failed giving rise to the need for authoritarianism?

- Why are the constitutional principles of equality, justice and fraternity tending to become subservient to the 'majoritarian' impulses of the electoral majority in a first-past-the-post system?
- What new impulses have made way for strident nationalism?

Where, in short, does the responsibility for the '*sin*' of letting down the ideological and administrative system lie? Who are the '*sinners*'?

Guilt, according to the philosopher Karl Jaspers, has categories: criminal, political, moral and metaphysical. Where would we be justified in placing it?

Dekhā to sab ke ser pe gunāhoñ kā bojh tha

(Every head bears the burden of sins)

II

Societies have changed course in the past either as a result of external aggression and cultural imposition or from internal ideological and spiritual convulsions.

Post-mortems are a gruesome business, more so of recent social and political happenings. Our generation took the post-independence developments as given. The Partition and its aftermath were indeed painful, but we took the decisions of our elders as irreversible even if their judgment was not infallible. We took pride in the Constitution given to us by the Constituent Assembly and often paid lip service to it forgetting Ambedkar's warning about a 'life of contradictions', and about his caution on conditions precedent for the successful working of democracy listed as (i) no glaring inequalities; (ii) need for a strong opposition; (iii) equality in law and administration; (iv) observance of constitutional morality; (v) no tyranny of majority over minority; (vi) functioning of a moral order in society; and (vii) a strong presence of public conscience.

Above all, we soft-peddled the quiet impulses in society directed at subverting these very egalitarian principles that sought to allow the principles of justice, equality and fraternity to take roots.

We did the same with institutions of the state—legislative, executive, judicial—so diligently crafted and premised on rule of law that links the notions of rights, development, governance and justice and is defined as the absolute supremacy of regular law, equality before the law, and access to justice.

Much earlier, in fact at the moment of birth, Josh Malihabadi had summed up the corrosive behaviour patterns in society:

Wahshat rava, anaad rava, dushmani rava
Halchal rava, kharosh rava, sunsani rava

(Abhorrence is valid, so is dishonour and enmity
Disturbance is valid, so is sensation and tumult)

Rishwat rava, fasaad rava, rehzani rava
Al qissa har woh shai ki hai nakardani rava

(Bribery is valid, so is disturbance and loot
In fact, everything that should not be done is valid)

So, across the board and in each of the critical areas of national activity, our performance as a people has often been wanting and at times abysmal. We professed but did not practice faith in a set of moral values and in institutions crafted to implement them. We undermined them by our behaviour and selfishness; rule of law, said a senior law officer in 2005, was 'under serious threat' and 'each institution is destroying itself from within' and that 'there are cancerous developments eating into the fabric of each institution. If these trends are not arrested, they are bound to be destructive of the Indian State in the long run'.[5]

We did make material progress. Many good schemes and programs for economic development were made but poorly implemented. Uneven development has characterized our performance. We are listed 130th in the Global Human Development Index (2018) and as the 12th most inequitable economy in the world.

There have of course been good patches and commendable performances, but these were not sustained. Collectively and perhaps unconsciously, we allowed the seeds of discontent to take roots.

In the recent election campaign, much was said with justice about rural distress, unemployment, declining levels of foreign investments and exports performance. The interesting thing is that opposition assertions about the poor state of the economy, belied by the government during the campaign, have been accepted as correct after the publication of results!

We witnessed the same process with other economic measures like the return of black money. Could there be better examples of chicanery?

Most of us would not have heard of Edward Bernays. He died in 1995 and was considered the father of propaganda in the United States. He wrote a short tract in 1928 entitled *Propaganda*. Its opening lines were:

> The conscious and intelligent manipulation of the organized habits and opinions of the masses is an important element in democratic society. Those who manipulate this unseen mechanism of society constitute an invisible government which is the true ruling power of our country.

Propaganda, he said, is of no use to the politician unless he has something to say which the public, consciously or unconsciously, wants to hear. He also observed that 'the engineering of consent is the very essence of the democratic process, the freedom to persuade and to suggest'.

The moulding of the public mind by a public figure or a demagogue is not an unknown phenomenon and has been witnessed in recent times. Much earlier, a poet had depicted the style that beggared all description:

> *Magar usko faraib-e-nargis-e-mastana aata hai*
> *Ulati hain safain gardish main jab parvana aata hai*

> (Her enchanting eyes, well versed in deception,
> bring about dislocation when unleashed)

Yet, the audience had to be conditioned to receive the message. This was done through a sustained process of indoctrination initiated at the pre-school, primary and secondary school levels in which culture itself was redefined and conflated with aspects of faith and selected versions of the past. A network of ideologically oriented groupings continued it at other levels in society. Their organization, resources and reach became formidable over time. Their approach, to borrow a phrase from a recent comment in the *Economist* magazine, is 'zealous, ideological and cavalier with the truth'.[6]

Created alongside was a simplistic and motivated version of the Partition blaming it on one community in a selective and slanted narration of recent history. An Indian version of 'Muslim-phobia' has been inducted in the social media discourse. In this manner an image of the 'Other' has been created to supplement the indoctrination of the minds.

This process of moulding the minds was known but not countered even when governments of other political orientation were in seats of power. This can only be attributed to an ideological vacuum or worse that seemed to have crept in, perhaps allowed to creep in. A late and simplistic corrective was of no avail and was laughed off. We lost our way and did not even realize it:

Na pucho ahd-e-ulfat ki bas ik khvab-e-pareshan tha
Na dil ko raah par laae na dil kā muddaā samjhe

(Do not enquire about the period of romance when the heart
could neither feel settled nor discern its purpose)

Secularism as a concept and as a practical instrumentality of statecraft has been subjected to sophistry and made a site for political and legal contestation without regard to its antecedent moral principles of equality, democracy, rights and freedom.

Thus, conceptually and in practice faith, history and culture were packaged and a particular orientation given to it. Ignored or underplayed was the critical point that the Indian identity was an amalgam of *identities* and that pluralism, and the attendant practices of tolerance and acceptance, was the basis on which Indian nationalism and the freedom movement took shape. The Indian reality of migrating groups seeking greener pastures since times immemorial was better depicted in a couplet:

Sar zamin-e-hind par aqwam-e-alam ke Firaq
Qafile baste gae hindostan banta gaya

(Caravans from the nations of the world kept coming, O Firaq
and India got settled)

III

Answers to our four questions are now clear. The *sin* is the betrayal of the core values of the Constitution; the *sinners* are those who professed those values but did not uphold them adequately and allowed a thoughtless use of franchise to become the instrumentality of betrayal.

It is easy retrospectively to identify the tactics resorted to. Although lack of performance and unfulfilled promises were glaring in the face of the voter, particularly the youth, it was ingeniously evaded and replaced by a toxic brew of 'national interest' and 'national security'. Its success, in the absence of sufficient facts, was facilitated by ideological indoctrination and the organization that accompanied it.

This orientation of the voter was not challenged. Instead, the ground for it seems to have been prepared over time by failures in governance and a slackening in the processes of commitment to the values of the Constitution.

Is it then surprising that the public felt disappointed, despondent and frustrated?

The implications of strident nationalism remain to be understood. Its momentary success, selectively targeted at an obdurate and ill-intentioned neighbour, is evident; less perceptible are its longer-term consequences. The pre-requisites of a 'Great Nation' vision are as yet invisible; the notion of an Akhand Bharat as depicted in a cultural organization's cartography has geopolitical and demographic consequences that may not have been thought through. India lives in a world of nation states in its own region and globally. The challenges of the future lie less in the realm of traditional interstate security and more in areas of human security—pandemics, water, environment, climate change, eradication of poverty. These require cooperation, adjustment of national demands and dictate a new mindset to address them.

Where then is the corrective? It lies in the foundational principles of the Indian polity and their diligent implementation. This is the only alternative to the hallucination induced by a 'majoritarian' ideology that threatens to overwhelm the plural, diverse, egalitarian and democratic landscape we relish and cherish. The hallucinatory virus, let it be admitted, may have seeped into the bloodstream and through it to the interstices of the heart and the mind; it would therefore require a sufficiently powerful antidote that has to have effective alternatives on national and global issues.

Can the amnesia, the compromises and the misperceptions of recent and not so recent past be overcome? Yes, only if a meaningful alternative is offered.

We do stand at the crossroads.

17

Journalism in Times of Strident Nationalism*

I

Boobli George Verghese was a journalist of eminence. To his contemporaries, he was more; a concerned citizen and a man of conscience who firmly believed that journalism at its best involved a ferocious scrutiny of power.

He lived and worked in post-independent India. He witnessed and at times participated in the crafting of a modern Indian State on a vision considered unique by the world—of building on the existential reality of a plural society, a democratic polity with a secular state structure. He crafted a place for himself in the world of the media and also had time to reflect upon the role of the Indian media in changing times.

He was perceptive enough to observe that

> as India's multitudinous but hitherto dormant diversities come to life, identities are asserted and jostle for a place in the sun. Issues of majority and minority, centre and periphery, great and little traditions, rural and urban values, tradition and modernity and all of Naipaul's million mutinies have to be negotiated and managed. This management of diversity within multiple transitions is a delicate and complex process aggravated by inexorable population growth.[1]

II

The media informs, educates even entertains. In a democracy, it plays an important role in the formation, projection and dissemination of public

---

* B.G. Verghese Memorial Lecture, March 2019.

opinion. It is, or should be, a guardian of public interest, an honest witness to events, a tool to hold government accountable to the people. It is meant to be a bridge between the people and the government by facilitating dialogue for the formulation and implementation of State policies in accordance with the wishes of the people.

A free, fair, honest and objective media is a potent instrument for enhancing transparency and accountability on all sides. Freedom of the media is thus one of the most important ingredients of democracy and reflects the character of the State. For the media to play its designated role, it must be impartial and unprejudiced in coverage of news and views connected with all segments of society. It must not be subservient to vested interests, nor be distorted by them. If it has a specific orientation, it must say so candidly.

Some months ago I had occasion to recall what a journalist of another generation had said on the role of the press in different societies. I seek your indulgence to recall it here:

> The role of the press in a democracy is different from that in a totalitarian state. Democracy is government by law; [a] totalitarian state is government by authority; in the former decisions are arrived at by discussion, and in the latter by dictation; in the former the press acts as a check on authority, in the latter it is the handmaid of authority; in the former the press makes the people think, in the latter to obey without question; in the former the press necessarily [has] to be free, as without [a] free press there is no free discussion, in the latter the press supports authority.[2]

This provides the rationale for journalism in a democracy. The Constitution and its Preamble make evident the nature of our democracy. It is dedicated to the attainment of Justice, Liberty, Equality and Fraternity for the People of India. Its various functions based on these principles are valid and essential, more so in a modern society whose size and numbers need means of communication other than direct face to face ones. This is sustained by law. The Supreme Court has held

> The fundamental freedom under Article 19(1)(a) can be reasonably restricted only for the purposes mentioned in Articles 19(2) and the restriction must be justified on the anvil of necessity and not the quirks and of convenience or expediency. Open criticism of Government

policies and operations is not a ground for restricting expression. We must practice tolerance to the views of others. Intolerance is as much dangerous to democracy as to the person himself.[3]

Yet, it has not been smooth sailing. Our democratic State structure dedicated to the pursuit of a development model premised on justice, equality and fraternity is in reality, as Rajni Kothari put it, 'characterized by the politicization of a fragmented social structure through a wide dispersal and permeation of political forms, values and ideologies'. Others have spoken of institutional decay and cancerous growth within them. One observer of the national scene has resorted to a line from the poet W.B. Yeats to describe the situation: 'the best lack all conviction while the worst are full of passionate intensity.' This passionate intensity often goes beyond the lines of democratic behaviour. Lost in the process is Ambedkar's focus on public conscience and the observance of constitutional morality. There has been some debate of late about this latter term but, as a former judge of the Supreme Court has observed, it comes under three aspects: equality, liberty and dignity.[4]

This general malaise across all sections of society has its media version. The World Press Freedom Index for 2018 based on a set of known parameters including media independence, transparency and violence against media persons has given India a ranking of 138 in a total of 180 countries. It was 136 a year earlier and 105 in 2009. Similarly, the Freedom of Press report of the Freedom House categorizes India as 'party free' with an overall score of 43 (out of 100).

As in other walks of life, journalism functions in time and space. A former editor of the *Guardian*, Alan Rusbridger, wrote last year about contemporary challenges to journalism and about the need for journalism to regain the trust of its readers by rethinking its methods and reconfiguring its relationship with the new kaleidoscope of other voices.

> The stakes for truth have never been higher he observed. In a revealing chapter entitled 'Do You love Your Country?' he sheds some useful light on the approach that Western democracies are tending to take on matters of press freedom. These techniques and practices have been replicated in our own country with our own versions of 'manufacturing consent.

Over the years, our media has grown in size and coverage. Despite its impressive numbers and diversity, phenomena like cross-media ownership, paid news and fake news, as also the declining role of editors and their editorial freedom, do raise questions about its objectivity and credibility.

Besides these, an unstated major premise is the pervasive *national mood of strident nationalism.*

How has this come about? What are its dimensions and implications?

We need to begin with a terminological clarification. Humans are social creatures and live in societies as citizens in nations in the international system. They owe allegiance to it by legal and emotional bonds which they seek to strengthen. These bonds in normal discourse are depicted as those of patriotism and nationalism; the terms often used interchangeably. Yet the two do differ in meaning and content, as pointed out by the essayist George Orwell whose descriptions bears citation in full:

> By 'nationalism' I mean . . . the habit of identifying oneself with a single nation or other unit, placing it beyond good and evil and recognizing no other duty than that of advancing its interests. By 'patriotism' I mean devotion to a particular place and a particular way of life, which one believes to be the best in the world but has no wish to force on other people. Patriotism is of its nature defensive, both militarily and culturally. Nationalism, on the other hand, is inseparable from the desire for power. The abiding purpose of every nationalist is to secure more power and more prestige, *not* for himself but for the nation or other unit in which he has chosen to sink his own individuality.[5]

More recently, some European leaders have described nationalism as 'ideological poison' and as 'betrayal of patriotism'. For this reason, informed opinion is now suggesting the need for striking a balance. An essay in the current issue of the journal *Foreign Affairs* highlights this approach:

> Benign forms of popular nationalism follow from political inclusion. They cannot be imposed by ideological policing from above, nor by attempting to educate citizens about what they should regard as their true interests. In order to promote better forms of nationalism, leaders will have to become better nationalists, and learn to look out for the interests of all their people.[6]

Strident nationalism, on the other hand, has no hesitation in transcending and transgressing individual rights guaranteed by the Constitution. It therefore has to be guarded against and its ideological premises contested.

III

The historical process of the making of modern India was depicted as a nation in the making by Bal Gangadhar Tilak and some others of that period. Nationhood, therefore, could not be taken for granted and had to be constantly developed and consolidated. This process was undertaken by the freedom movement which provided a platform for its articulation and called it nationalism in all its diverse identity and plurality.

This nation in the making exercise necessarily had many dimensions. It meant freedom from constraints as also freedom to act in pursuit of certain desired objectives. The struggle to be free to decide our own destiny involved, in the first place, a moral and ethical judgment about the desirability of freedom. Next to it was the question of methodology; how to achieve this objective and how not to proceed in pursuit of it.

Leaders and opinion-makers of that period drew sustenance from diverse sources. The consolidation of the British rule also resulted in the emergence of a class of Indians who imbibed modern education and familiarized themselves with many of the principles that were being articulated in the philosophical, political and legal debates in the world beyond our borders. Both these streams of thought influenced those who led our freedom movement; both impacted on the ideas of Mahatma Gandhi.

How did Gandhiji express his 'belief in ordered moral government of the universe' in practical terms? He asserted, 'It is not nationalism that is evil; it is the narrowness, selfishness, exclusiveness which is the bane of modern nations, which is evil.'[7] He focused on the emotive power of nationalism to forge unity in the regional and communal diversity of India.

Rabindranath Tagore on the other hand called Nationalism 'a great menace' and 'one of the most powerful anesthetics that man has invented'; he expressed himself emphatically against 'the idolatry of nation'. Nehru on his part was opposed to bringing religion into nationalism.

Alongside, the 19th-century renaissance movements lead to an attempt to conflate ideas of Hindu cultural nationalism with mainstream nationalism. This was succinctly expressed by Sri Aurobindo in his famous *Uttarpara* speech of 30 May 1909: 'I say no longer that nationalism is a creed, a religion, a faith; I say that it is the Sanatan Dharma which for us is nationalism. The Hindu nation was born with Sanatan Dharma, with it moves and with it grows.'

Later versions of this approach have taken the shape of Hindutva as a concept of cultural revitalization and political mobilization. Hindutva, wrote Savarkar, 'is not a word but a history. Hinduism is only a derivative, a fraction, of Hindutva. Hindutva embraces all the departments of thought and activity, of the whole being of our Hindu race'.[8] Savarkar's effort was to define the two main coordinates of the Indian nation, its territoriality and its culture, and to demonstrate their congruence. Some years later, the ingredients of this concept were spelt out with greater specificity by Golwalkar who also expressed his opposition to a federal structure and desired an amendment to the Constitution to bring about a unitary form of government.

Thus, *Hindutva* has emerged as a concept of cultural revitalization and political mobilization. Its approach of ethnic specificity, in the words of sociologists D.L. Sheth and Ashis Nandy, 'seeks to subjugate and homogenize the ethnic pluralities by establishing the hegemony of an imagined cultural mainstream'.[9] It has generated social violence by some adherents of this approach.

These principles, depicting Indian nationalism in terms of the faith of the religious majority, have serious negative political implications for sections of the citizen body and are in violation of the principles of the Constitution. In the typology of democracies in social science literature, it would convert our liberal democracy based on the principle of equality into an ethnic one whose characteristics were spelt out in some detail by the sociologist Sammy Smooha on the basis of Israel's experience: (i) the dominant national discourse recognizes an ethnic group as forming the dominant core nation; (ii) the State separates membership in the single core ethnic nation from citizenship; (iii) the State is owned and ruled by the core ethnic group; (iv) the state mobilizes the core ethnic group; (v) non-core groups are accorded incomplete individual and group rights; (vi) the State allows non-core groups to conduct parliamentary and extra parliamentary struggles for change; (vii) the State perceives non-core groups as a threat; and (viii) the State imposes some control on non-core groups.

Smooha goes on to define some of the conditions that lead to the establishment of an ethnic democracy; these include the core ethnic group's numerical majority; it is committed to democracy; has the support of a Diaspora; and enjoys international legitimacy.[10] It is evident that many of these conditions are tending to prevail in our own land today and the model cited above may have been considered by some as worthy of emulation as in the case of the proposed Citizenship (Amendment) Bill pending in Parliament.[11]

IV

One consequence of this approach is the ineptitude and bias in governance and departures from the rule of law; another is the stridency in the advocacy of this brand of nationalism accompanied by intolerance of dissent. Both find their reflection in journalism in ample measure.

Violence against journalists remains a matter of serious concern. It has two aspects: firstly, violence by those in segments of militant pubic who do not want coverage of misdeeds, the Gauri Lankesh case being the most condemnable instance of it; and secondly by the authorities in the shape of local security forces who do not want the media to report strong-arm tactics used against public expressions of outrage in specific happenings. Correctives to the latter are few and rarely prompt, as in the Hashimpura killings case of 1986. In most of these, there is usually State complicity in acts of omission or commission. Both transgress what the law permits; both violate the rule of law.

Some writings in the media are candid about a crisis of credibility, internal constraints, curtailment of dissent and an atmosphere of intimidation highlighted by specific instances of violence. This, overt or covert, trend is attributed by one commentator to lack of economic security: 'If you challenge the government you run the risk of losing your job. Yet for many this is not just their livelihood but the anchor of their (and sometimes their families') existence.'[12] Some pronouncements by government personalities occasionally suggest derision of the media. The phenomenon of fake news, 'alternate facts', and trolling has added to it in good measure. A former Chief Election Commissioner commented on the adverse impact 'in a big way' on voter behaviour in elections and the need 'to bring in a robust mechanism for conduct of social media platforms'.[13]

The Editors Guild took note of the deteriorating situation on 8 August last year and issued a statement titled 'An increasingly challenging environment on freedom of the press.' It

> condemned the manner in which the right to practice free and independent journalism is seen to be undermined by a combination of forces—some media owners' inability to withstand political covert or

from the political establishment and frequent instances of blocking or interference in the transmission of television content that is seen to be critical of the government.

It cited specific instances, decried 'all attempts on the part of the government to interfere in the free and independent functioning of journalists, either put under pressure directly, or through the proprietors'. The statement urged media owners 'not to cow down to political pressure,' described as 'Owellian' the interference with TV signals and demanded that corrective action be taken. It decried the tendency 'on the part of the government and the political class to 'use selective denial of journalistic access as a weapon.'

Recent events have produced Indian versions of 'embedded journalism' and of *'gussa'* (anger) of the public. It has led to what has been called 'news-distorting nationalism of rating-hungry TV news channels'.[14] Credible media observers have noted that 'a part-communal, part-pseudo-nationalist poison has seeped deep into India's collective thinking' and poses 'a very real threat to Indian democracy'.[15] The casualty in the process is credibility. These domestic versions of 'skewed notions of romantic patriotism or tribal allegiance' have also contested our propensity for 'democracy and rational thought'[16] and propel us to agree with the historian Ramachandra Guha's observation that 'while we may all wish to be patriots, writers (as well as television anchors) must never become propagandists for a leader, party or government'.[17] A participant in recent discussions has put it bluntly: 'Not only is the media celebrating existing immoralities, it is also scaling new heights of impropriety. Crudity is the new definition of refinement—the mainstream media's vulgarity has destroyed the norms of Indian democracy that once prevailed in the public domain.'[18]

Textbooks on journalism emphasize that the benchmarks for the media are accuracy, independence, impartiality, humanity and accountability. Somewhere towards the end of his *First Draft* George Verghese observed that

a good or great newspaper or channel is for its readers, listeners and viewers, part university, part government, both teacher and overseer . . . We need to ask ourselves whether the Indian media has departed, or dare depart from that ideal, if it wants to remain true to its mission.

I leave it to this audience to guess what he may have to say from his lofty perch about journalism in this age of strident nationalism.

18

Citizenship*

Since time immemorial, humans came together in societies and sought to bestow identities on themselves. The Code of Hammurabi (circa 1750 BCE) talked of patricians, plebeians and the slaves; so did Aristotle's *Politics* (340 BCE) of citizens, aliens and slaves. Kautilya's *Arthashastra* spoke of Aryans of the four varnas and non-Aryans of various categories. Beyond these preliminaries, it was Aristotle who raised the critical question: 'Who is a citizen, and what is the meaning of the term?' His answer was emphatic: 'He who has the power to take part in the deliberative or judicial administration of any state is said . . . to be a citizen of that state.'[1]

Throughout history, geographical entities also developed methods of signalling for themselves and for others the limits of their areas of influence and allegiance. These came to be known as boundaries and within them affiliation and allegiance of individuals and groups was signalled through symbolic and concrete acts of acknowledgement of authority.

In the case of India and notwithstanding our antiquity as a civilization, these boundaries varied with the fortunes of empires. It was the freedom movement and its outcome in August 1947 that paved the way for the transition to a nation state in the modern sense.

The period of British rule also created an existential reality in the shape of those Indians who were descendants of persons who had emigrated in the 19th century mostly as indentured labour to different parts of the British empire. These indentured labourers were found principally in Ceylon, Burma, Malaya, South Africa, Zanzibar and Fiji. They numbered around four million. Gandhiji had lived and worked among them in South

---

* *Seminar* magazine No. 713, January 2019.

Africa; leaders of the freedom movement were at all times supportive of their cause, but also advised them to integrate in their host societies on a basis of equality.

When the Constituent Assembly commenced its work in December 1946, its approach was premised on a single citizenship for the Union of India. Some months later, the Partition and its aftermath of large-scale violence and displacement of multitudes, compelled attention to its implications. Competing visions of an emerging India and its citizen body were thus intensely debated in the Constituent Assembly; the Constitution proclaimed on 26 November 1949 was its outcome. Its Preamble enunciated the guiding principles and moral values; the opening phrase *We the People* signalled the identities embedded therein. The task before the constitution-makers was to spell out the ambit of these opening words. How, specifically, is the circle to be drawn?

Consequently, it was essential to dwell on the concept of citizenship and spell out the normative principles for defining national identity through the circles of inclusion and exclusion. The national movement had formulated a concept of citizenship that was differentiated. Every dimension of it was contested and bore the imprint of recent happenings, particularly of the Partition and its aftermath. The record shows a new way of thinking about the relationship between the individual and the State.

In legal terms and in international practice, citizenship of a modern State is determined on the basis of two principles: *jus soli* (by birth) and *jus sanguinis* (blood-based decent). In actual practice, and in many States, rules governing citizenship by marriage or naturalization have tended to dilute the applicability of these principles.

India chose the *jus soli* principle. However, and 'given its multi-ethnic society and the absence of a single ethno-cultural basis for nationhood' and because 'the Indian nation was substantially a political entity under construction', dilutions followed. The debates in the Constituent Assembly showed that 'an ultimately progressive settlement in favour of jus soli could not eliminate the ever-present threat of encroachment from jus sanguinis'. As a result, 'the Indian Constitution adopted a secular *jus soli* conception of citizenship but the idea of the "natural" citizens, usually Hindu and male, strongly inflected the debate on it'.[2] This is clear from the wording of Articles 5, 6 and 7: 'If Article 5 was an enunciation of citizenship for ordinary times, Article 6 and 7 were articulations of citizenship for extraordinary times with the former applicable to those who migrated to

India from Pakistan and the latter (with some exceptions) to those who migrated from India to Pakistan.'[3]

The Constitution prescribed the citizenship status at its commencement and left it to Parliament under Article 11 to regulate the right of citizenship. The final shape to these contestations thus emerged in the Citizenship Act, 1955. It indicated five processes by which citizenship could be acquired: by birth, descent, registration, naturalization and incorporation of territory. A sixth type was added in August 1985 after the Assam agitation. The Act defined 'illegal immigrant'; it provides for termination of citizenship as also for conditions under which its deprivation can be undertaken.

It has been observed that the Citizenship Act and the Rules and Orders pursuant to it, indicate an effort to use it as a tool 'to construct a uniform a pan-Indian identity'. However, it also shows that 'a citizenship that was deeply marked by ethnic and majoritarian ascriptions was becoming the order of the day and the central government authorized to arbitrate on this issue was increasingly conceding the ground towards such an end'.[4] Subsequent developments made this evident. Thus, the Act of 1955 has been amended by the Citizenship Amendment Acts of 1986, 1992, 2003, 2005 and 2015; the changes and modifications to them together shed much light on the direction being taken.

The emerging pressures manifested themselves on the periphery of the nation state. The most significant amendments to the Citizenship Act have been to Sections 3 (citizenship by birth) and 6 (citizenship by naturalization); these were to address concerns about illegal immigration from Bangladesh. Section 7 (citizenship by incorporation of territory) has been amended to provide for overseas citizenship of India. After the turn of the century, they are also reflective the developing self-perception of the Indian State in the comity of nations.

The first impulse for accommodation emanated from the situation in Assam following the massive wave of immigration from Bangladesh that impacted on the demographic structure of the State in religious terms. A report by the Governor of Assam in 1998 citing a threat from 'almost exclusively Muslim' illegal migrants from Bangladesh was cited as the reason.[5] The agitation by the All Assam Students' Union brought forth the IMDT (Illegal Migrants Determination by Tribunal) Act, 1983 which provided for the detection and expulsion of illegal immigrants. Its political objective was to check unrest in sections of the public and address the vulnerabilities of Muslim migrants. It achieved limited success; it did not check the agitation and was struck down for being discriminatory by the Supreme Court in 2006 in *Sarbananda Sonowal* v *Union of India*. The reasons cited in the judgment, including reference to Article 355 of the Constitution, are emphatic.

Earlier, an amendment in 2003 to Section 3(2)(ii) of the Citizenship Act denied citizenship rights to children of illegal immigrants. It has been opined that in these amendments to rules 'religion was made an explicit ground for granting citizenship'.[6]

A different approach was adopted in the case of Hindu migrants from Pakistan coming into Rajasthan and Gujarat in 1965, 1971 and 1992; the number of the latter was around 17,000. 'Citizenship Camps' were held by District Collectors for them and Rule 8A of the Citizenship Rules 1956 was specifically amended to accommodate 'Minority Hindus with Pakistan citizenship'.

Another dimension to the citizenship debate was added by the question of overseas Indians, recent migrants as well as descendants of those who went earlier and now number around 31 million. Those often referred to as Non-Resident Indians (NRIs) have come to the notice of public opinion and have been articulated upon by public figures. Around the turn of the century a political input added to it and the NDA government set up a committee to examine all aspects of the matter. The L.M. Singhvi report concluded that

> India, because of its size, population and strategic location is ambitious to establish itself as a global player. In this context the role played by Indian Diaspora has, over the period of time, become important and is emerging as an important factor in promoting certain foreign policy goals. Initially, the Indian government was conscious of the potential of People of Indian Origin (PIO). Till 2000 there was no definite policy vis-à-vis the Indian overseas. Recent initiatives taken by the government have given strong signals of the Indian government's intentions to continue to engage the Indian Diaspora giving it a vanguard role in India's quest to emerge as a regional and global power.[7]

The report went on to suggest 'dual citizenship in a limited form with limited rights and to specific countries.'

These aspects were reflected in the Citizen (Amendment) Act 2003 and invited criticism on ground of 'class bias' in favour of recent migrants to the developed countries.[8] The underlying politics came to the fore after the general election of 2004. Addressing the Pravasi Divas gathering at Mumbai in January 2005, Prime Minister Manmohan Singh announced that the government would amend the 2003 amendment to the Act and 'extend the facility of dual citizenship to all overseas Indians who migrated from India after January 26, 1950' instead of restricting it to the 16 mentioned in the 2003 amendment, subject to the same condition that their countries allowed it under their laws. This was reflected in the Amendment Act of 2005. This enlargement of the ambit was immediately criticized by the principal opposition on the ground that it ignored 'national security consideration' by opening the door to those Indians who migrated to Pakistan and Bangladesh after 1950 and to Bangladeshi infiltrators.[9]

The change of government in 2014 brought forth the Citizenship (Amendment) Bill, 2016. Its stated major premise was the assertion in the Bharatiya Janata Party's (BJP) 2014 Election Manifesto (page 40) that 'India shall remain a natural home for persecuted Hindus and they shall be welcome to seek refuge here'. This seems to reflect in some measure Israel's Law of Return for the Jewish people and its opening proclamation that 'every Jew has the right to come to this country as *Oleh* (an immigrant)'.[10]

The primary objective of the present Bill is (a) to provide for the acquisition and determination of Indian citizenship by certain categories of illegal immigrants: 'persons belonging to minority communities, namely, Hindus, Sikhs, Buddhists, Jains, Parsis and Christians from Afghanistan, Bangladesh and Pakistan'; (b) to amend the residence requirement from eleven to six years for this category; and (c) make possible cancellation of OCI cards if its holder violates a law of India.

On 6 January 2015 an Ordinance was issued on the ground that 'pending the consideration of the Bill circumstances exist which render it necessary to take immediate action' in regard to the required period for registration and naturalization and for Overseas Citizens of India and Persons of Indian Origin Schemes. The urgency of the matter, according to some comments in the media, emanated from a time-related commitment made by the Prime Minister during his US visit in 2014.

The Bill has been referred to the Standing Committee for the Ministry of Home Affairs. Its report is awaited. In the meantime, opposition to it has emanated from various quarters on the ground that it makes illegal migrants eligible for citizenship on the basis of religion. This violates Article 14 of the Constitution which guarantees right to equality and violates the Basic Structure principle, that while religious persecution could be a principle for differentiation, it cannot be articulated in a manner that dilutes the secular foundations of citizenship in India and goes against constitutional morality.[11] The nobility of intent underlying the Bill is belied by its selectivity in terms of neighbouring countries and religious minorities confronting difficulties; thus the rationale for leaving out Ahmadiyyas in Pakistan, Rohingyas in Myanmar and Uyghur Muslims in China is unclear.

More specifically, public and student groups in north-eastern states (Assam, Arunachal Pradesh, Mizoram and Nagaland) have objected to it on the ground that it would upset the demographic balance and impact adversely on indigenous segments of the population in the region. Alongside is the highly emotive question of the National Register of Citizens (NRC) and issue of the 4 million residents of Assam whose citizenship status awaits a decision.

It has also been observed that provisions for the cancellation of the provisions of Overseas Citizen of India (OCI) are wide-ranging and could be susceptible to misuse.

Unlike a good majority of the countries of the world, India has not signed the 1951 UN Convention on Refugees and its 1967 Protocol and has, instead, dealt with refugee problems (including the massive inflow from East Pakistan in 1971) on an ad hoc basis. This, while facilitating political and administrative arrangements of the moment, does impact on a principled approach to the problem.

The resulting situation has been aptly summed up by a scholar

> While *jus soli* remains the governing principle of citizenship in India, citizenship laws and jurisprudence have come to be manifestly inflected by elements of *jus sanguinis*. Whether it is the issue of "illegal immigrants" from Bangladesh on the eastern border of India, or that of "minority with Pakistan citizenship" on the western border, the law and the rules have tended to view these very differently seeing the latter (but not the former) as people with a rightful claim on Indian citizenship. This accenting of Indian citizenship with *jus sanguinis* is reflected also in the expansive approach latterly adopted towards the Indian diaspora.[12]

Behind and beyond this legal tweaking, the question of their impact on the core values of the Constitution and of the idea of India envisaged therein remains a disturbing one.

19

Reimagining Parliament

Hopes and Perils

I

The creation of a rule-based accountability system, and the formulation of the rules themselves, is as old as the first human groups who concluded that living together is preferable to separate individual existence. This has been the rationale down the ages of village councils and of bigger bodies. Experience has taught humanity that accountability is an essential ingredient of the exercise of authority and the latter without the former is not conducive to public good. Thus has evolved the institution known today as Parliament or legislative assembly.

Since the human being desires to live in freedom, it is but natural that this legislative-cum-accountability organization should reflect its own choice. This is what Gandhi ji meant when he said in 1922 that Swaraj would not be a gift of the foreign rulers but spring from 'the wishes of the people of India as expressed through their freely chosen representatives.' It found expression in the programme of action of the Indian National Congress as also in the debates of the Constituent Assembly. From this emerged the principle that the power and authority of the sovereign people of India 'are derived from the people.' This was enshrined in our Constitution, prefaced by its rousing Preamble.

Democracy as a system of governance based on a constitution limits the majority and protects the minority. It thus has wider moral implications than mere majoritarianism which is likely, sooner or later, to degenerate into elective despotism. Pluralism therefore is the soul of democracy. 'A true democracy', it is said, 'is surely one in which the existence of the power of the many is conditional on respect for the rights of the few.' There is no place for 'a crude statistical view of democracy'.

Our Constitution prescribed universal adult franchise on the first-past-the-post (FPTP) system and the first General Election of 1951–1952 was held on this basis. The voter turnout was 44.87 per cent. The two Houses commenced their work in May 1952. Since then, seventeen elections for the Lok Sabha have been held and the voting percentage in the last one, 2019, was 67.4 of whom 68 per cent were women.

It is evident that the democratic system has settled in, and the Indian voter is participating in these elections in increasing numbers. The electoral process has been deepened qualitatively by the 73rd and 74th Amendments. Over decades, the electoral machinery under the charge of the Election Commission of India has done a commendable job of organizing these elections at all levels. The process has been helped by the extensive use of technology to simplify the nuts and bolts of the electoral system.

On the positive side, therefore, the score card makes good reading. The institution of electoral democracy has been put in place, has been tested periodically, and found to be fundamentally efficacious. No less relevant are the changes in the participatory profile of the electorate and the impetus given to it by the social awakening of the 1990s. These have deepened the process of both participation and representation; more on this count however needs to be done to ensure better representation of women and some deprived segments like religious minorities.

Parliamentary democracy and the Parliament of India in its two Houses and the State Legislatures are the creations of the Constitution. They are entrusted to discharge within their prescribed domains the responsibilities of (i) accountability of the executive; (ii) law making; (iii) controlling the national finances and approving taxation proposals; and (iv) discussion of matters of public interest and concern. In addition, the Parliament has some electoral and judicial functions.

At the conclusion of this work, Dr Ambedkar argued powerfully for social democracy and said it cannot last unless there lies at the base of it, social democracy; he defined the latter as

> a way of life which recognizes liberty, equality and fraternity as the principles of life. They form a union of trinity in the sense that to divorce one from the other is to defeat the very purpose of democracy. Without equality, liberty would produce the supremacy of the few over the many.

Without fraternity, liberty would produce the supremacy of the few over the many. Without fraternity, liberty and equality could not become a natural course of things.[1]

He warned the Constituent Assembly that 'the Constitution can provide only the organs of the state such as the Legislature, the Executive and the Judiciary. The factors on which the working of those organs of the state depends are the people and the political parties they will set up as their instruments to carry out their wishes and their politics'.[2] Who can say how the people of India and their parties will behave?

The experience of seventeen general elections have brought to light some drawbacks of the system and on the basis of experience gained, the need for correctives has also been felt. Particularly relevant is the 255th Report of the Law Commission of India in 2015 that focused on election financing, paid news, political advertising, and introducing internal democracy and transparency within political parties.

On the functional side, some questions do arise:

- How well have the parliamentary institutions, beginning with the Parliament of India, functioned?
- Have the functions of executive accountability, law making and public debate been discharged in adequate and requisite measure?
- Is the voting public satisfied with the performance?

The answer to the first question has to be empirical as well as qualitative. What is it that the Parliament is required to do? What has been the frequency of meetings of the two Houses of Parliament, and of the State legislatures? How effectively have they, as instruments of accountability and legislation, delivered? What has been the response of the legislatures to matters of public concern in normal and abnormal times?

The constitutional provisions, and the statistical data, tell the story in good measure. The Constitution provides that sessions of Parliament should not be separated by more than six months at a time. It is also stipulated that sessions and their duration are decided by the President of India on the advice of the government of the day and other political parties or individual Members have no say in the matter.

The record shows that the frequency of meetings of Parliament has declined progressively. In the 1950s and 1960s the Lok Sabha met for an average of 121 days a year; the average for the Rajya Sabha in this period was ninety-four. This figure declined to an average of seventy-two in subsequent decades. The data for state legislative assemblies, often in single digits, makes dismal reading. Allowance also has to be made for time lost due to 'disruptions' that have now become endemic. In both the 14th and the 16th Lok Sabha, for instance, about 24 per cent of time was lost through disruptions. Nor was the functioning of the Rajya Sabha any better.

The malaise was described by former Speaker of the Lok Sabha the late Shri Somnath Chatterjee 'as politics of intense confrontation (gaining the) the upper hand with the result that disruption of the proceedings of the House through sloganeering, coming into the well of the House, walk-outs etc have greatly eroded people's faith in the efficacy of this great institution'.[3] 'Petulant children' is how the then finance minister Shri Pranab Mukherjee described the disrupters. On the other hand, eminent parliamentarians in both Houses sought to justify disruptions as valid parliamentary tactics.

Recommendations of the Committee on Ethics in both Houses have suggested correctives but with little success. In the realm of Rules, the presiding officers of both Houses have the authority to ask an unruly Member to withdraw for the day; they can also ask a defaulting Member to 'withdraw for the remainder of the Session' provided a motion to this effect is carried in the House. In addition, the Lok Sabha through its Rule 374A (made in December 2001) gives the Speaker the authority to expel a member for five days for causing 'grave disorder' by coming into the well of the House. The desired results, however, have not been forthcoming because these rules were premised on individual defaulters, not groups. A meaningful recourse to parliamentary etiquette thus becomes an essential corrective.

The first challenge then to restore the sense of purpose of Parliament is to restore the duration of its sittings to around 100 days a year and by making its members imbibe in word and deed the purpose for which they are elected by their constituents. The primary responsibility for this rests with party and group leaders without whose knowledge and consent disruptions do not take place.

The legislative functions of Parliament are substantive rather than pro forma. In the nature of things, a great majority of legislative proposals emanate from the executive and unquestionably embody its collective wisdom and experience. The need nevertheless to subject them to scrutiny of legislators cannot be dispensed with nor can their right to seek a wider scrutiny through expert and public opinion. This was the rationale of having Standing Committee scrutiny, a device that is now being resorted to with declining frequency.

Close observers of the functioning of our Parliament have opined that over the years there has been a decline in its effectiveness as an institution of accountability and oversight. One simple reason is time availability. The fact that in earlier years sessions were of longer duration meant that more time could be given for each of the primary functions of the Houses. Legislative proposals emanate from the executive and their impact on different segments of society need public inputs both from the elected representatives and from different segments of civil society. Hasty legislation inevitably resulted in faults or oversight that led to legal or political challenges.

Since one of the primary functions of Parliament is accountability of the executive, its mechanisms become a matter of critical importance. The first among them is the use of the Question Hour. It is an individual right and can be exercised on a daily basis within the framework of procedures. Questions can be Starred or Un-starred; the former, to be answered orally, allows follow up supplementary questions. They quiz the executive on a wide range of policy matters as also on specifics. Notices of these are given in advance and are answered in the form of written replies. In actual practice, this form of accountability is often diluted by verbosity in oral answers. The prescribed procedure requires both questions and answers to be 'short, crisp and to the point' and should not be an occasion for making statements. Both, regrettably, are observed in the breach with the result that the efficacy of the Hour as an instrument of accountability is diluted. This is in sharp contrast to the efficacy of the Question Hour in other parliaments. There have nevertheless been occasions when 'innocent' questions have opened the doors for wider investigations.

The British House of Commons, since October 1961, has the practice of a weekly Prime Minister's Question Hour. Its effectiveness has been commented upon favourably. Biographical accounts of some incumbents of that high office have shed interesting light on the efforts made by the individuals to seek 'a crutch'[4] before facing the House. Our own Parliament has not been tempted to risk this innovation and often, but not always, questions relating to the head of government's portfolios are answered by junior ministers.

Apart from the daily Question Hour, there are a great many other procedural devices through which the executive's accountability is ensured. Short Duration Discussions, Calling Attention and Special Mentions are admissible procedures that can be resorted to, given the time and inclination of the executive of the day to allow other viewpoints to be voiced.

The Parliament has a set of Standing Committees to facilitate its work. These are (i) committees to enquire (on privileges and petitions); (ii) committees to advise (Business Advisory committees and the Committee on Rules); (iii) House Keeping Committees; (iv) committees on scrutiny and control (Committees on Public Accounts, Estimates, Government Assurances, Subordinate Legislation, Public Undertakings, Welfare of Scheduled Castes and Scheduled Tribes and the Departmentally Related Standing Committees). In addition, ad hoc committees are set up to report on bills and motions.

One of the functions of Parliament is to scrutinize the functioning of the departments of the government in the context of their budgetary demands. In 1993 and taking note of the need for it, the system of Departmentally Related Standing Committees (DRSC) was instituted and twenty-four such committees (twenty-one from Lok Sabha and ten from Rajya Sabha) were instituted. These examine Bills, budgets and specific matters referred to them pertaining to the work of the department. Their work pertaining to proposed pieces of legislation has been somewhat uneven. While 60 per cent of the Bills introduced in the 14th Lok Sabha were referred to them, the same figure for the 15th Lok Sabha was seventy-one but declined to twenty-seven for the 16th Lok Sabha.

The proceedings of the two Houses of Parliament are controlled and guided by the Speaker in Lok Sabha and Chairman in Rajya Sabha. Both are elected offices whose holders do not require rare qualities 'but common qualities in a rare degree'.

Do the legislatures at central and state levels function enough? Do they spend sufficient time on deliberation, legislation and accountability of executives? Is their functioning in keeping with established norms and in line with public expectations? Do they, by their functioning, set a model or a pattern of behaviour for the public especially the youth to emulate? Are correctives possible, or has the system irretrievably lost its way?

Records shows that the notional time allocation is different from time actually utilized for the conduct of business. A uniquely Indian contribution to parliamentary practice known as 'disruption' has contributed to it and data is available about the time so lost. It reflects poorly on our seriousness as a people to adhere to agreed norms of behaviour.

II

Debate on our democracy has also focused on the meaning of political representation and the paradox emerging from it. Who represents? Who is represented? How can the system be made more representative? How should we ensure that every segment of our very diverse society is reflected in the elected body?

Apart from the less than satisfactory score on functioning within the prescribed procedures, students of Indian polity have raised questions about (a) the social composition of Parliament and (b) the changing concepts of representation. The first is reflected in the community and caste-wise composition, the educational and occupational background of the Members and in the decisive transformation of the social base post-1990. Available statistical data and academic studies sustain it. The second, no less relevant, is the changing public perception of what constitutes representation.

A modern democracy is representational in nature and hence determining the modes of representation and making it operational become critical. In the aftermath of Independence, we chose adult franchise and the FPTP system; and the data of the electorate's participation in early general elections tells its story candidly. The political discourse subscribed to 'unity in diversity' but the intent in the early period was on the former rather than the latter. It has been opined by Professor Hiren Mookerjee that 'the first two parliaments were dominated by men who were quite patriarchal . . . and felt that their social background did not affect their views and perceptions and sense of responsibility as representatives'. The nature of representation started changing in the 1970s and underwent drastic transformation in the post-1990s. Questions of representation of diversity, and of federalism, came to the fore and cannot be wished away.

Alongside are questions about whom the representatives represent. Since 'caste remains a key variable' of our social structure and has been a vehicle of socio-political change, a great many studies have been undertaken on the caste and community backgrounds of state-level elected representatives to examine how caste-based representation has translated into politics in a dynamic perspective. They indicate a distinctive 'evolution of the caste profile of the Hindi belt MPs' and 'the growing politicization of the OBC, largely due to their mobilization in favour of reservations resulting in a transfer of power from upper castes to OBC politicians'; 'this process is even more pronounced at the state level among some of the larger states of the Hindi belt'.[5] The outcomes vary since the arithmetic of caste varies from state to state. The caste/class transfer of socio-economic democratic power however remains an existential reality of Indian polity.

The emergence of social media, a rival claimant to representative power in civil society, is a global phenomenon of recent origin and has emerged as both complementary and antithetical to question or supplement the representativeness of Parliament. It has manifested itself in both forms in our polity. An obvious reason for this is that 'while Parliament has become increasingly representative in descriptive terms, it has also simultaneously become unresponsive in terms of legislation and governance and has tended to avoid accountability by closing ranks'.[6]

III

It would be fair to measure Parliament's functioning on three counts: (i) as a legislative institution in terms of its functioning; (ii) as an instrument of control over the functioning of the executive; and (iii) in terms of present-day realities and the role of civil society organizations and institutions. A decline in terms of its assigned responsibilities is much too evident and credible observers have opined that we are now more a symbol than substance of a vibrant democracy. So are the shortfalls as an instrument of control over the executive. Particularly noticeable is the tardiness in galvanizing the functioning of the Standing Committees; one observer has described their irrelevance as 'breath-taking'. The responsibility for both principally, but not wholly, rests with the executive of the day and can be induced through collective action of the political parties combined with public pressure. Similarly,

- Attendance by Ministers in meetings of the Standing Committees should be made obligatory and should not be confined to Secretaries of the Government.
- The two Houses of Parliament should revert to the earlier practice of sitting for 90–100 days.

- There should be a binding mechanism to check disruptions and time lost should be recouped within a specified period.
- To accommodate civil society concerns, rules and procedures for the functioning of the Petition Committees of the two Houses should be reviewed.

The imperative to retrieve the institution is evident to adherents of democratic values and of the Constitution. The apprehension that a dormant Parliament could become the first stage to its oblivion is real and lends credence to allegations of India becoming 'the world's largest illiberal democracy'. The primary objective of proposed correctives should in some measure be to induce Parliament to accommodate in its functioning the realities of our times, restore its primacy in the functioning of institutions of the Indian State, and convince a younger generation that it remains relevant.

India is and claims to be the largest democracy in the world. We are an active participant in the deliberations of the Inter Parliamentary Union (IPU). Some years ago this body had developed and circulated a self-assessment toolkit to (a) evaluate individual parliaments against international criteria for democratic parliaments; and (b) to identify priorities and means for strengthening Parliament. The toolkit focused on six questions:

- The representativeness of Parliament
- Parliamentary oversight over the executive
- Parliament's legislative capacity
- The transparency and accessibility of Parliament
- Parliament's involvement in international policy

Thus, both domestic debate and international norms beckon us to undertake a self-assessment. Therein lies the corrective.

An observation in another context yet relevant universally is to be noted: Parliamentary democracy, evolved by time, fashioned by chance and fashioned by experience, still places the possibility of an ever better system, in our hands. Free and fair elections, reform by statute rather than by force, government for the many without forgetting the few, the liberty of the individual made possible by the collective endeavour, not arbitrary tyranny but the rule of law; the shared sovereignty of the people—these are worth taking pride in, protecting and enhancing.[7]

In our case, however, it was adopted by choice, perhaps implanted, with all the risks of rejection. Is this what is happening? A look at the data on the functioning of State legislatures (Articles 168–212 of the Constitution) sustains the apprehension of a system failure and self-abdication.

In a lecture in December 1952, Ambedkar listed seven conditions on 'Conditions Precedent for the Successful Working of Democracy': (1) no glaring inequalities in society; (2) a strong opposition; (3) no tyranny of majority over the minority; (4) equality in law and administration; (5) observance of constitutional morality; (6) a functioning of moral order in society; and (7) public conscience. He concluded by mentioning some cases of failure and said, 'We ought to be very cautious and very considerate regarding our own future.'

Seven decades later, we have to concede that we are on a slippery slope. We have practiced electoral democracy mechanically without making it fully representative. Our electoral procedures and practices have accentuated, rather than diminished, social cleavages. We have allowed money power in all its manifestations to distort the electoral outcomes. Our political process depicts a declining observance of constitutional morality. Our society exhibits a disturbing disregard for moral order and public conscience and, in the words of an eminent academic, the lines between legality and illegality, order and disorder, state and criminality, have come to be increasingly porous.

Our system is in dire need for rejuvenation—and our commitment to the principles and values of the Constitution.

SECTION THREE

INDIAN MUSLIM PERCEPTIONS AND THE INDIAN CONTRIBUTION TO THE CULTURE OF ISLAM

20

Militant Islam*

I

The historian Ira Lapidus has described the history of Islamic societies as 'a dialogue between the realm of religious symbols and the world of everyday reality, a history of the interaction between Islamic values and the historical experience of Muslim people that has shaped the formulation of a number of difficult but inter-related Muslim Societies'. Elsewhere in his monumental work he describes the impact European intervention had on these societies: 'In each case the European impact was different'; it 'upset the equilibrium of institutions', threw up new power elites whose responses to the new situations and pressures varied from place to place. In this wide-ranging endeavour, the modernism of elites and the intelligentsia vied with the reformism of the ulema and thus produced an 'alternative concept of reconstruction of their societies, each a variation upon past orientations towards the relationship of state and religion'.[1]

The recent history of these societies, and particularly of Arab Muslim societies, thus becomes a critical element in addressing the intellectual and the societal evolution of the thought process relating to the role and efficacy of the new states which took shape in these lands principally in the 20th century. In this context the failure of the Arab state to deliver internally, and the trend towards 'a reinterpretation of the Islamic tradition in a way that lends itself to a revolutionary meaning',[2] signalled the ascendancy of those who came to be known as the fundamentalists. The process started with Hasan Al-Banna in Egypt who was followed by other Egyptian thinkers like Abdul Qadir Awdah, Sayyid Qutb, Mohammad Al

---

* DPG Seminar on War and Peace in Islam, February 2002.

Ghazali and Yusuf Al-Qaradawi. Elsewhere in the Arab world, the trend
was contributed to by Mustafa Al Sibai and Said Hawwa of Syria Hassan
Turabi of Sudan and Rashid Al-Ghanaushi of Tunisia. The intellectual
progenitors of the trend in the Indian subcontinent were Abul Hasan Ali
Nadvi in India and Abul Ala Maudoodi in Pakistan. In Iran, Ali Sheriati
and Khomeini generated impulses which led to the establishment of the
Islamic Republic in 1979. In each case the thinkers concerned delved into
the vast repertoire of Islamic history, and selected tokens of Islamicity
to sustain the advocacy of an alternate political order which would make
possible the application of the sharia; in each case this selection was 'a
political act'.[3]

A great deal of terminological confusion has crept into the debate.
Observers of the Islamic world have used the terms Islamic Resurgence,
Islamic Revival, Islamic Fundamentalism, Islamism, Political Islam,
Islamic Activism and Militant Islam, to describe the phenomena.
Writing in 1992 John Esposito expressed a preference for 'Islamic
revivalism and Islamic activism'.[4] Oliver Roy has used Islamism and
Political Islam interchangeably.[5] Others, including Laura Guazzone, have
shown a preference for Islamism.[6] Youssef Choueiri describes Islamic
Fundamentalism as a 'vague term' which covers the revivalism of the 18th
and 19th centuries, the reformism of the 19th and 20th centuries and
radicalism of the past five decades.[7] The Egyptian sociologist Saad Eddin
Ibrahim, on the other hand, has a marked preference for Islamic Activism
which he defines as 'collective socio-political action aiming at changing
the status quo in the direction of what is believed to be the proper Islamic
order'.[8] Contemporary Islamist writers like Yusuf Al Qaradawi describe
themselves as *Islamiyyum* and reject the use of the expression political
Islam describing it as 'part of a plan set by enemies of Islam to distort and
divide Islam'.[9]

Islamic revivalism, reformism or radicalism did not emerge in a vacuum
and bears the imprint of history. This history, since the 18th century at
least, is one of interaction of Muslim societies in Asia and Africa with
European imperialism. The pervasive impact of this was aptly described by
Cantwell Smith:

> The fundamental malaise of modern Islam is that something has gone
> wrong with Islamic History. The fundamental problem of modern
> Muslims is how to rehabilitate that history: to set it again in full vigour so

that Islamic society may once again flourish as a divinely guided society should and must. The century stems from an awareness that something is awry between the religion which God has appointed and the historical development of the world He controls.[10]

In the Arab world this spiritual crisis was renewed with extraordinary vigour in the aftermath of the 1967 Arab–Israeli war. The war and the Arab defeat vividly demonstrated that the Arab State, hard in appearance, was in fact not a strong one. The defeat dealt a deathblow to the carefully nurtured, and passionately held, concept of Arab nationalism and pan-Arabism. 'What the 1967 defeat did was to force an audit during a moment of great stress and clarity. And what a spectacle it was!'[11] In this audit-induced soul-searching, the lead was taken amongst others by the Syrian leftist intellectuals Sadeq Al-Azm and Ali Ahmad Said 'Adonis', who questioned the fundamentals of Arab identity. The public mood, however, sought solace in religion. The Muslim Brotherhood in Egypt, persecuted by Jamal Abdul Nasser, got a fresh lease of life and the teachings of Hasan Al Banna and Sayyid Qutb suddenly gained a wider readership. By 1974 moderate dissent of the Islamic variety had given way to acts of violence against the State; these have continued unabated though with varying degrees of intensity. Furthermore, and given the centrality of Egypt in the intellectual and cultural life of the Arab world, these trends of Egyptian thinking and action have been emulated elsewhere.

II

Islamic militancy has been defined as 'actual violent behaviour committed collectively against the state or other actors in the name of Islam'.[12] Persons or groups undertaking these acts are generally described as radical Islamists. Who are these groups and the persons constituting them? What is their social origin? What is their militant ideology and how is it distinguished from the traditional or moderate fundamentalist Islam? Answers to these questions are to be sought in the writings of leading Islamists of the contemporary era as well as in case studies of individual groups and in an analysis of the principles espoused by them.

A coherent account of modern Islamists needs to begin with Hasan Al Banna (d. 1949), who founded the Muslim Brotherhood in 1928 and defined 'the parameters of its mission, purposes, and method'.[13] He drew a distinction between religion per se and the religious establishment, condemned the latter for its supine attitudes, emphasized the centrality of the mosque as a place of worship, a place of education and as a hospital for spirituality and the mentally and physically sick. He outlined the ideology of the movement in five clauses: 'Allah is our God; the Messenger is our model; the Qur'an is our constitution; Jihad is our means; and martyrdom in the Way of Allah is our aspiration. These can be condensed further into five words: modesty, recitation (or Qur'an and Hadith), prayer, military preparedness, and ethics.'[14] The goals of the movement were identified as the liberation of the Islamic fatherland from foreign domination and the establishment of a free Islamic state which would reform education, wage war against poverty, ignorance, disease and crime and create an exemplary society with the help of deep faith, precise organization and uninterrupted work.[15]

The last of the Six Tracts is devoted by Al Banna to Jihad. 'Allah has imposed Jihad as a religious duty on every Muslim, categorically and rigorously, from which there is neither evasion nor escape'; it is 'prescribed' in the Qur'an in the same manner and in the same language as the injunction on fasting. Consequently, abstention from, or evasion of, jihad is 'one of the seven mortal sins'.[16] It is conceded that striving through good conduct, or the utterance of 'a word of truth in the presence of a tyrannical ruler' is also amongst the forms of jihad, 'but nothing in them confers on their advocate the supreme martyrdom and the reward of the striver in jihad unless he slays or is slain in the way of Allah'.[17]

Al Banna's ideological discourse, focusing as it did on religion, history and political organization in the context of Egypt in the interwar years, allowed no room for rapprochement between Islamism and the West and left an indelible mark on subsequent thinkers and leaders of Islamic movements; it was particularly so in the case of Sayyid Qutb whose formulations 'lie at the core of much of contemporary Islamist thinking and organization'.[18]

Qutb (d. 1965) whose personal intellectual history saw the transition from a liberal to an extremist on account of the political repression in Abdel Nasser's Egypt, begins with a doomsday scenario: 'Mankind today is on the brink of a precipice' due to a loss of values both in the capitalist West and the communist East. There is, therefore, the need for 'a new leadership' which would 'preserve and develop the material fruits of the creative genius of Europe'. Islam is the only system which has the relevant values but 'Islam cannot fulfill its role except by taking concrete form in a society, rather, in a nation; for man does not listen, especially in this age, to an abstract theory which is not seen materialized except in a living society'; hence the need to revive Islam to attain the leadership of the world. This can only be done through 'a new faith and a way of life which on the one hand conserves the benefit of modern science and technology, and on the other, fulfils the basic human needs on the same level of excellence as technology has fulfilled them in the sphere of material comfort'.[19]

To bring this about 'we need to initiate the movement of Islamic revival in some Muslim country' for which 'there should be a vanguard' which 'should know the landmarks and the milestones of the road towards this goal'.[20] In this exercise both Arabism and nationalism are rejected, as are the modern concepts of territoriality, ethnicity and sovereignty: 'the nationality of the Muslim by which he is identified is not the nationality determined by the Government' and 'the fatherland is that place where the Islamic faith, the Islamic way of life, and the shariah of God is dominant'.[21]

This dominance cannot be achieved by preaching alone since those who have usurped the authority of God are not going to give up their power merely through preaching; hence the need to use 'the movement' though which 'material obstacles are tackled' particularly 'that political power which rests on a complex yet interrelated ideological, racial, class, social and economic support'. Only thus would 'the freedom of man on earth be achieved'.[22] Qutb clarifies that 'it is not the intention of Islam to force its beliefs on people but Islam is not merely a belief' but a way of life. Therefore, it is *'jihad bis saif* (striving through the sword) which is to clear the way for striving through preaching in the application of the Islamic movement'.[23] This jihad is not restricted to a defensive posture only since an Islamic community 'has a God-given right to step forward and take control of the political authority'.[24]

Interestingly enough, Qutb claimed to have benefited in his understanding of Islam through the Indian scholar Maulana Abul Hasan Ali Nadwi, and he wrote a foreword to one of Nadwi's books. Qutb described the book as a refreshing example 'of how history can be recorded and interpreted from the wider Islamic point of view'. From such an analysis Qutb drew the conclusion that Islam as a faith inspires leadership whose 'real mettle is tested and proven only when it assumes responsibility. It can lead the caravan of life. It cannot be a camp follower'.[25]

In a sense, therefore, Qutb postulated a theory of revolution which declared all existing societies as Jahili (based on ignorance since they are devoid of the concept of Tawhid—the Oneness of God) and hence in imperative need of change through jihad. Also dismissed in the process are the traditional ulema and the traditional jurisprudence (Fiqh) and the quietist perceptions which throughout Islamic history signalled a preference for tyranny if the alternative was anarchy and which advocated consensus building as a valid method of addressing new situations. The revolutionary activism advocated by Qutb, however, was no innovation and was in fact grounded in the 13th–14th-century theologian and thinker Ibn Taymiyya's advocacy of resistance to illegitimate power.

The ideas of Hasan Al Banna and Sayyid Qutb spread across the Arab and Islamic world but would have remained confined to theological and intellectual circles had not the Arab defeat in the Six Day War induced general dissatisfaction and spiritual agony. A widespread perception that 'the Arabs had turned away from God, and God had turned away from them' induced even the Government of Egypt to distribute to the armed forces, a mere two months after the defeat, booklets explaining the meaning of jihad.[26] Government pronouncements, similarly, became laced with religious idiom. This retreat from professed modernity, intended perhaps to be tactical and temporary, failed to assuage popular sentiments and was to result in far-reaching developments.

III

The emergence of military groups amongst the Islamists, and the strategic and tactical approach developed by them, does not indicate uniform patterns. The process, therefore, is better comprehended through country-wise (and group-wise) case studies. For this purpose, it would be useful to analyse developments in a select group of Muslim societies, Arab and non-Arab, in the past three decades. For this purpose, Egypt, Algeria, Iran and Indonesia could be considered as broadly representative of different trends.

Egypt: Knowledgeable scholars have identified the Islamic revival in Egypt as multi-layered and at four levels: (a) growing religiosity among the populace at large; (b) growing social and political criticism by mosque preachers; (c) the activities of mainstream Islamic revivalist movements (e.g., the Muslim Brotherhood) with their focus on education and the gradual building up of Islamic institutions; and (d) activities of neofundamentalist splinter groups having a more militant ideological outlook combined with a belief in the necessity of changing the whole social order.

The most prominent amongst the latter are Al Takfir wa al-Hijra (Excommunication and Emigration), Al Najun min al-nar (The Saved from the Inferno organization), and Al Jihad. All of them indulged in acts of violence including assassinations and were dealt with harshly by the Egyptian State at the time. However, the authorities also tried to co-opt them and their mass base for political gains against the leftist elements on the Egyptian political scene.[27] Sociologists have analysed the structure of these groups and have found that the founder-leaders had several, common characteristics: 'age, modern scientific education, previous membership of the Muslim Brotherhood, prison experience, and disposition towards secret organization'. They also had a great deal of charisma, were eloquent and were considered exemplary Muslims well versed in matters of understanding national and international issues. The typical members of these groups could be described as 'young (early twenties), of rural or small town background, from the middle or lower middle class, with high achievement or motivation, upwardly mobile, with a scientific or engineering education, and from a normally cohesive family'.[28] This bears a remarkable similarity to those who joined radical leftist movements in an earlier period.

Most recent observers of the Egyptian scene have noted that the two decades of militancy have now been replaced by a new phenomenon in which 'the central pillars of the state—the universities, the professional unions or syndicates, the ulema at al Azhar, the courts—have become the central players in the grassroot religious revival' which is authentic and 'poses a far greater challenge to Western interest then the militant movements now on the decline'.[29]

Algeria: The origins of the Islamist impulse in Algeria can be traced to the movement against French rule led by the Association of Algerian Ulema formed by Abdul Hamid Ibn Badis in 1931. The Association's motto was 'Islam is my religion; Arabic is my language; Algeria is my Fatherland'. In the revolutionary phase of the struggle for independence the battle cry was 'Muslim Algeria' and not simply 'Arab Algeria'. The struggle itself was declared to be a jihad and the leaders of the revolution, secular as well as religious, used Islam 'as a strategic weapon'. This perception was kept up after independence. The one-party government of Front de Liberation Nationale (FLN), with its monopoly of power, sought to reconcile the conflicting imperatives of Arabization and Islamization on the one hand, with those of development on socialist lines and of the Western orientation of the elite, on the other. This effort failed and was aggravated by the failure of the Algerian State to deliver on the economic front. The initial troubles took the shape of a cultural clash, in late 1970s, between Arabophone and Francophone students. By early 1980s populist Islam was making considerable headway. The impact of Egyptian Islamism was evident and so was the nomenclature adopted by the various Islamist groups; Al Jihad, Al Taqfir wa al Hijra, Al Dawa wa al Tabligh, etc. Each of these professed to draw its inspiration from Al Banna and Saiyyid Qutb. Eventually the Algerian Islamist leaders, Abbasi Madani and Ali Beljadj came together to form the Islamic Salvation Front (FSI) in 1989. The new organization was far from cohesive and was 'a melting pot for very diverse factions which have little more in common than Islam and a desire to put an end to a political situation in Algeria based on arbitrariness and economic inequality'.[30]

The FIS sought to 'set itself up as a global and general alternative for the solution of all ideological, political and economic and social problems within the framework of Islam'.[31] It showed its intolerance of the less radical Islamist groups by issuing a fatwa condemning to death the leader of the Algerian Hammas. After its success in the municipal elections in 1990, FIS enforced a strict code of morality for the public. It also denounced Sufi symbols like tombs of saints. It adopted a radical posture in foreign affairs and supported Iraq in the Iraq–Kuwait War. Earlier, it had lent support to the Afghan Mujahedeen. The moment of crisis for the FIS came in 1992 when, after its victory in the first round of elections to the National Assembly, the Algerian army as well as other secular groups and trade unions showed a determination 'to find an effective strategy to prevent the second round of elections'.[32] The groundwork for this was undertaken several months earlier when representatives of North African governments had met and established a task force to combat 'radical Islam'.[33] What followed was a military intervention in the name of preserving State security and stability: 'The military's crackdown drove the FIS to change from a legal opposition to a combative, and, in some segments, revolutionary, movement.'[34] The FIS soon split into moderate and radical factions. Included in the latter were many 'Afghans' (Algerians who had fought on the side of the Mujahideen in the Afghan resistance). They announced their identity as the Armed Islamic Group or Groupe Islamic Armé (GIA) and engaged in a no-holds-barred conflict with the Algerian army, a conflict which continues to this day though with lessened intensity. It has left deep scars on all sections of Algerian society.

Iran: The Iranian Revolution of 1979 demonstrated the validity of Trotsky's dictum that 'the masses go into a revolution not with a prepared plan of social reconstruction, but with a deep feeling that they cannot endure the old regime'.[35] The Revolution astonished the world because an opposition armed only with slogans, leaflets and audio cassettes overthrew a ruler with formidable national and international resources at his disposal and in a period of impressive though lopsided economic growth. Some of the intellectual inspirations for the change came from the Sorbonne-trained Islamist Ali Shariati. The leftist groups and the trade unions provided the manpower for street demonstrations. The real catalyst, however, was the personality of Ayatollah Khomeini and the network of the Shia clergy which he was able to motivate and mobilize into action. The Revolution, somewhat like the French Revolution, went through different stages including a power struggle with some of its initial supporters (Mujahedi-e-Khalq), a stage of Terror, and a long Revolutionary War with Iraq. In the final analysis this effort at establishing an Islamic State resulted in a dictatorship of the clergy which then sought to elevate itself above the normal injunctions of faith. The government, asserted Khomeini in 1988, 'which is part of the absolute vice-regency of the Prophet of God is one of the primary injunctions of Islam and has priority over all other secondary injunctions, even prayer, fasting and hajj'.[36] After the death of Khomeini, Iran went through a Thermidorian phase leading to the birth of a Second Republic in which the transition was made 'from the age of revolutionary passions to that of revolutionary reason' and sought 'renewed legitimacy'— democratic and religious—through the election of May 1997 which brought Mohammad Khatemi to power on a promise of rejuvenating civil society.[37]

The Iranian Revolution, and the foundation of the Islamic Republic, provided tremendous impetus to Islamic movements the world over (despite the virtually unbridgeable sectarian divide). Despite this, the euphoria faded soon enough in the Arab and the Islamic world; the exceptions to this were the Hizbullah in South Lebanon, the Islamic Jihad in Palestine and some groups in war-torn Afghanistan. This living experience with Triumphant Islamism also demonstrates its limitations:

The consolidation of the regime after 1979 and its continuation after Khomeini's death provide much material for analysis of what the practice of Islamism is in terms of political and social control. It also illustrates the greatest failing of the Islamist movement in general: namely, their lack of an economic programme.[38]

Indonesia: The Islamic movement in Indonesia took shape in the struggle against Dutch rule. The Muslim parties, particularly Masjoomi and Mohammadiyah, enjoyed the strongest influence in the early period after independence and secured 44 per cent of the votes cast in the election of 1955. At the same time some of the Muslim militant groups linked to the resistance in the pre-independence period and affiliated to Masjoomi continued to hold their own in parts of the country; one such group was the Hizbullah which declared an Islamic State ('Darul Islam') in parts of West Java and continued to function till 1962.[39] The Islamist groups were also used by the government in its struggle against the Indonesian Communist Party in 1965–1966 period. In the initial stages of Soharto's Presidency, the authorities as an act of policy differentiated 'between the religious and political activities of Islam, encouraging religious activities, but proscribing attempts to develop a powerful political base'.[40] This was not altogether successful and the government's 'cultural solution' was considered unacceptable by many who drifted towards political Islam under the influence of the writings of Al Banna, Sayyid Qutb and Maudoodi. These elements 'believe that violence is necessary to achieve their goal of establishing an Islamic state and is also justified in eliminating unislamic elements in the existing state and society'. These fundamentalists are 'generally drawn from the modernist rather than the traditionalist stream and see themselves as continuing the struggle pioneered by the Darul Islam and part of the Musjoomi'.[41] Their activities included sporadic acts of violence which, however, failed to take the shape of an organized movement.

IV

Despite the high profile developed by them in the past two decades, the assertions and interpretations advocated by the proponents of 'Militant Islam' have not gone unchallenged and have been disputed in both in theological and in political terms by scholars, political activists and governments. This critique has essentially emanated from two directions: (a) liberal modernists and (b) moderate Islamists. The first group endeavours to deconstruct the Arab-Islamic mind in order to highlight its historical character and the impact it has had on the development of Islamic jurisprudence (Fiqh) and particularly on the concept of the Islamic State. The Islamic moderates, on the other hand, have faulted the radicals on their comprehension and their interpretation of the classical texts and have pointed out that excessiveness and extremism in matters religion are violative of the Qur'anic injunction (2:143) of 'an Ummah justly balanced'; they also draw attention to a Hadith (saying of the Prophet): 'Beware of excessiveness in religion. People before you have perished as a result of such excessiveness.'[42] Such excessiveness is contrary to human nature, is short-lived, and jeopardizes other rights and obligations; it manifests itself in bigotry, intolerance and harshness and each of these is expressly forbidden by Qur'an and Sunnah.[43] This excessiveness is caused by 'a lack of knowledge of—and insight into—the purposes, spirit and essence of *din* (religion)'. This lack of knowledge and of the context in which specific injunctions were given results in self-presumption and conceit which is the root cause of undesirable innovation (bi'ah) which in turn leads to 'internal schism and general disintegration' of the Ummah.

Moderate Islamists and mainstream Ulema point out that many of the basic premises of the militants are based on misconception and on an excessive reliance on allegorical texts. The misconceptions are based on an inability to appreciate 'the difference between absolute (or perfect) *iman* and limited (or nominal) *iman*; between perfect Islam and limited (or nominal) Islam; between major *kufr* leading to non-Islam and *kufr* of disobedience; between major *shirk* and minor *shirk*; between hypocrisy of belief and hypocrisy of action'.[44] With regard to the allegorical text, it is asserted that emphasis on these and a disregard on the categorical ones is and has always been a major cause for misunderstandings on religious maters and is emphatically contrary to what is said in the Qur'an (3:7):

He it is Who has sent down to you (Muhammad) the Book; in it are verses of basic or fundamental (meaning); they are the foundation of the Book; others are allegorical. But those in whose hearts is perversity follow the part thereof that is allegorical, seeking discord, and searching for hidden meanings, but no one knows its true meaning except Allah.[45]

Having identified these theoretical and practical shortcomings in the arguments of the militants, the moderate Islamists also highlight the reasons leading to the emergence of the militant mindset. In the process they hold the Arab regimes, and their repressive policies, responsible for the situation. They express the view that the Islamic awakening amongst the youth is genuine and should therefore be carefully channelled rather than repressed. They complain, with justice, that the authorities in West Asian states did not begin to pay attention to religious youth until the latter began to oppose, on religious grounds, some of the policies of their respective governments.

V

An eminent scholar has observed that if we are to understand anything at all about what is happening in the Muslim world 'then there are two essential points that need to be grasped. One is the universality of religion as a factor in the lives of Muslim peoples, and the other is its centrality'.[46] Islam thus is both the most effective form of consensus and of basic group identity amongst the masses.[47] The brief survey in this essay suggests that Islamic militancy in recent times arose out of genuine resentment emanating from alienation and deprivation and in a quest for authenticity. The militants seek to obtain this authenticity through the Islamic model of a utopia which may never have existed but is nevertheless an integral component of the Islamic political imagination. The question of deprivation, on the other hand, is real and widespread but cannot be addressed in the absence of a viable economic programme and of an alternative developmental model which, so far at least, the radical Islamists have failed to put forward.

Islamic militancy in most Muslim countries is on the decline at the moment and has received a major setback in the aftermath of the 11 September 2001 events. The militants have noted that their endeavours at the local or national levels are now likely to be thwarted through a good measure of regional or international cooperation. The battle for the minds and hearts would nevertheless need to be waged convincingly. This would require the incorporation of the recent experience of Arab (and non-Arab) Muslim societies where, in the words of Fouad Ajami, the intellectual edifice of secular nationalism and modernity built up over a generation has been lost and in which 'the generational fault-line between secular parents and their theocratic children'[48] is clearly identifiable.

What then are the options in the face of this evident re-Islamization of society notwithstanding the failure of the militant Islam model?

The uneasy coexistence with the existing regimes could continue, with marginal accommodation. How far can this accommodation be stretched? Would not the regimes continue to draw a line in quest of self-preservation? Would not the present situation recur every time the line is touched?

The regimes could, autonomously, opt for participatory governance, co-opt moderate Islamist elements and expose them (on the Jordanian model) to the vagaries of electoral politics where pragmatic adjustments rather than doctrinaire assertions would hold sway. The moderate Islamists now accept that 'the tools and guarantees created by democracy are as close as can ever be to the realization of the political principles brought to the earth by Islam to put a leash on the ambitions and whims of rulers'.[49]

Muslims living in non-Muslim majority societies now show a growing awareness of the benefits of secularism and are debating to a lesser degree the question of incompatibility between Islam and secularism.[50] Over a period of time these perceptions could assist the development of civil society norms, including secularism, in Muslim majority societies themselves. This would, however, require a change in the paradigm of expression, perhaps along the lines advocated by the Indonesian Islamist leader Abdur Rahman Wahid. The experience of Iran in recent years highlights the difficulties which would be encountered in any such endeavour.

In the final analysis, therefore, questions arising out of Islam's encounter with modernity would need to be answered by the Muslims themselves. The need of the hour is to strike the right balance and even radical Islamists cannot with ease ignore a fatwa by the 14th-century theologian Ahmad Ibn Taymiyya:

An evil may be tolerated in two cases: if it would lead to avoiding a worse evil that cannot be averted otherwise, and if it will bring about an interest that can neither be abandoned nor be brought about otherwise. An interest or a benefit may be abandoned in two cases: if it involves the loss of a better interest, or if it entails an evil that is much larger. This is what related to religious balances.[51]

The exercise of translating this into social and political action would be interesting but not devoid of pain. Ibn Taymiyya cites with approval the adage that 'a wise man is not one who can tell good from evil, but is one who can tell the better of two good things and the lesser of two evils'.

21

Islam and the Democratic Principle*

Islamic cosmology begins with Creation. The Qur'an dwells on the purpose of Creation. It was for 'just ends' (s.xv. 85, xvi. 3, xliv. 39, xlv. 22, xlvi. 3), and for obedience to God (viii. 20). The question of disobedience, and its implications, is addressed through the story of *Iblis* (s.xxxviii. 71–78).[1] Questions pertaining to governance, to the legitimacy of the ruler, to the rights and duties of both the rulers and the ruled and to the conditionality of allegiance have thus been of abiding concern to Muslims and Muslim societies. Each of these is a traditional theme; each also has a contemporary ring about it. Tradition and modernity thus emerge as two facets of the same coin and the challenge, in Daniel Brown's perceptive phase, is to 'see tradition as a beam of light, refracted by the prism of modernity'.[2]

Scholars have long debated the Islamic concept of governance. They have scanned the texts, the exegesis and the annals of history. Some have lifted the veil, so to speak; others have reinforced it. As a consequence of the latter, what was evident and obvious became shrouded and disputed. Valuable time was lost and enlightened speculation—the hallmark of a vibrant community—was abandoned in favour of frigid and misleading emulation.

Muslims constitute one-sixth of humanity and are to be found in most parts of the world. Islam to them is a living reality in a religious and social sense and Islamic precepts on societal matters, therefore, impact on their perceptions relating to public issues. Consequently, the image of a pristine model of the political entity, and of governance, has a practical relevance in every age. It is thus essential to ascertain what was specifically ordained and to do so by revisiting the basic texts.

---

* Khuda Bakhsh Memorial Lecture, February 2003.

The Qur'an reveals its own essence and purpose in the second sura: 'This is the Book; in it is guidance sure, without doubt, to those who fear God' (ii. 2). This guidance is given in over 6000 verses; of these, the following relate to questions of governance:

- 'The Believers are but a single Brotherhood.' (xlix. 10)
- 'Ye are the best of Peoples, evolved for mankind, enjoining what is right, forbidding what is wrong, and believing in God.' (iii. 110)
- 'O ye who believe! Fulfil (all) obligations.' (v. 1)
- 'O ye who believe! Obey God, and obey the Apostle, and those charged with authority among you. If ye differ in anything among yourself, refer it to God and His Apostle, if ye do believe in God and the Last Day.' (iv. 59)
- 'Those who hearken to their Lord, and establish regular prayer; who (conduct) their affair by mutual Consultation; who spend out of what We bestow on them for Sustenance.' (xlii. 38)
- 'It is part of the Mercy of God that thou dost deal gently with them. Wert thou severe or harsh-hearted, they would have broken away from thee: so pass over (their faults) and ask for (God's) forgiveness for them; and consult them in affairs (of moment). Then, when thou hast taken a decision, put thy trust in God.' (iii. 159)
- 'It is not fitting for a Believer, man or woman, when a matter has been decided by God and His Apostle, to have any option about their decision: if anyone disobeys God and His Apostle, he is indeed on a clearly wrong Path.' (xxxiii. 10)
- 'O ye who believe! Stand out firmly for justice, as witnesses to God, even as against yourself, or your parents, or your kin, and whether it be against rich or poor: for God can best protect both. Follow not the lust of your heart, lest ye swerve, and if ye distort justice or decline to do justice, verily God is well acquainted with all that ye do.' (iv. 135)

These sections of the Text prescribe general principles for the conduct of personal and public affairs. By implication, they relate to the organization of the political life of a community and principally to its method of functioning; the latter is to be undertaken through public consultation (*Shura*) prior to decision-making. These principles were implemented by the Prophet himself in the conduct of the political affairs of the city-state of Madinah and of the Islamic community. As such, they constituted a model.

A number of questions need to be addressed. What was the nature of the model and its operational details? Was it recommendatory or prescriptive? To what extent was it emulated in the period immediately after the Prophet and in subsequent ages? Above all, what conclusions can be drawn from the historical record?

* * *

Historically speaking, the Muslims were a religious community before they became a political one. Social cohesion therefore existed at the moment of birth of the political community and the Prophet of Islam combined in his person the twin roles of being the religious and the political head of the community. The Constitution of Madinah clearly stated that points of contention in the community were to be 'referred to God and to Mohammad'.[3] This was sui generis. After him the community was confronted with compelling questions: who was to be the leader, how was he to be identified, what powers were to be conferred on him, whom would he consult and with what frequency, what—in case of need—would be the corrective mechanism? The spatial dimension complicated matters. The dramatic expansion in those early years of the Muslim domains beyond the confines of the Arabian Peninsula resulted in transforming the city-state into an empire and this had a profound impact on the nature and functioning of the Islamic State. Thus, a careful scrutiny of the historical record relating to that period is essential—more so because tradition and reverence often discourages us from doing so.

It is significant that the Prophet did not nominate a successor. In a process that was Madinah-centric, Mohajir-centric, and contentious, Abu Bakr al-Siddiq was selected as 'Khalifa Rasul-Allah' (Vicegerent of the Prophet of God). Those outside were not consulted. Details of the proceedings of this electoral college are given by Ibn Hisham and Tabari.[4] Two years later Abu Bakr nominated Umar ibn al Khattab as his successor: 'I have entrusted your affairs to him who I feel is the best of you';[5] his choice was approved by public acclamation in Madinah. Ten years later Omar, on his part, entrusted the choice of the next Khalifa (Caliph) to a council of six that was to limit its search to its own members and operate within draconic rules of procedure to ensure unanimity.[6] Finally the procedure for the selection of the fourth Caliph was somewhat akin to the one adopted for the first, except for the friction and violence that preceded it and left an indelible mark on community perceptions.

The conclusion is inescapable that the earliest—and the most revered—period of Islamic history did not produce a pattern or a set procedure for the selection of the political leader of the community. What it did produce, unambiguously, were prescriptions and practices about how the leader of the community should conduct himself and what rights accrued to the ruled—both as obligations emanating from religion itself. The primacy, obviously, was given to the practice of the Prophet himself. Then came the administrative practices of the first four Caliphs and particularly of Omar and Ali. All of them displayed an acute awareness of the duties of the ruler.[7] It is this that accounts for the imprint of that period on the political imagery of the Muslims.

The record shows that in keeping with the prevailing Arab tribal custom, opinion did not favour the hereditary principle, even though it acknowledged the importance of lineage as well as the hierarchy of tribes. It was accepted that 'the chief must be a man of wisdom and sound judgement';[8] in terms of moral excellence, however, compromises were sometimes made. In the year 660 CE, when Muawiyah bin Abu Sufyan was contending for the office in succession to Ali ibn Abi Taleb, a field commander of the latter posed a question to his troops: 'O people, choose between submitting to a leader of error or fighting without a leader'; the response was 'no, we choose instead a leader of error'.[9] Two centuries later the jurist al-Jahiz described the year of Muawiyah's assumption of office as 'a year of schism, coercion, oppression and violence, a year in which the imamate became a monarchy after the fashion of the Chosroes and the caliphate a tyranny worthy of a Caesar'.[10] After nineteen years of rule Muawiyah, having consolidated a monarchical structure, could pretend to emulate the precedent of Abu Bakr to nominate his successor and unabashedly bestow the choice on his son Yazid despite his poor public image. His death bed remarks to his son summed up his achievement on this score: 'O my son, I have spared you the effort, made things smooth for you, subdued enemies for you, subjected the necks of the Arabs for you, and created unity for you.'[11]

The change was formal as well as substantive. The Arab armies that subdued the Byzantine and the Sasanian empires also imbibed some of the style of governance of these two world powers. Mohammad Shaban has explored the economic implications of the imperial venture.[12] Aziz Al-Azmeh has traced the 'unrestrained, even playful, experimentation with the prerogatives, privileges, and enunciations of kingship, which were directly and personally exercised' by the Umayyad rulers. The Abbasids added to them in considerable measure.[13] The practical impact of the change in the designation of the office—from Khalifa Rasul-Allah to Khalifat Allah (Vicegerent of God)—made in the period of the second Khalifa, began to be felt in Muawiyah's reign when, among other prerogatives, he assumed the power of life and death over fellow Muslims.[14]

A change so substantive, within a generation, is difficult to comprehend. Was the legendary Arab love for freedom, and for tribal autonomy, exchanged for the benefits accruing from being collectively the masters of an empire? Did they view as sacrosanct the Shura-model as a principle of governance? If so, why was it not sustained; if not, what was the need to continue the fiction of the Caliphate? The imperative for the latter, it would seem, lay in the need for legitimacy and legitimization. Did this concern for legitimacy confine itself to the process of selection of the ruler only, or did it extend itself to the manner of governance also?

The chronology of events is relevant. The Umayyads (660–750 CE) ruled but did not propound a theory of Khilafah (Caliphate). A conceptual framework for the office in fact emanated from the opponents of the dynasty, the Khawarij and the Zaydis, both of whom (but from diametrically opposite positions) insisted on the Khalifa-Imam possessing the required personal qualities; they also asserted the right (arising out of the contractual nature of the commitment) of the community of Believers to withdraw allegiance in case of poor or sinful governance. The Abbasids, who took office on pretence of greater piety but soon imbibed the work and lifestyle of their predecessors, faced a similar situation. The resulting confusion in the minds of the pious therefore called for a juridical exercise that would 'justify the transfer of power from the orthodox caliphs (the *rashidun*) to the Umayyads and from the latter to the Abbasids and also to defend the internal peace of the Muslim community under the historic caliphate'.[15] Concern for stability thus became the primary concern.

The Sunni theory of the Caliphate, developed in the 8th and 9th centuries CE by a number of eminent publicists and jurists, took final shape when effective power had begun to ebb from the Khalifa-Imam into the hands of local rulers. It thus had to accommodate itself to three developments that had not been catered for in the original concept: (i) the transition from a Caliph selected through consultations to one assuming office through the hereditary principle; (ii) the qualitative enhancement in the powers exercised by the Caliph unilaterally and (iii) the eventual decline in the military power of the Caliphs resulting in the transference of actual power to local rulers who subscribed notionally to the supremacy of the Caliphs. The absence of institutions to manage the empire contributed to it so did over-reliance on military means and a failure to develop a viable tax structure for the provinces. When the Caliph Mu'tadid came to power in the year 892, 'there were no reserves in the central treasury for the first time in its history'.[16]

Amongst those who pronounced on the subject, the most prominent name is that of Abu al-Hasan al-Mawardi (974–1058 CE). The purpose of the Imamate or Supreme Leadership is 'upholding the faith and managing the affairs of the world'. He regarded the office as obligatory and prescribed seven conditions of eligibility. Appointment to it could be made in two ways: 'selection by electors, or appointment by a predecessor. There is considerable disagreement among scholars on the number of electors necessary for the valid investment of a sovereign'. Confining himself to historical precedents, he said the number could range between one and six who could even be designated by the predecessor; he does however make a mention of the view that the selection should be 'no fewer than the generality of electors throughout the land in order for his election to be unanimously approved and his authority universally accepted'. The public duties of the Khalifa—ten in number—are mentioned, and if carried out necessitate allegiance and obedience; at the same, lack of justice (including sinfulness and suspected unorthodoxy) and physical disability could render him unqualified to continue in the post. A procedure for removing an incumbent from office, however, is not spelt out. Al-Mawardi cites with approval a remark of the second Caliph, Umar, about the requisite qualities: 'strong but not violent; flexible but not weak; frugal but not niggardly; and generous but not extravagant'.[17]

It is another matter that at the time al-Mawardi was writing, the Caliph had ceased to exercise effective political power and the prescriptions of the jurist therefore were essentially aimed at bringing the holder of actual power within the framework of Islamic legitimacy. Allowance is therefore made for legitimizing the local rulers who establish themselves forcibly; thus, fear of injury to public interest was considered reason enough for 'the investiture of the usurer'. The same dilemma confronted Al-Ghazali

(1058–1111 CE) whose thinking on the subject is dominated by a fear of civil war and disturbance leading to disorder and anarchy. The choice, he said, is between giving up all the civic institutions of the imamate in view of the latter's lack of effective power or in continuing on the assumption that the office continues: 'The concessions made by us are not spontaneous, but necessity makes lawful what is forbidden—which is to be preferred, anarchy and the stoppage of social life for lack of a properly constituted authority, or acknowledgement of the existing power whatever it may be? Of these two alternatives, the jurist cannot but choose the latter.'[18] This practice, of adopting theory to the requirement of the times, was continued by Fadl Allah Khunji (d. 1521) who unequivocally stated that the holder of effective power was the Imam irrespective of how that power was acquired.[19] The 'right' thus created formed the basis of the exercise of absolute power by the Muslim rulers in India, Persia and Turkey. In such a context, proper governance acquired a different connotation altogether. Its primary purpose became the maintenance of public order and the avoidance of anarchy. By implication, therefore, tyranny became a secondary issue— undesirable yet unavoidable.

Three centuries later another eminent thinker, Shah Wali Allah Dehlavi (1703–1762 CE), reviewed the resulting situation:

> Those holding the office of *khalifa* often tend to be cruel and oppressive, following their whims and vagaries. They may abuse their authority and corrupt the populace by an unbridled exercise of power in disregard of the latter's rights. In such circumstances the disadvantage of the office of *khalifa* may exceed its anticipated advantages. In pursuing this policy, they often fall back on false claims of following the right course and of giving consideration to some supposed public policy. It was, therefore, necessary that certain basic rules were laid down whose violation would be condemned and the rulers could be subjected to impeachment on account of their violation.

Despite this trenchant criticism his preference remained for a quietist approach. The ruler should be allowed to continue in office as long as the system of Prayers remains undisturbed because 'violence and strife' involved in removing him would do greater harm. Two sayings of the Prophet were cited in support of this approach.[20] Thus on one hand the aberration was sanctified while on the other the norms of proper governance, prescribed and observed in period of the Prophet and his immediate successors, were relegated to a less essential area of concern. In the process, as Muhammad Asad rightly observed, 'a glorious beginning was allowed to lapse into oblivion, to the detriment of Islam and of the social development of its followers'.[21]

A similar concern for legitimacy in theory but acquiescence in practice—though based on different premises and proceeding on a different process of reasoning—runs through the Shia schools. The initial contestation, immediately after the death of the Prophet, related to the selection of the first Caliph. While the Sunnis vested the authority for leadership in the community as a whole, the Shias 'preferred to accept the leadership of only those who derived their authority directly from the person of the Prophet and in this way enjoyed divine sanction'. In the initial period and until the death of Husain (680 CE) the focus was on 'on a well-defined trend of thought, an ideal of polity, and on an underlying principle of religious adherence'. Thereafter, 'disagreements arose over the specific criteria for deciding who the divinely inspired leader was, and this led to the internal division of Shia Islam'.[22] Imam Jaafar as-Sadiq sought to refine the concept of the Imam by 'dividing the Imamate and the caliphate into two separate institutions until such time as God would make an Imam victorious' and by endowing the Imamate with two basic characteristics: that the Imamate is a prerogative bestowed by God on a chosen person from the family of the Prophet who transfers it to another by an explicit designation, and that the Imam is a divinely inspired possessor of a special sum of knowledge of religion that he transfers to his successor.[23] Despite this, differences persisted and resulted in the emergence of three principal schools: the Zaydiyya, the Ismailiyya and the Imamiyya.[24] These differences impacted on Shia perceptions of governance but did not, until recently, disturb the quietist approach of legitimizing political authority.[25]

The abolition of the Caliphate by the Turkish National Assembly in 1924 put an end to this legacy of over a millennium. More importantly, the Egyptian scholar Ali Abd ar-Raziq argued in 1925 that the Caliphate had no basis in the Qur'an, the Traditions or consensus and that Islam leaves the Muslims free to choose whatever form of government they find suitable to ensure their welfare.[26] He said,

> There is nothing in the religion which prevents Muslims from competing
> with other nations in the field of social and political sciences, and from

demolishing that antiquated order which has subjugated and humiliated them, and to build up rules of their state and the organization of their government on the basis of the most modern achievement, of human reason, and on the most solid experiences of nations as to the best principles of government.[27]

Abd ar-Raziq, however, was ahead of his times and the trend of thought, following the controversy relating to his ideas, tended to proceed in the opposite direction. Thus Rashid Rida, while acknowledging the impossibility of reviving the Caliphate, uses *ijtihad* to promote the concept of an Islamic State. This idea formed the basis of the political philosophy of the Muslim Brotherhood School of thinkers—principally Maudoodi and Sayyid Qutb—who considered Islam and democracy to be incompatible. Others in the Islamist camp, like Malek Bennabi of Algeria (d. 1973), sought to adopt Islamic values to modernity and argue that 'if there exists a democratic tradition in Islam, then it ought not to be sought in the letter of the constitutional text, but rather in the spirit of Islam in general' which shows humanistic cultural development: 'Islam offers genuine democracy because it is a synthesis between political democracy and social democracy.' The present predicament of the Muslims, he said, is of their own making.[28]

Rachid Ghannouchi of Tunisia, a disciple of Bennabi, has developed the theme further in recent years to suggest that if Islam is the final Divine Revelation, then it is only appropriate that no final prescriptions are given for matters that are of a changing nature and Muslims can devise suitable solutions for them by flexibility and constructive thinking (*ijtihad*). This means

> a distinction between the areas that have to be filled by Divine commandments and the areas that were intentionally left vacant so as to be filled with what is needed to cope with changes through *ijtihad* but within the framework of *aqida*.[29]

Two others of his assertions are significant: in the first place 'Muslims require genuine modernity no less than anyone else. Genuine modernity entails human emancipation and establishing the right of freedom of choice; the propagation of scientific and technological progress; the establishment of a democratic system and reassertion of the sovereignty of the people'. Secondly, in the absence of a government on the pristine Islamic pattern, 'the second best alternative for Muslims is a secular democratic regime' which is 'less evil than a despotic system of government that claims to be Islamic'.[30] Still others like Fazlur Rahman stressed that the Qur'anic precepts visualize 'the Muslim society to be relentlessly egalitarian and open, unstained by elitism and no secretiveness and that the internal life and conduct of society pivots around mutual active goodwill and cooperation'. Consequently, 'the participatory association of the ummah in the political and legislative decisions affecting the life of the community can neither be rejected nor postponed' and those who suggest this 'are wittingly or unwittingly guilty of rendering Islam null and void'.[31]

The Imami doctrine, too, confronted conceptual reinterpretation. Ayatollah Khomeini, drawing upon the approach of the 19th-century *mujtahid* Mulla Ahmad Naraqi, argued for the assumption of power by the ulema as the only legitimate basis for governance in the period of the occultation of the 12th Imam. Such a government, he said, is 'constitutional in the sense that the ruler is subject to a set of conditions in the governing and administering of the country, conditions set forth in the Qur'an and the Sunna'.[32] The Constitution of the Islamic Republic of Iran sought to encapsulate this within the framework of a democracy; in the process, it highlighted the contradiction between its democratic and anti-democratic elements, arising chiefly from the conflict between two notions of sovereignty embodied in the document.[33]

The debate in the 20th century settled the question of incompatibility with regard to democracy and made some dent in the traditionalist perceptions concerning secularism. The discussion, however, remained confined to matters pertaining to rulers; little was said on the form and content of governance. One reason for this, perhaps, was the absence of the concept from the 'active vocabulary' of public administration, and of international covenants. Developments on the global scene and the democracy wave that swept many parts of the world towards the end of the Cold War, however, induced analysis of the functioning of political communities within their boundaries and within a wider framework of relations and forces. Questions relating to the observance of human rights norms surfaced on the national and international agenda, and so did matters pertaining to the status of women, the rights of the child, the treatment of ethnic, linguistic or religious minorities, intolerance or discrimination on grounds of religion or belief, the right to development and a host of other themes. The Vienna Declaration and Programme of

Action on Human Rights promulgated that democracy, development and respect for fundamental rights and freedoms 'are interdependent and mutually reinforcing'. The Millennium Summit of the United Nations called for 'a new ethic of stewardship'. The World Bank developed governance indicators. The UNDP proclaimed a convergence between human rights and human development in pursuit of human freedom; hence 'effective governance is central to human development'. The Arab Human Development Report defined good governance as 'participatory, transparent and accountable. It is also effective and equitable and it promotes the rule of law'. Cumulatively, new norms of legitimacy surfaced on the horizon and the view took shape—but not without resistance—that national sovereignty should not be a shield against excesses in governance.

How should Muslim thinking respond to these, 21st century, norms of governance? In the first place, do these contradict or contravene the core values of governance as prescribed by Islam: consultations before decision-taking, an open process of governance, social justice, duties of rulers, rights of the ruled and a right of dissent leading up to allegiance being withheld? Secondly, do they circumscribe the freedom of Muslims to practice their faith? The answer to both is in the negative. If so, the suggested norms should find wide acceptance. This, however, is not the case yet and a range of arguments, ranging from culture-specificity to local traditions, are put forth to evade a responsibility and a course of action that is unambiguously prescribed by religious law and happens to coincide in great measure with contemporary standards. This has resulted in a wider onslaught, from many quarters and from motives that are far from altruistic, on the value system of Islam.

Progress in societies is a function of challenge and response. The challenge of the age is to expand autonomously the vistas of freedom and responsibility. In 1996 Mahathir Mohamad of Malaysia said that since Islam was for all times and for every part of the world, the Muslim quest for guidance from religious texts has to be in the context of the present times.[34] In 1997 a call for the creation of an Islamic civil society, whose citizens 'would enjoy the right to determine their own destiny, supervise governance, and hold the government responsible', was made by Mohammad Khatami of Iran; others, in a spirit of introspection, spoke more ambiguously about 'the need to set the Islamic house in order'.[35] The impact was minimal. A deeply embedded neo-patriarchal pattern of governance, understandably, would not contemplate with relish the loss of patrimony; and yet, change must come if Muslims are to distance themselves from their present predicament.

A more persuasive argument for change relates to security and stability. This too has been espoused by Khatami: 'It is necessary to explore the relationship between freedom and national security and the positive effect of the former on the latter, and the destructive effect of the lack of freedom on social stability.'[36] In another part of the world Abdurrahman Wahid of Indonesia said the challenge is to develop an integrated educational system; also, a new approach to the understanding of Islamic law in order to reconcile the apparent contradiction between its formalistic precepts and 'the universal values that we not only endorse but also proclaim to be at the heart of our faith'.[37] These new dimensions to the imperative for change are suggestive of an emerging awareness of the magnitude of the exercise that must be undertaken. A new impulse, in the shape of the external pressure for change, is a complicating factor as is evident from the United States policy announcement of 12 December 2002 urging the Arab public to find strong leaders who would 'find a balance between faith and an open political system'. Would not externally induced change distort the process, sap self-confidence and generate negative reactions over a longer term?

The benchmarks of good governance—participation, transparency, accountability and rule of law—are a part of the Islamic precepts of proper governance. Hesitation with regard to them, on the part of any Muslim society, emanates from extraneous and non-Islamic reasons. Such attitudes are harmful to the citizens of the societies concerned and hamper their collective progress. These situations call for urgent affirmative action. In 1961, Muhammad Asad felt the 'moment of free choice' had arrived for the nations of the Muslim world. He was of course wrong because he made no allowance for the 'infra-historical rhythm' (to borrow Abdullah Laroui's phrase) of Muslim societies.[38]

A change of rhythm is the categorical imperative of our times. Is it too much to suggest that this be done in order to rejuvenate the creative impulse that characterized the civilization of Islam for so long, so well?

Postscript

Some readers of this essay, published in the *Khoda-Bakhsh Library Journal* (volume 131, January–March 2003, pp. 1–18) raised a question about the gap between theory and practice: 'Why has democracy not taken root in most Islamic Countries?' An answer to this is to be sought in the conceptual framework of the debate, as also in its location in time and space.

The democracy debate is an aspect of modernity. It has been argued that democracy is a two-sided process: concerned, on the one hand, with the reform of state power and, on the other, with the restructuring of civil society. It thus entails 'the interdependent transformation of both state and society . . . If one chooses democracy, one must choose to operationalize a radical system of rights'.[39] This debate, in most Muslim societies, came to the fore in a practical sense in the post-colonial period. The civic discussion about the form of government also coincided with, and in most cases was subsumed in, the wider debate about Islam and modernity. In this endeavour three impulses hindered deliberations on the form of government: the desire to adhere to tradition; the conviction that the principle of *Shura* was comprehensive and sufficient; the belief that the concept of popular sovereignty contradicted the dictum that sovereignty over the universe resided in God. The first impulse hindered a critical choice: a decision by Muslims on what exactly is to be conserved, what is essential and relevant for the erection of an Islamic future, and what is fundamentally Islamic and what is purely 'historical'.[40] The second impulse ignored the experience of governance in all periods of Muslim history after the initial, earliest, one. Nor were modalities of participatory governance explored in depth and sufficient attention paid to Mohammad Iqbal's observation that Muslims never effectively developed the elective principle.[41] The third impulse showed signs of being unduly influenced by the 19th to early 20th-century juristic concepts of sovereignty and displayed little awareness the manner in which the Pluralistic Theory of the State, and international law, had transformed the concept of the State and therefore of sovereignty.[42]

The distortion of the theoretical framework, combined with the imperative to justify the status quo, thus became a principal determinant and led in Muslim lands to 'the adoption of a culturally defensive posture'.[43] Consequently, the requirement 'to reformulate the orthodox content and create institutions to ensure the (1) the solidarity and the stability of the community and the state and (2) the active, positive and responsible participation of the public at large in the affairs of the government and the state'[44] was not availed of. Instead, the debate remained enmeshed in contours of what constitutes an *Islamic State*, in the metaphysical dimensions of the concept of sovereignty and in Western *secular* democracy being the antithesis of Islam. Vested interests, in the shape of the ruler or of the ruling elite, became the principal beneficiary of this social and intellectual mobility. Religion was principally used as a mobilizing force to preserve the status quo. The effort to use it as a transforming factor remained confined and ineffective until the advent of Islamist thinkers and activists. The latter led one scholar to note that 'religious resurgence and democratisation are the two most important developments of the final decades of the twentieth century'.[45] A contemporary jurist, who assessed the twin impulses in the context of the classical theory, concludes that 'there are some differences between the Islamic system of rule and a modern democratic state. Yet, there is enough in common between them to justify the characterisation of the Islamic State as a qualified democracy'.[46]

The pattern in practice, nevertheless, was not uniform. A desegregation of 'Muslim societies' presents a 'spectrum of experiences'. A common fallacy is to treat the 'Muslim' and the 'Arab' as synonymous terms and draw conclusions that are generally erroneous. Statistically speaking, 85 per cent of the Muslims of the world are non-Arabs and over 70 per cent of Muslims live in Asian States. The presence or absence of democratic governance in Arab or West Asian lands cannot, therefore, be reason enough for a generalized statement about the compatibility or otherwise of Islamic or Muslim society and democracy. On the contrary, a wider geographical paradigm—inclusive of Asian in particular—contradicts such a perception and presents a differentiated picture of successes and partial successes; this is sustained by the recent history of countries like Bangladesh, Indonesia, Iran, Malaysia, Pakistan and Turkey.

Despite these, impediments remain and shed light on the pace and limitations of democratization. They relate principally to two critical areas: the first of these pertains to the domain of the sacred and the secular and the second to the acceptance and implementation of a modern system of rights. The secular paradigm of an earlier generation failed and led to re-Islamization. Similarly, the question of a *modern* system of rights cannot be dealt with in the classical—and religiously sanctioned—framework of *haqq Allah* (Right of God) and *haqq al-abd* (Right of Man).[47] The social milieu, and the equation of forces in society, inevitably plays a role in the process of State formation. If the State construction is on a collision course with the social dynamics of the political process, then reconciliation requires skills that are firmly embedded in civil society. The focus thus inevitably shifts to the civil society.

In the Arab world, a change of approach and expression is noticeable in the Alexandria Statement on Arab Reform Issues of March 2004. It summed up the requirement for genuine democracy 'without ambiguity':

> This genuine democracy requires guaranteed freedom of expression in all its forms, topmost amongst which is freedom of the press, and audio-visual and electronic media. It calls for adopting free, regular, centralised and decentralised elections to guarantee freedom of power and the rule of the people. It also requires the highest possible level of decentralisation that would allow greater self-expression by local communities, unleashing their creative potentials for cultural contributions to human development in all fields. This is closely linked to achieving the highest level of transparency in public life, to stamping out corruption within the framework of establishing good governance and support for human rights provided according to international agreements. The rights of women, children and minorities, the protection of the fundamental rights of those charged with criminal offences and humane treatment of citizens are on top of the list.

Specific political reforms and the adoption of international norms and covenants are incorporated in the document. So is a suggestion for cultural reforms that would jettison negative values like 'submissiveness and obedience' with positive ones of 'independence and dialogue'. The statement suggested the reform vision can only see the light of day if civil society and government work together to bring it about.

Empirical analysis indicates that this reform vision has yet to be realized in adequate measure. Some have attributed this to the methodology of thought:

> The Muslim mind . . . has remained a prisoner of those concepts and basic approaches that doom it to remain bound by past mistakes and digressions and bereft of the ability to penetrate, distinguish, and amend its own course, or plumb the depth of issues confronting it. Thus it is unable to boldly chart a course for the future, for it sits bound and blindfolded in a dusty corner of the distant past.[48]

This line of argument rejects both the 'imitative historical model' and the 'imitative foreign model' and advocates instead an innovative Islamic model adapted to the requirements of the present. It is valid to the point of advocating change.[49] The critical impulse, however, relates to the extent of change and of innovativeness; unless it is sufficiently far reaching, the chances of it getting away from the gravitational pull of tradition will remain in question.

22

Convocation Address at the Jamia Millia Islamia University*

I

Ba naam-e-khudavand jaan aafareen
Hakeem-e-sokhan dar zubaan aafareen

(In the name of God the Merciful
In the name of the Lord soul-offering
Wise one, speech crafting in the tongue
Lord forgiving, apt to help)

—Opening lines of Saadi's *The Bustan*

A diplomat by profession, an academic by courtesy and the holder of a public office perhaps by the fall of the dice is called upon by you not only to participate in the most solemn of occasions in the academic calendar of a university, but also to share the inadequacy of his thought process with this audience. Prudence would have counselled restraint; my own association with the Jamia, however, induced me to take the bold step of venturing into the unknown.

A few weeks ago, and while trying to restore some order in the books in my study I came across a little booklet on the founders of Jamia Millia Islamia, penned by an old teacher of mine, Syed Mohammad Tonki. It contains a perceptive remark:

---

* Address at the Convocation Jamia Millia Islamia University, 30 October 2007.

Jamia ki aik haisiyat tahreek ki hai aur doosari aik idaare ki.Tahreek main woosat-e-amal o fikr aur aik tarah ki hamagirihoti hai; iddara mahdood daaire main rah kar khaas haalatke mud-e-nazar kaam karta hai aur apni baqa ke liye samet-taaur fikr o amal ko samait-ta hai.

(Jamia has one identity as a movement and another as an institution. The movement has space to work and has togetherness. The institution works [functions] in a limited circle under specific conditions for its continuance and work.)

The first identity created the second; having done so, it expected the second to carry the banner of its progenitor. This is one aspect of the matter. My purpose today, however, is to probe some of the un-stated premises of the first in the hope that these might shed light on what continues to be a teasing question for Muslim thinkers in India and elsewhere—that of reconciling tradition and modernity in all its ramifications in the social and political life of the community.

II

In its most obvious sense, the foundation of Jamia was a protest against the political conformity of Aligarh in the context of the period immediately after World War I. Maulana Mahmood Hasan saheb described it as *hukoomat-e-waqtiyah ki parastish* (devotion to the government of the day). This protest was not a flash in the pan, did not happen by accident, and was not confined to a narrow section of opinion. Instead, it emanated from a basic premise that perceived the established political order as unjust.

Did the protest go beyond it? If so, how far did it go and with what content? An essay by Dr Zakir Hussain in 1938 sheds light on his perception of Jamia's primary purpose:

Jamia ka sub se bara maqsad yeh hai ki Hindustani Musalmanon ki future lifeka aisa naqsha tayyar kare jis ka markazmazhab-e-Islam ho aur us main Hindustan ki quami tahzeeb ea woh rang bhare jo aam insani tahzeeb ke rang main khap'e.

(Jamia's biggest purpose is to create a sketch for the future of Indian Muslims whose centre be the Islamic faith that fits into normal Indian culture.)

The focus of this was on challenging the perceived dichotomy between the requirement of faith and those of developing an Indian cultural identity in the most comprehensive sense. Zakir saheb conceded that this objective was somewhat opaque in the minds of the Jamia fraternity. Some others at Jamia spoke in the same vein. Abid Hussain urged the need to create an alumnus who is '*insan-e-kamil, sachcha Musalman aur pacca Hindustani*'. Perhaps there was, in the background, a resonance of Syed Ahmad Khan's concept of *amal-i-saleh* (good deeds). Taking the argument further, Mohammad Mujeeb dwelt on the sources of the Indian sense of unity. Written in 1962, his perception remains relevant four and a half decades later:

> We can become united only if we create within ourselves individually and in consonance with our dispositions and our taste an overriding passion for a unity which can bear the moral burden of the wrongs we have committed and the mistakes we have made. The acceptance of this approach to unity will be a spiritual effort and can succeed only if it receives sustenance and power from the traditions of religiousness which are a part of our history. The state by declaring itself secular has thrown out a challenge to each and every citizen to show that he can enrich civic life by drawing inspiration from the institutional religion which he professes.

The citizen responded to it in varying measure. The core question of Indianness, however, does stand settled.

The objective of creating an identity comprehensive enough to encapsulate both Indianness and Muslimness in the plural, democratic and secular ethos of contemporary India also required creative thinking addressed to changing situations of a modernizing India. The task of converting this into a plan of action became, and remains, the principal challenge to contemporary Muslim thinking. Underlying any such endeavour is the tension between the twin concepts of tradition and modernity. To what extent have these been addressed?

In this context, an observation of the former Pakistani diplomat and author, Professor Akbar Ahmad, is to be noted. 'The postmodernist age in the 1990s' he wrote in 1992, 'hammers at the doors of the Muslim ijtihad; Muslims ignore the din at their peril. Before they creak open the door, however, they must know the power and nature of the age and for that they must understand those who represent it.'[1]

Does this suggest the inevitability of a single, unavoidable, pattern of response? If so, it overlooks the diversity of the Muslim situation and the resultant complexity of the response patterns. The Muslim world has expanded beyond its traditional boundaries; the inherited paradigm of Muslims living principally in Muslim-majority societies, and thinking in terms of those societies, has now acquired different dimensions. Muslim communities in India, China and Russia have sought to develop locally relevant response patterns; the same is true of Muslim communities in the United States and in the member States of the European Union. None of these have been devoid of pain. There is therefore relevance in the Swiss philosopher and academic Tariq Ramadan's observation that while globalization causes the old traditional points of reference to disappear, it at the same time awakens passionate affirmations of identity. As a result, he notes, Muslim communities in the West are 'living through a veritable silent revolution'.

Awareness of identity and the desire to develop it is one aspect of the matter; the capacity to actualize is another; a third is the desire to strike a balance between identity and what Professor Ramadan has called an authentic dialogue with fellow citizens aimed at mutual enrichment. It is here that empirical evidence is of crucial importance. How much of an effort was made (and is being made) to give a comprehensive response to the challenge? What areas of community life were addressed? What obstacles were encountered? What was the success achieved?

Some answers to these questions are now available, thanks to the Sachar Committee Report on the social, educational and economic condition of the Muslim community in India. The Committee set out to collect 'authentic information' particularly on equity-related questions and succeeded in quantifying the extent of deprivation. It reported that 'the topic of education was raised most frequently in the representations (made to it), followed by reservation, employment and security related issues'. It identified with some precision the areas of State failure, suggested urgent corrective action, and recommended that this 'should sharply focus on inclusive development and the 'mainstreaming' of the community while respecting diversity'.

The default by the State in terms of deprivation, exclusion and discrimination is to be corrected by the State; this needs to be done at the earliest. Political sagacity and public opinion play an important role in it. Besides it, however, there is another default; here I refer to the inadequacy of the autonomous effort by the community itself in relation to its social perceptions. How has this been approached? Is there a veritable silent revolution underway in the thinking of the Indian Muslim?

Firqa-bandi hai kahein aur kahein zaatain hain
Kya zamaane main panaph-ne ki yahi baatain hain?

(There is groupism or caste divisions. Is this the way to prosper in life?)

It is evident that significant sections of the community remain trapped in a vicious circle and in a culturally defensive posture. Tradition is made sacrosanct while the rationale of tradition is all but forgotten. *Jadeediyat* or modernity has become a tainted expression. Such a mindset constrains critical thinking necessary both for the affirmation of faith and for the well-being of the community. The instrumentality of adaptation to change—ijtihad—is frowned upon if not ignored altogether. Forgotten is its purpose, defined by the late Sheikh Abul Hasan Ali Nadwi as 'the ability to cope with the ever-changing pattern of life's requirements'. Similarly, al Ghazali's delineation of the ambit of Maslaha—protection of religion, life, intellect, lineage and property—provides ample theoretical space for focused thinking on social change.

III

Has this focused thinking, resulting in corrective action, taken place? One could scrutinize a few of the most obvious examples. Syed Ahmad Khan was acutely aware of the problems in an era of painful change. He confronted the view that ijtihad is no longer necessary:

> We must remember that circumstances keep changing and we are faced daily with new problems and needs. If therefore we do not have living mujtahids, how shall we ask those who are dead about questions which were not material facts of life in their time. We must have a mujtahid of our age and time.

Despite this, he was diffident in regard to follow up action and his concept of amal-i-saleh remained devoid of the requisite degree of practical comprehensiveness. Similarly, the poet Dr Mohammad Iqbal, stressed the need to reconcile the elements of permanence and change in Muslim societies and the resultant necessity of ijtihad in every generation. Modern Islam, he said, is not bound by the 'voluntary surrender of intellectual independence':

Taqleed se naakara na kar apni khudi ko
Kar ooski hefazat ki yeh gauhar hai yagana

(Do not lose your identity in imitation
Guard it because it is unique.)

In practical terms, however, Iqbal leaned on the side of caution; his philosophical legacy, in the words of Fazlur Rahman, has not been followed largely because he has been both misunderstood and misused by his politics-mongering followers.

The one exception to such an approach was Maulana Azad who advocated a move away from a narrowly juristic view in favour of a mental renaissance to achieve the highest moral and spiritual values of Islam. In opting for this approach, he, as Mohammad Mujeeb put it, stood absolutely alone and could not gather a following.

As a result, and despite the quantification of the extent of social backwardness, community effort to ameliorate it has remained confused and inadequate.

Let us look at the situation in its totality. Muslims in India today number about 150 million and constitute a significant segment—13.4 per cent—of Indians. 51.9 per cent of this population is below the age of twenty and 60.6 per cent below the age of twenty-five. Muslims have the highest child sex ratio of any social group in the country—986 girls per 1000 boys. They are more urbanized than the general population. On the other hand, the literacy rate among Muslims is 59.1 per cent, against a national average of 65.1; it is even lower in the case of female literacy. There are 40.7 per cent of Muslims in the OBC category (15.7 per cent of the total OBC population of the country) and a small segment in SCs. The incidence of poverty among urban Muslims is even higher than among the urban SCs/STs, is well above other OBCs, and is almost double of the national average. These figures speak for themselves in terms of the imperative for correcting social imbalances resulting from social immobility.

In the face of multiple challenges, is prioritization possible or even desirable? Should education precede social reforms or follow it? Should both wait for a lessening of threats to physical security and the obvious manifestations of exclusion? How is the collective will to be generated for simultaneous, across-the-board, movement?

IV

What is the way out? It would seem, given recent history and prevailing perceptions, that the following are unavoidable:

Develop a clear understanding of the modern world and the social and intellectual forces emanating from it. Sufficient evidence of this is available, in the Indian context, in the course of a citizen's daily life.

Seek conceptual clarity about tradition and modernity. Tradition is a double-edged sword; it is used both to deny change and to justify it; alternative uses of tradition are thus a major battle ground. Some years ago, Abdul Hamid Abu Sulayman, a Saudi Scholar had drawn attention to the 'psychological impediments' that have impeded the Muslim mind in the analysis of 'its intellectual legacy or what it holds as sacred'. The argument on tradition and modernity requires to be turned around; a formulation by another scholar therefore merits attention: 'Rather than viewing modernity as a source of light, dispelling the darkness of tradition, we should instead imagine tradition as a beam of light, refracted by the prism of modernity.'

Comprehend the concepts of ijtihad and Maslaha in the light of contemporary Islamic thought in different parts of the world and a willingness to use them to address contemporary problems in Indian Muslim society. The Algerian scholar Mohammad Arkoun, for instance, has urged the need to rethink the historical situation so that 'critical thought, anchored in modernity but criticising modernity itself and contributing to its enrichment through recourse to the Islamic example' could open a new era in social movements. The manner in which Asian Muslim societies like Indonesia, Malaysia, Iran and Turkey have addressed the questions of knowledge and gender deficit needs to be studied, perhaps emulated.

Undertake a structured effort, on the basis of the above, to confront the evils of ignorance and stagnation through a sustainable programme of education and social reform. Such an effort would need to focus on autonomous correction of social customs hampering progress, particularly the ones with a tenuous base in religion; the priority areas of attention would need to be on primary and middle levels of education, on the education of girls, on vocational training and on a wide-ranging awareness programmes relating to rights of citizens and the facilities available to them by law but often denied in practice.

Reinvigorate the traditional practice of charity through focused philanthropy and impart a new dynamism to the management of Awqaf to derive maximum benefit for the community. There are, according to the Sachar Committee, a total of 4.9 lakh registered Wakfs in the country with a current market value of about Rs 1.2 lakh crores (1,200 billion). Some of these properties are in adverse possession and the State must help retrieve them; the majority of them are misused by individuals and institutions; if put to 'efficient and marketable use they can generate at least a minimum return of 10 percent which is about Rs. 12,000 crores per annum'.[2]

Collect and publicize success stories, of individual and community initiatives, that do exist in different parts of the country.

None of the above would be a substitute for, or dilution of, well documented and justified demands for affirmative action by the State within the framework of Articles14, 15(4) and 16(4) of the Constitution and the various programmes announced by the Government pursuant to the Sachar Report. Instead, they could become a critical foundation on the basis of which maximum benefits can be derived from these schemes.

We need to remember that in any form of therapy, patient cooperation is essential.

We have to remind ourselves that in the India of today, time is of critical importance.

We could recite with benefit a couplet of relevance:

Aghyar mehr mah se bhi aage nikal gaye
Uljhe huwai hain subh ki pehli kiran main hum

(Others have gone between the moon and the sun
Yet we are still entangled in the first rays of the sun)

What may be the modality of change? Who can be its flag bearers? The bourgeoisie, wrote Karl Marx, has historically played a most revolutionary part in changing societal relations. The Muslim middle class, however, is weak and hesitant as an agent of social change. The literacy and development gap in regard to Muslim women adds to this handicap; so do perceptions of physical and economic insecurity.

The agents of change would thus have to be new grass-root community leaders principally emanating from the youth who constitute the biggest segment in terms of numbers and who are better placed to understand its demands and aspirations. Their effort would need to focus both on legitimate demands on the State and on the mobilization of internal resources of the community for the empowerment of the marginalized. Above all, it would need to imbibe the advice given by Maulana Azad in October 1947:

Tabdiliyon ke saath chalo, yeh na kaho ki hum is taghghur ke liye tayyar na thei.

(Move with changes, do not say we are not ready for change.)

I conclude where I commenced: the role of Jamia Millia Islamia. Its achievements in recent years have been noteworthy. It has shown itself receptive to new ideas and creative practices. The institution is now a part of the academic landscape of the country. Having reached thus far, could some in the Jamia community now also think of a larger mission that is, in a sense, part of its original mission, so eloquently enunciated by Zakir sahib? Success in such an endeavour would benefit Indian Muslims and enrich India itself.

Lastly, I felicitate the young women and men who have been formally honoured today and who are leaving the precincts of the academia to enter a harsher world. They need to retain at all times their enthusiasm and optimism. They must remember that the horizon of knowledge is ever receding; the quest for it, therefore, does not end with a university degree. On the contrary, it is the first step in a grand participatory venture of building a new India.

23

Convocation Address at the Aligarh Muslim University*

I

Ba naam-e-khudawand jaan aafareen
Hakim-e-sokhan der zubaan aafareen

(In the name of the Lord, soul-creating,
Wise one, who endowed the tongue with speech)

A torrent of emotions gathered over half a century and more overwhelm a speaker who returns to familiar surroundings of youth, and of later years, to be the chief guest at the most solemn of university ceremonies. Stray thoughts compete for attention and the balance between the past and the present is sought to be swayed.

An Old Boy of considerable seniority wrote recently that nothing ignites nostalgia among Aligarh Muslim University (AMU) alumni the way the Tarana does, adding that I doubt if any other educational institution on earth has an anthem that can equal the lyrical quality of the AMU Tarana. I subscribe to this personally. I also cannot erase from my mind the intellectually accommodating ambience of the campus in the mid and late 1950s, the architectural magnificence of the university mosque, of the buildings around the Strachey Hall, and above all the captivating image of the university cricket ground. The nostalgia is overpowering.

I extend my felicitations to the students graduating today. They owe their success to their own industry and dedication. They should know that

---

* 29 March 2014 at Aligarh.

the pursuit of knowledge does not end with the portals of the university. Their journey in life now begins. Whether they enter the job market or go on to pursue further studies, they must remember that there is no end to education.

I felicitate the personalities who have been awarded the Honoris Causa. This institution recognizes and applauds their contributions to the public good.

Convocations are occasions to acknowledge intellectual excellence and achievement. They should also be moments of introspection about the purpose of education, its role in society and in the life of the nation. This is that rare, fleeting, moment in life when the individual can afford to steer clear of peer pressure, pursue one's convictions, sail into the unknown and chart unconventional paths. Many famous names in AMU's past did just that.

The uniqueness of this institution is evident. It is a university, a place where men and women gather to seek knowledge in all its manifestations. They do so because, as Ibn Khaldun would have said, 'the pasture of stupidity is unwholesome for mankind' and 'the evil of falsehood is to be fought with enlightened speculation'; hence the need both for critical insight, and for lifting the veil of ignorance.

There is another aspect of uniqueness evident to all. It is *Muslim*, meaning by it an inheritor not only of the sum total of human knowledge but also particularly of the segment bequeathed by the civilization of Islam. This weight of twin legacies is what propelled the founding fathers of this institution.

A third characteristic, taken for granted and yet worthy of mention, is location. It is in *India*, one of the cradles of human knowledge whose inputs into, and interaction with, the world of Islam enriched both. Nor can the location-specific ethos developed at Aligarh for over a century and more be ignored; it may be emulated but cannot be duplicated. An institution of higher learning and a cultural entity is not easily given to being a commercial or philanthropic franchise.

Thus, the challenge emanating from being posited, notionally, on a tripod was demanding at all times. In different stages of the University's history its responses to these were fairly reflective of its intellectual capacity and its commitment to the values and objectives it had prescribed for itself. The record, to my mind, is a mixed one.

Today, the challenge has acquired greater intensity. The imperatives of the 21st century would sustain and accelerate the pattern, perhaps add new dimensions to it.

The question that I pose to myself, and to all of you, is a simple one: is the AMU prepared and equipped to respond meaningfully, in thought *and* deed, to these challenges?

II

Universities are not a modern novelty. They have existed in all civilizations. Recorded history traces their existence in ancient Greece and ancient India, and in Egypt, Morocco and Europe in medieval times. They emerged whenever human thought processes evolved to the point of asking questions that go beyond primary needs of human existence. They are expected to offer a depth and breadth of vision not available in the rush of everyday life. A university is a place that not only produces knowledge but also produces doubt; a place that is creative and unruly, home to a polyphony of voices. It also has a practical objective: to impart skills to get a job or a better job, to improve prospects in life. For the latter reason, their concerns and curricula have to respond in good measure to the requirements of the age.

Two decades earlier the historian Paul Kennedy penned a volume entitled *Preparing for the Twenty-First Century* and concluded that three elements would be critical to the effort. He listed these as i) the role of education; ii) the place of women; and iii) the need for political leadership.

Each of these, I submit, is relevant to this campus and to us both as a nation and a society in all its diverse segments. Each remains relevant two decades later; in fact, the passage of time has reinforced the urgency of achieving a high degree of success in each.

I begin with education. The shortfalls are evident. Despite educational attainment by segments of society, the base line of literacy at the dawn of freedom in 1947 was 12 per cent. It reached 74 per cent in 2011 and is still below the global average of 84 per cent. Inscribing the Right to Education as a Fundamental Rights, and the Right to Education Act of 2009, has certainly enhanced enrolment but is yet to translate itself into quality education. As a result, school-leavers often do not have the capacity to imbibe college and university learning. Nor have they benefited yet from the new schemes of 'vocationalization' of secondary education. This also holds true for areas of technical and professional education.

Consequently, and in order to accommodate the less prepared, undergraduate teaching often begins at sub-standard levels. Its impact is pervasive. Mediocrity thus prevails, with both the teachers and the taught wallowing in it. The overall impact of the resulting picture is adequately reflected in the various employability assessments in the public domain as also in the modest quantity of scientific research emanating from institutions of higher education and research. These make depressing reading.

This is to be contrasted with the levels of educational requirement in the 21st century. Two ingredients of it are critical: the first relates to globalization of standards and the second to the upgradation of skills. Both need a level of teaching and assessment that should be comparable or nearly comparable to the best in the world. Both, I submit, are lacking in our institutions of higher education today.

Why have we come to such a pass? One reason is the conversion of our universities into degree awarding machines for the benefit of youth who do not receive sufficient guidance on career options at the school leaving stage and therefore drift through a degree course aimlessly. The other reason, linked to the first, is the lack of focus on quality teaching, on evoking the interest of the students in subjects of their choice, in encouraging them to explore its dimensions and in inculcating the habit of thinking for themselves. Learning by rote from made-easy books and focusing on 'model' answers to standard questions that examiners set mechanically year after year, thus becomes the hallmark of an average student. Little or no effort is made by the teacher to induce critical and innovative thinking. The curiosity latent in every young mind is not awakened.

If the student is the innocent victim of this scheme of things, the teacher often is an accomplice. In an essay on the functions of a teacher, Bertrand Russell had written that 'no man can be a good teacher unless he has feelings of warm affection towards his pupils and a genuine desire to impart to them what he himself believes to be of value'.[1]

Teaching, in other words, should be a calling of aptitude and choice rather than of necessity. There is a dire need for inculcating this motivation in our colleges and universities.

Perhaps the malaise has deeper roots. A major role is played by societal values. Our society is passing through a callously materialistic phase, one in which money has become the measure of all things. Eminent scientist and Bharat Ratna awardee Professor C.N.R. Rao spoke recently about the disinclination among youth to pursue scientific research and innovation and opt instead for more lucrative callings. This trend does not further the requirement of the best minds devoting themselves to fundamental scientific research.

Correctives are thus imperative and have to begin here and now. We have to go beyond being affluent 'hewers of wood and carriers of water', or being 'IT coolies', and acknowledge that we are living in a highly competitive global knowledge society with receding horizons in which mediocrity means irrelevance.

These same receding horizons beckon us to continue to study our societal environment and retain our focus on areas of social sciences, humanities and languages, particularly those in which the AMU developed excellence over decades. An involvement with modernity does not imply an abandonment of the past; on the contrary, modern tools of learning can be used with benefit in the pursuit of all disciplines, as is being done in the best universities of the world.

So, the way out of the present crisis lies in re-emphasizing the need of seeking excellence. Here no quarters should be asked for, none given. The plea for affirmative action for socially and educationally backward is a valid one; the requirement, however, is for *opportunity*, not lack of performance.

A century ago, Allama Iqbal had suggested the corrective:

Is dour main taleem hai amraz-e-millat ki dawa
Hai khoon-e-fasid ke liye taleem misl-e-naishtar

(Education is the cure for the ailments of a community
It is like a surgical knife that drains putrid blood)

Yak lahza ghafil gushtam wa sad saalah raahum door shud

(I was negligent for a moment and my journey became a hundred years'
longer)

It is the time now for all segments of Muslim society in our country, and those of it in the AMU, to address this challenge without further loss of time. Success will be rewarded by a place in the ranks of the march of humanity in the 21st century; failure will lead to becoming inconsequential.

III

Human endeavours do not take shape in a vacuum. The societal ambiance is invariably critical. Change is an unavoidable ingredient of all societies. We cannot be an exception, nor can we be irrationally selectively. Maulana Azad's advice of October 1947 should be recalled a generation later:

Azizo, upne ander aik bunyadi tabdeeli paida karo . . .
Tabdeelion ke saath chalo, yeh na kaho ki hum is tagayyur ke liye tayyar nahin thai'.

(Friends, make way for real change in yourselves . . .
Move with the change; don't say you're not ready for it.)

One aspect of change pertains to the place of women in society. It is inextricably linked both to education and to the dead weight of history and social custom. It remains a blind spot for segments of our people. And yet it must be admitted that half the population, half the potential workforce, and those who give first lessons in education and manners to the younger generation, cannot be excluded from the benefits of modern education and denied the opportunity to contribute to nation building efforts.

The Constitution guarantees equality to all citizens and prohibits discrimination on grounds of sex. Despite this, attitudes and practices particularly in regard to education and participation in the work force, both of Muslims in general and Muslim women in particular, persist. The Sachar Report of 2006, and subsequent studies, quantifies this in ample measure. The gap between the present levels and the national average needs to be bridged at the earliest.

The Muslims of India, in their self-perception, prioritize their problems: physical security, education and employment. Each of these is within the ambit of affirmative action; some positive steps have been taken, more remains to be done. A younger generation, confident and assertive, seeks the right to equality and its share in decision-making.

The dead weight of tradition, poverty and communal politics has resulted in Muslim women facing three handicaps. These relate to: (a) literacy; (b) economic power resulting from work and income; and (c) autonomy of decision-making. The net result is a pattern of structured disempowerment. There is nothing in the tenets of faith that permits it; on the contrary, rights and obligations are equally enjoined.

Social customs usually represent the crystallization of occasion-specific requirements; they are neither sacred nor immutable. Experience of other traditional societies shows that practical correctives can be introduced without transgressing values. Aligarh, where the first steps were taken in 1906 for the education of Muslim girls, must now help realize the 21st-century targets of gender parity.

The same holds for political leadership. A citizen by definition participates in civic affairs and should be allowed to do so. I recall what I learnt as a student in this institution. Pericles, in ancient Athens, said ordinary citizens are 'fair judges of public matters' and that 'instead of looking on discussion as a stumbling block in the way of action, we think it is an indispensable preliminary to any wise action at all.'

The validity of this for our world of universal adult franchise is evident. The deepening of the democratic process within our polity, and the emergence or crystallization of local, regional or sectional demands, compels both a wider understanding and a conscious development of the capacity to reconcile and accommodate competing requirements within the ambit of the Constitution. The political churning currently underway is perhaps also part of a global turmoil induced by rising expectations and globalization of values and facilitated by the revolution in communication techniques.

The civic training of young citizens, therefore, has to begin early and should be facilitated in educational institutions. AMU's annals record the names of freedom fighters and public figures baptized on this campus. By the same logic, freedom is not synonymous with anarchic behaviour or arbitrary demands undermining the very purpose or ethos of the institution. At the same time, the right to associate has to be within the limits of public order, decency and morality. Those who wrote grammars of democracy in earlier or modern times, did not visualize anarchy as a valid option.

IV

An important aspect of this university's ethos is its assertion of identity within the framework of diversity that characterizes modern India. Both are critical ingredients; both are cherished; both bestow a uniqueness that encapsulates a thousand years of history of the Indian subcontinent; both require careful navigation through treacherous rapids characterized by assimilative urges on the one hand and isolationist pressures on the other.

Any discourse on identity needs to begin with the ground reality. Ours is a plural society, a secular polity and a State structure that is democratic and based on rule of law. Plurality is thus an existential reality. Each ingredient of the mix is important. We steer clear of notions of assimilation and adaptation, philosophically and in practice. Instead, the management of diversity to ensure the integration of minds and hearts is accepted as an ongoing national priority. By the same token, every citizen has to contribute to it. Segregation, seclusion or self-imposed isolation is un-civic and a transgression of the spirit of a plural society.

The objective is, and should be, to go beyond tolerance of the *Other* and move towards *Acceptance* of those who may be different. It would bring forth, in the words of Canadian scholar Will Kymlicka, 'three interconnected ideas: repudiating the idea of the state as belonging to the dominant group; replacing assimilationist and exclusionary nation-building policies with policies of recognition and accommodation; and acknowledging historic injustice and offering amends for it'.[2]

This imposes obligations on the State to promote equal treatment. This is enshrined in our Constitution; the challenge is to universalise and deepen its implementation.

The duty of the citizen is to be a participant in the process, assist it and actively seek his/her rights:

Yeh bazm-e-mai hai yaan kotah dasti main hai mahroomi
Jo barh ke khood utha le haath main meena usi ka hai

(This is an assembly of drinkers where tardiness means defeat
The drink belongs to him who seizes the initiative and takes it)

V

It is in this landscape that I go back to my earlier question: of AMU's preparedness in thought and deed to the emerging challenges of the 21st century. I have touched upon some aspects of the challenge. The answer is not with me; I do know it is with the youthful segment of the audience before me. Will they rise to the occasion? Will they eschew mediocrity for excellence and pursue it in curricular and extracurricular fields? Will they help promote gender parity? Will they become active participants and builders in a new, changing India that is taking shape before us?

There are times in lives of individuals and people when the imperative is to go beyond stale logic and pessimism of the intellect and lean instead on the optimism of the will. Such an occasion beckons you today. I repeat what I had said on an earlier occasion here:

> *Agar aflak ke tare torne hain to perwaaz ki taaqat paida karni hogi; sirf guftaar kaafi nahin hai*

(To reach the stars you have to acquire the capacity to fly;
Just talking about it is not enough)

I wish you all success in this endeavour and remind you of what a poet of our times had aptly said:

> *Dekh zindaan se pare, rang-e-chaman shour-e-bahaar Raqs karna hai to phir paaon ki zanjeer na dekh*

(Look beyond the confines of prison if you wish to see the colours of spring;
Do not look at the shackles on your feet if you wish to dance.)

24

Indian Muslims

Quest for Justice*

I

Needless to say, and like many other compatriots, I have over the years followed in some measure the work of this consultative body.

The Mushawarat was formed in response to a perceived need to defend and protect the identity and dignity of the Muslim community in India in terms of the rights bestowed by the Constitution of India on the citizens of this land. This objective remains relevant though some of its ingredients may stand amplified or modified today.

The Muslims of India constitute a community of 180 million, amounting to a little over 14 per cent of the population of the country. They are, after Indonesia, the second largest national grouping of followers of Islam in the world. Their contribution to the civilization and culture of Islam is in no need of commentary. They were an integral part of the freedom struggle against the British rule. They are dispersed all over the country, are not homogenous in linguistic and socio-economic terms and reflect in good measure the diversities that characterize the people of India as a whole.

The Independence of India in August 1947, and the events preceding and following it, cast a shadow of physical and psychological insecurity on Indian Muslims. They were made to carry, unfairly, the burden of political events and compromises that resulted in the Partition. The process of recovery from that trauma has been gradual and uneven, and at

---

* Inauguration of the All India Majlis-E-Mushawarat Golden Jubilee in New Delhi on 31 August 2015.

times painful. They have hesitantly sought to tend to their wounds, face the challenges and seek to develop response patterns. Success has been achieved in some measure; much more, however, needs to be done.

In the past decade, work has also been done to delineate the contours of the problem. The Sachar Committee Report of 2006 did this officially. It laid to rest the political untruth in some quarters about the Muslim condition and demonstrated that on most socio-economic indicators, they were on the margins of structures of political, economic and social relevance and their average condition was comparable to or even worse than the country's acknowledged historically most backward communities, the Scheduled Castes and Scheduled Tribes. It specified the development deficits of the majority of Muslims in regard to education, livelihood and access to public services and the employment market across the states.

In the same vein, Expert Group reports were prepared in 2008 on the need to develop a Diversity Index and establish an Equal Opportunity Commission.

Taken together, these and other studies bring forth sufficient evidence to substantiate the view that 'inequality traps prevent the marginalized and work in favour of the dominant groups in society'.[1]

More recently the Kundu Report of September 2014, commissioned to evaluate the implementation of decisions taken pursuant to Sachar recommendations, has concluded that though 'a start has been made, yet serious bottlenecks remain'. It makes specific recommendations to remedy these. It asserts that 'development for the Muslim minority must be built on a bed-rock of a sense of security.'[2]

It is evident from this compendium of official reports that the principal problems confronting India's Muslims relate to

- identity and security;
- education and empowerment;
- equitable share in the largesse of the State; and
- fair share in decision-making.

Each of these is a right of the citizen. The shortcomings in regard to each have been analysed threadbare. The challenge before us today is to develop strategies and methodologies to address them.

The default by the State or its agents in terms of deprivation, exclusion and discrimination (including failure to provide security) is to be corrected by the State; this needs to be done at the earliest and appropriate instruments developed for it. Political sagacity, the imperative of social peace, and public opinion play an important role in it. Experience shows that the corrective has to be both at the policy and the implementation levels; the latter, in particular, necessitates mechanisms to ensure active cooperation of the State governments.

The official objective of *sab ka sath sab ka vikas* is commendable; a prerequisite for this is affirmative action (where necessary) to ensure a common starting point and an ability in all to walk at the required pace. This ability has to be developed through individual, social and governmental initiatives that fructify on the ground. Programmes have been made in abundance; the need of the hour is their implementation.

II

The foregoing pertains principally to governmental action or lack thereof. Equally relevant is the autonomous effort by the community itself in regard to its identified shortcomings. What has it done to redress the backwardness and poverty arising out of socio-economic and educational under-development? How adequate is the response in relation to the challenge?

A century back the lament was emotive:

Firqa-bandi hai kahein aur kahein zaatain hain
Kya zamaane main panaph-ne ki yahi baatain hain?

(There is groupism or caste divisions.
Is this the way to prosper in life?)

Today, we have to admit that both 'firqa bandi' and 'zaat' identity is a ground reality. The imagery of Mahmood and Ayaz standing shoulder to shoulder in the same line is confined to the mosque; so are the injunctions on punctuality, cleanliness and discipline. Each of these is violated beyond the confines of the congregational prayer. Corrective strategies therefore have to be sought on category-differentiation admissible in Indian State practice and hitherto denied to Muslims (SC status) or inadequately admitted (segments of OBC status). Available data makes it clear that a high percentage of Muslims falls into these two broad categories.

It is evident that significant sections of the community remain trapped in a vicious circle and in a culturally defensive posture that hinders self-advancement. Tradition is made sacrosanct, but the rationale of tradition is all but forgotten. Jadeediyat or modernity has become a tainted expression. Such a mindset constrains critical thinking necessary both for the affirmation of faith and for the well-being of the community. The instrumentality of adaptation to change—ijtihad—is frowned upon or glossed over. Forgotten is its purpose, defined by the late Sheikh Abul Hasan Ali Nadwi as 'the ability to cope with the ever-changing pattern of life's requirements'. Equally relevant is Imam Al-Ghazali's delineation of the ambit of Maslaha—protection of religion, life, intellect, lineage and property. Both provide ample theoretical space for focused thinking on social change without impinging on the fundamentals of faith.

It is here that the role of Mushawarat becomes critical. As a grouping of the leading and most respected minds of the community, it should go beyond looking at questions of identity and dignity in a defensive mode and explore how both can be furthered in a changing India and a changing world. It should widen its ambit to hitherto unexplored or inadequately explored requirements of all segments of the community particularly women, youth, and non-elite sections who together constitute the overwhelming majority.

This effort has to be made in the context of Indian conditions and the uniqueness of its three dimensions: plural, secular and democratic. Some years ago A.G. Noorani, a close observer, had posed the problem:

> To deny discrimination and pretend all is well is to fly in the face of facts. But agitation against discrimination can arouse the very emotions that foster discrimination. The solution of the Muslim problem lies in a resolution of this dilemma by devising a form and content of agitation which heals old wounds and inflicts no new ones. This resolution can be achieved by regarding discrimination as what it is; a problem of Indian democracy to be resolved within the framework of national integration.[3]

This would necessitate sustained and candid interaction with fellow citizens without a syndrome of superiority or inferiority and can be fruitful only in the actual implementation of the principles of justice, equality and fraternity inscribed in the Preamble to the Constitution and the totality of Fundamental Rights. The failure to communicate with the wider community in sufficient measure has tended to freeze the boundaries of diversities that characterize Indian society. Efforts may be made to isolate the community; such an approach should be resisted.

The Indian experience of a large Muslim minority living in secular polity, however imperfect, could even be a model for others to emulate.

One last word. The world of Islam extends beyond the borders of India and Muslims here, as in other lands, can benefit from the best that may be available in the realm of thought and practice. Some years ago, I had occasion to read the Algerian-French philosopher Mohammed Arkoun and was impressed by his view that our times compel us to rethink modernity so that, as he put it, 'critical thought, anchored in modernity but criticizing modernity itself and contributing to its enrichment through recourse to the Islamic example' could open up a new era in social movements.[4]

Would future generations forgive us for failing to explore these options?

'Verily never will God change the condition of a people until they change it themselves with their own souls.'[5]

And so, the task before Mushawarat in the foreseeable future should remain a threefold one: to sustain the struggle for the actualization in full measure of legal and constitutional rights; to do so without being isolated from the wider community; and to endeavour at the same time to adapt thinking and practices to a fast-changing world.

25

India and Islamic Civilization

Contributions and Challenges*

I

Allow me to begin with some recollections. In the 1980s of the last century, I spent four happy and purposeful years in this city, a resident of Mugga Way, travelling across the length and breadth of the continent, dividing my time fairly evenly in robust discussions with Australian friends, watching cricket, learning to play golf, endeavouring to rejuvenate Indo-Australian relations and highlighting the communality of interests that characterize it. Some of this was acknowledged in a reference made to me in the House of Representatives on 6 April 1989 and in a Report of the Senate Standing Committee on Foreign Affairs, Defence and Trade later that month. Since then, our two countries have travelled a good distance and today have a vibrant relationship.

The recollections of those years are vivid in the minds of the Ansari family. I was therefore happy to receive today's invitation from my old friend, Professor Amin Saikal, to talk to this learned audience on a subject that, one way or another, is of relevance to humanity in terms of history, culture and contemporary geopolitics.

Professor Saikal had suggested a lecture 'on any aspect of the civilization of Islam' and utilizing this leeway I propose to focus today on the interaction that characterized the role played for over seven centuries on the soil of India by people of Muslim faith. Today, they constitute the third, perhaps the second, largest community of Muslims in the world.

---

* Australian National University, Canberra, 2018.

They are geographically dispersed, linguistically heterogeneous, unified in faith, influenced by its culture as well as by local cultural practices and are citizens of a vibrant democracy. By the same logic, they are called upon to respond to contemporary domestic and global challenges having an impact on them.

A look at the map is helpful. India as a geographical entity was not *terra incognita* to the Arabian Peninsula or other lands of western Asia where Islam had its first followers. This was particularly true of contacts with the trading communities of the coastal regions of western and southern India; records show that an established trade route existed well before the advent of Islam. So was the presence of Indian trading communities in those lands and tradition records Prophet Mohammad's familiarity with persons 'who looked like Indians'.[1] India was thus a known land, sought after for its prosperity and trading skills and respected for its attainments in different branches of knowledge. Long before the advent of Muslim conquerors the works of Al Jahiz, Ibn Khurdadbeh, Al Kindi, Yaqubi and Al Masudi in the 9th and 10th centuries testify to it. Alberuni in early 11th century studied Indian religion, philosophy, sciences, manners and customs and produced a virtual encyclopaedia remarkable for its detail and objectivity. In fact, a closer reading of his short second chapter 'On the Belief of Hindus in God' might have saved centuries of misperceptions arguably on theological grounds.

The new faith came to India through diverse channels—through traders in the south and through conquerors and travellers in north-west. A historian has noted that 'the presence of Muslims in India can be traced to three different sources: conquest, immigration and conversion with the mingling of different stocks taking place in a manner that was beyond social or political control', adding that the vast majority of Indian Muslims are converts and that the main agency for conversions were the mystics, principally in the 15th and 16th centuries.[2]

The imprint of this interaction is writ large and was delineated many years back with some precision by another historian, Tara Chand. Indian culture, he wrote,

is synthetic in character. It comprehends ideas of different orders. It embraces in its orbit beliefs, customs, rites, institutions, arts, religions and philosophies belonging to society in different stages of development. It eternally seeks to find a unity for the heterogeneous elements which make up its totality. At worst its attempts end in mechanical juxtaposition, at best they succeed in evolving an organic system.[3]

Heterogeneity was the core of this process. It was a characteristic of the social, cultural and philosophical landscape. Interaction with its own people who had opted for a new faith produced a variety of responses, conscious and sub-conscious. One aspect was formal and political; another was social and intellectual. The first adapted to the ground reality, benefited from it and in turn induced the second.

What was the ground reality? In a general sense and right through the medieval period of Indian history two sets of readings are available: the imperial system in northern India and the more modest principalities in the south that developed their own distinctive identities before eventually succumbing to the political pressure from the north.

It is a historical fact that for almost seven centuries from the 11th to the 18th century the State system in India was headed by persons who professed to be Muslim. Despite this at no stage in this period was the State theocratic nor was Islam declared to be the State religion; instead, the norms of governance were regal in a non-denominational sense. Practice thus drew a clear distinction between rules emanating from the *Sharia* and those from *Zawabit* or *Jahandari* (secular State laws). Overtime, the imprint of the structure of Indian society was visible and so was adaptability. Professor Richard Eaton has observed that 'the Indo-Islamic traditions that grew and flourished between 711 and 1750 served both to shape Islam to the regional cultures of South Asia and to connect Muslims in those cultures to a worldwide faith community'. He adds that 'it is precisely this double movement between local cultures of South Asia and the universal norms of Islam that makes the study of Indian Islamic traditions so rewarding'. He also notes that 'even within South Asia, one finds enormous variations of Islamic traditions not only across social classes and over time, but also across space'.[4]

II

Adaptability and accommodation, and attendant creativity, can thus be depicted as two dimensions of Muslim culture as it developed and flourished in the Indian subcontinent. This was reflected on a wide canvas in many segments of social life. A survey of these in a single lecture can only be illustrative. I therefore propose to explore this in four areas: statecraft, social life, creative arts, and spirituality.

I begin with statecraft. There is a consensus among historians that 'it is a mistake to see the Mughal Empire either as an Islamic state, in which Sharia prevailed, or a Muslim state in which the Muslims, as an entire community, were part of the ruling class'.[5] Thus a doctrine of 'supra-religious sovereignty' became the operative norm. This was reflected, among other things, in 'the composition of the Mughal governing class where, by 1707, the Rajputs and other Hindus came to have a share in the resources as well as positions of authority within the state roughly to the extent of a third of those available'.[6]

The same was also true of earlier dynasties. The classic text on the medieval Indian theory of kingship is Ziauddin Barani's 14th-century work, *Fatawa-I Jahandari*, on the techniques and rules of government. It is based on an examination of the working of the institutions of Delhi kingship for over ninety-five years. Its postulates were amplified and re-enunciated in the 16th century by Mughal Emperor Akbar's chief secretary Abul-Fazl Allami in his monumental work *The Ain-I-Akbar*, which itself is part of a larger work *The Akbar Nama*.

Barani's principal dictum was that the institution of monarchy was necessary for social order and the enforcement of justice and that 'the king should have the power to make State laws 'even if in extreme cases had to override the Shariat'.[7] Barani defined *Zawabit* or State laws as 'rules of action which a king imposes as an obligatory duty on himself for realizing the welfare of the state and from which he never deviates'.[8] Abul Fazl's observations on the subject followed and amplified a line of thought no different from the earlier Indian prescriptions of Kautalya's *Arthashastra* written in 4th century BCE.

Two instances recorded by historians substantiate the Mughal approach. Responding to a letter from the Persian king Shah Abbas I, Jalaluddin Akbar said,

> We must be king to all people who are the treasures of God and have mercy for everybody no matter what their religion and idea is (since) the state of each religious group has two alternatives: either he has made the right choice or if he has made a mistake in choice, he must be pitied not blamed.[9]

Several decades later, Aurangzeb, notwithstanding his anxiety to restore the primacy of Sharia in state matters, wrote to one of his officers: 'What have worldly affairs to do with religion? For you there is your religion and for me mine.' In another letter, he observed: 'What concern have we with the religion of anybody? Let Jesus follow his own religion and Moses his own.'[10]

The same was the policy in the Deccan kingdoms where in the philosophy of governance the necessity of a pragmatic approach towards the subjects of the state prevailed. Thus, in the Qutb Shahi kingdom of Golconda, 'very little differentiation was made between the Hindus and the Muslims so far as the affairs of the state were concerned' and 'the whole outlook of the state as centered in the person of the Sultan was non-communal'.[11]

The resulting situation has been summed up by another historian:

> Thus the Akbarian concept of a state based on peace and harmony with votaries of all religions, a composite ruling class representing basically the regional ruling elites and a section of middle bureaucracy, and promotion of a culture based on the poly-cultural traditions of the country combined with Persian and Central Asian culture had struck deep roots and could not be dislodged, despite the efforts of some narrowminded theologians enjoying state support.[12]

This approach to governance reflected in the social life of society. While religious communities, and caste sections within each, lived in segments, compulsions of daily life led to normal cooperation. A study of the pre-Mughal period has observed that 'it was somewhat difficult to distinguish the lower classes of Muslims from the masses of Hindus' and that even in the case of conversions 'the average Muslim did not change his environment which was deeply influenced by caste distinctions and a general social exclusiveness. As a result Indian Islam slowly began to assimilate the broad features of Hinduism'.[13] Records show that 'there was in principle no change in the basic pattern of life and thought between 1350 and 1600'.[14] Thus, 'The blending of social customs was prompted by necessity but it was not hindered by sectarian or caste considerations. The result was a cultural pluralism that continued for centuries.'[15]

In an essentially feudal order, any assessment of social life has to be in terms of social classes. The condition of the poor was aptly described by a 17th-century Dutch trader who observed that 'the common people lived in poverty so great and miserable that the life of the people can be depicted or accurately described only as the home of stark want and the dwelling place of bitter woe'.[16] Those at other steps of the social order, middle classes and higher nobility, were better off. The empire had 120 cities and around 3200 towns. Trade and commerce flourished though by the middle of the 18th century the direction of external trade changed and some of the traditional centres of foreign trade suffered considerable losses.[17]

Developments in creative arts were distinctive and constitute a significant phase in the annals of Indian art. The period saw the arrival of a new style of architecture reflected in the mosque and the tomb in the religious domain and the palace, pavilions, town gates, gardens and landscape architecture in the secular domain. The combination of scale, detail and good taste is breath-taking.

The same was the case with painting in which the refined Persian style was combined with the lively vision of Indian artists. The Hindu art of mural painting underwent a remarkable change with the arrival of the Mughals. The themes of the paintings were varied and often focused on religion and mythology. Towards the later part of the Mughal rule, the Rajput School and Pahari School of painting began to develop under local patronage. Though Rajput school was indigenous by nature, after coming in contact with Muslim painting it was completely transformed and gave birth to Kanga School of painting in the 18th century.

Particular effort, under royal patronage, was made to translate religious texts and other major Sanskrit works into Persian. The cultural intermingling in Persian and Sanskrit literatures was a characteristic of the age and has been dwelt upon by scholars.[18] Akbar had the *Mahabharata,* the *Ramayana,* and the *Atharvaveda* translated in Persian. Yet another area of excellence was the writing of history and so was calligraphy, vividly visible to visitors on the panels of the Taj Mahal.

Nothing characterized medieval Indian society as well and as comprehensively as the broad realm of spirituality. The 11th and 12th centuries were a period of vigorous Sufi tradition in Khurasan (eastern Iran and western Afghanistan) that was transmitted to northern India and later to other areas. This coincided with the growth of the Bhakti movement that stood for intense personal devotion and complete surrender to God and in the unity of the godhead and brotherhood of humans. It began in South India in the 7th–8th century to bridge the gulf between the Shaivas and Vaishnavas. The Bhakti preachers disregarded the caste system. It is in the life and teachings of Kabir (b. 1440), Guru Nanak (b. 1439) and Chaitanya (b. 1485) that the Bhakti movement may be considered to have attained its zenith.[19] Their teachings had an impact on the development of local languages. The two trends imbibed each other's thoughts, traditions and customs. Both minimized the differences and distinctions between the Hindus and the Muslims and promoted mutual understanding and had a perceptible impact in the cultural domain.[20]

The liberal ideas and unorthodox principles of Sufism had a profound influence on Indian society.

> By the thirteenth century, Sufism had become a movement and it would not be an exaggeration to say that it brought Islam to the masses and the masses towards Islam . . . The Sufis made an intuitive choice of the common ground of spirituality between Hindus and Muslims and opened the way for a mutual appreciation of aesthetic values which could revolutionize the whole cultural attitude of the Muslims.[21]

The liberal principles of Sufi sects restrained orthodox Muslims in their attitude and encouraged many Muslim rulers to pursue tolerant attitude to their non-Muslim subjects. Most Sufi saints preached in the language of common man. This contributed to the evolution of various Indian languages like Urdu, Punjabi, Sindhi, Kashmiri and Hindi. The impact of the Sufi Movement was deeply felt on some renowned poets of the period, like Amir Khusrau and Malik Muhammad Jayasi who composed poems in Persian and Hindi in praise of Sufi principles.

A later manifestation of this, at a philosophical level, was Dara Shikoh's attempt to identify the convergence of the two faiths. In his tract 'The Confluence of the Two Oceans', he 'thirsted to know the tenets of the religion of Indian monotheists . . . and did not find any difference except verbal in the way they sought and comprehended the Truth'. Another example is a mid-17th-century work, Mir Du'l-feqar Ardestani's *Dabistan-e-Mazahib*, described by a scholar as the greatest book ever written in India on comparative religion.

III

This manifestation of Muslim life and thought in India over many centuries depicts adaptability, creativity and diversity. It is sui generis. This is reflected in scholarly assessments: 'Indian Islam has been remarkable for its identification with India without ceasing to be Islamic'[22] It adds 'color to the bizarre pageantry of India'.[23] A study on Muslim practices in medieval Punjab cites Barbara Metcalf's observation that 'Islam in India has found its expression in both local and cosmopolitan contexts and both these levels have shaped Muslim religious thought and practices'.[24]

This situation underwent a drastic and traumatic change with the advent of British rule and brought forth a multiplicity of responses from social groups and religious leaders ranging from religious reform to militancy. Resistance to the creeping foreign control took the shape of a series of peasant revolts in different regions. The theologian Shah Abdul Aziz proclaimed resistance as religiously valid. The uprising of 1857 was thus the culmination of a process in whose aftermath serious introspection about the Muslim condition took divergent routes, all focused on education. Barbara Metcalf has written in some detail about 'the diversity of Islamic movements' that surfaced and has cited with approval Albert Hourani's judgement that the 18th century was 'the Indian century of Islam'.[25] On the one side, new theological institutions of repute like Darul Ulum at Deoband and Nadwatul Ulema at Lucknow were established while on the other Syed Ahmad Khan and his colleagues struggled against odds to bring to segments of the community modern education in the shape of the MAO College that later became the Aligarh Muslim University. Individuals apart, however, modernism made limited headway unlike the reformist currents engendered by the Brahmo Samaj in Bengal and the Arya Samaj in Punjab.[26]

Politically, Muslim approaches to British rule after 1857 ranged between general allegiance (to seek some modest benefits), to protestations on specific issues and occasional resort to revolutionary language and behaviour. After World War I Mahatma Gandhi's effort to forge a broad Hindu-Muslim front by linking and supporting the Khilafat Movement with the Non-Cooperation Movement met with some success but could not be sustained. The record shows that in the late 1920s and 1930s leaders of the freedom movement with varying viewpoints struggled with competing impulses on the political and societal challenges confronting them. Scrutiny also shows that a lesser dose of cultural bias and a greater element of cultural accommodation may have brought forth greater harmony and, perhaps, prevented the tragic happening of 1947. The political perceptions and manoeuvres accompanying it did not have the support of most of the religious scholars, exemplified by Hussain Ahmad Madani of Deoband.[27]

Ten years after the event, the resulting situation was graphically expressed by the McGill scholar Wilfred Cantwell Smith:

> The Indo-Muslim community, battered by outward circumstances and gripped inwardly by dismay, has stood disconcerted, inhibited by effective self-recognition and from active vitality. And yet not only is the welfare of that community at stake, now and for future generations it is at stake. Also the histories of both India and Islam will in part turn on the success or failure of this community in solving its present problems, on its skill and wisdom in meeting the challenge of today.[28]

Three factors, he observed, would impact on this response: size, past tradition and involvement in 'the transcending complex of India'.[29]

The process of recovery from the trauma has been gradual and uneven, at times painful, and was and continues to be influenced by three impulses: autonomous initiatives, policy correctives and stated or unstated impulses to discriminate.

Indian Muslims have hesitatingly sought to tend their wounds, face the challenges and seek to develop response patterns. Success has been achieved in some measure; much however remains to be done. Educational levels remain below the national average and are particularly noticeable in regard to women where the slow pace of social reforms also results in low social mobility and workforce participation.

Autonomous correctives are one aspect of the matter; interaction with the larger community of citizens is another and requires candid dialogue and careful calibration without a syndrome of superiority or inferiority. The failure to communicate with the wider community in sufficient measure has tended to freeze the boundaries of diversities that characterize the Indian society.

In 2005 the government appointed a committee to delineate the contours of the problem. Its findings, the Sachar Committee Report, showed that on most socio-economic indicators—education, livelihood, access to public services and employment market across the states— Muslims were on the margins of structures of political, economic and social relevance and that their average condition was comparable to, or even worse than, the country's most backward communities whose condition is officially acknowledged.[30] This was followed by the Report of the National Commission for Religious and Linguistic Minorities (the Ranganath Mishra Commission) in 2007. Another report, in 2014, evaluated the implementation of the decisions taken and concluded that though 'a start has been made, yet serious bottlenecks remain' and asserted that 'the development of the Muslim community must be built on the bed-rock of a sense of security'.[31]

It is evident from the compendium of official and civil society reports that the principal problems confronting India's Muslims relate to (a) identity and security; (b) education and empowerment; (c) equitable share in the largesse of the state; and (d) fair share in decision-making. Each of these is a right of the citizen in terms of the plural, secular and democratic dimensions of the Indian polity. The defaults by the State are therefore to be corrected at policy and implementation stages by the State at the federal and state levels. Political sagacity, the imperative of social peace, and an informed and educated public opinion play an important role in this.

Is this being done in sufficient measure in word and deed? There are questions in the minds of many citizens about it, about our commitment to the core values of pluralism and secularism, about our capacity to resist the onslaught of ideas and practices that militate against values of justice, liberty, equality and fraternity prescribed for us by the Constitution.

The urgency of giving this a practical shape at national, state and local levels through various suggestions in the public domain is highlighted by enhanced apprehensions of insecurity amongst segments of our citizen body, particularly Dalits, Muslims and Christians. The objective of various groups indulging in strong-arm tactics 'is to make minorities feel unsafe and insecure, to force them to become furtive and fearful while practicing their faith or celebrating their festivals and thereby destroy India's pluralist heritage'.[32] These, along with other manifestations of distress in different social segments and regions, tend to suggest that we are perhaps a polity at war with itself in which the process of emotional integration has faltered and is in dire need of reinvigoration.

This rejuvenation is unavoidable given Indian society's living experience of diversity and plurality, tolerance and coexistence. The challenge today is to educate opinion about the consequences of intolerance, of narrow nationalism and of illiberal democracy and to ensure that it does not become pervasive by associating with fellow citizens who wish to retain secular principles and practices.

The Muslims of India, inheritors of a rich legacy, cannot but be a part of this process as actors and as beneficiaries. They recall with pride

Abul Kalam Azad's advice to them in October 1947 on the morrow of
the Partition: 'Come, let us vow that this is our land, we are for it, and
that basic decisions about its destiny will remain incomplete without our
voice.' They are committed to the Constitution and to the constitutional
procedures for grievance redressal. They are concerned over rising incidents
of intolerance and violence but there is no inclination in their ranks to opt
for ideologies and practices of violence. This is reflective of their moorings
in a composite society and their non-alienation. They retain and reiterate
their claim of being citizens, endowed with rights and duties bestowed
on them by the Constitution, and 'a form of citizenship that is marked
neither by a universalism generated by complete homogenization, nor by
particularism of self-identical and closed communities'.[33]

Despite some shortcomings and occasional aberrations, the Indian
model of accommodation of diversity in a country with a complex societal
make up remains a relevant example for a globalizing world that requires
all members of its citizen-body to go beyond mere tolerance to acceptance
of diversity in all aspects of life. Imperatives of ultra-nationalism and
geopolitics in recent decades have resulted in projecting the Muslim as 'the
new Other' and this Otherness is being perceived as a spectre haunting
the world very much like radical ideologies of earlier ages. This drift
into apprehension and intolerance has to be resisted and reversed; sanity
demands that all of us pull back from the precipice and anchor thought and
action on civic virtues national and global.

26

The Role of Women in
Making a Humane Society*

I

At a first glance, today's theme is self-evident and in no need of commentary. Women constitute about half of humankind and should therefore share the same responsibilities as men.

The term 'humane' according to the dictionary is compassion or benevolence; a humane society is therefore one that avoids pain or suffering to fellow humans. Sociologists consider a society humane if it is motivated by the most desirable of human values. It implies a society dedicated to the principles of justice, equality and fraternity and one in which its members are recognized and respected as human beings without differentiations of religion, race, caste, sex or place of birth.

This, in relation to the female half of humankind, implies that women get justice, equality and fraternity in equal measure in the societies they live in.

Does this correspond to reality? Data published by a UN Women report shows:[1]

* Gender inequality is a major cause and effect of hunger and poverty. About 60 per cent of chronically hungry people are women and girls.
* Women make up more than two-thirds of the world's 796 million illiterate people.
* Almost 70 per cent of employed women in South Asia work in agriculture, as do more than 60 per cent of employed women in sub-Saharan Africa.

* September 2017, Kozhikode.

- In most countries, women in rural areas who work for wages are more likely than men to hold seasonal, part-time and low-wage jobs.
- Women also receive lower wages for the same work.
- A large gender gap remains in women's access to decision-making and leadership.

Some questions inevitably arise: Why has this come about? What lends legitimacy to it? Does this situation benefit women as a human species or the societies they live in? Can women inequality in most spheres of human activity place them to be equal beneficiaries of the benefits of a humane society? How can it be corrected?

These and related questions need to be answered, in this conference, and on all platforms where human progress is discussed. The Concept Note's focus is on the status and role of women 'in the Muslim world'. This includes Muslim women in India since demographic data shows that the world's second largest Muslim population, amounting to around 189 million, resides in India.

II

I begin with the wider Indian scene. Jawaharlal Nehru had once said that 'you can tell the condition of a nation by looking at the status of its women'. The June 2015 Report of the High Level Committee on the Status of Women in India, headed by Professor Pam Rajput, was candid in its assessment and I would like to quote from its chapter on the 'Socio-Cultural Landscape':

> Indian women are born into and raised in a socio-cultural environment that is highly discriminatory, patriarchal and hierarchical, in which economic, political, religious, social and cultural institutions are largely controlled by men. This environment has evolved over centuries through various social practices and institutions that are governed by patriarchy. Through a combination of family, caste, community and religion, among others, patriarchal values and ideas are constantly reinforced and legitimized.

It adds that 'the first lesson in hierarchy, subordination and discrimination are learnt in the family'.

Thus, for purposes of analysis, the question of status in society requires determination at three levels: as citizens, as women and as women members of a specific religious grouping.

The rights of citizens are enshrined in our Constitution. It not only grants equality to women and prohibits discrimination but also recognizes their marginalization and empowers the State to adopt measures of positive discrimination in their favour. This has been reinforced by Supreme Court which has held that the equality clause does not speak of mere formal equality before law but embodies the concept of real and substantive equality which is an essential ingredient of social and economic justice.

As against this, the Gender Inequality Index of the 2016 Human Development Report of UNDP ranks India at 125 in a list of 159 countries.

Since it is nobody's case that Muslims in India are altogether immune to the social impact of Indian society including some of its ailments, a working hypothesis could be to accept these shortfalls as generally representative of the ground situation; at the same time, care is to be taken not to treat Muslim women as a monolithic category since like other large communities, it is also highly differentiated and heterogeneous. The Sachar Committee Report sheds much light on this.

A number of academic and field studies are available on the general condition of Muslim women as well as in different socio-economic segments. One study examined them in three categories: education, workforce participation and social mobility. Allow me to summarize its findings:

Education

- In 2009–2010, 34.7 per cent (rural) and 19.8 per cent (urban) Muslim women have never attended school.
- Nineteen per cent (rural) and 11 per cent (urban) have illiterate husbands.
- Less than 10 per cent have completed schooling.

Workforce participation

- Out of the total numbers of Indian women who participated in the workforce, 70 per cent are Hindu women and 29 per cent are Muslim women.
- Two-thirds of Muslim women are self-employed or engaged in home-based labour and have a low level of earning.

Social mobility

- 75 per cent of Muslim women need their husband's permission to engage in almost all activities.
- Many are unaware of government schemes.
- 20 per cent have access to media.

These, and other actual or alleged drawbacks, are often attributed to tradition based on socio-religious beliefs and practices. It is therefore essential in the first place to distinguish religion per se from practices attributed to it by tradition in individual societies.

The principle of equality and justice between men and women in terms of their rights and obligations is emphatically stated in *Sura Al-Ahzab*. This is reiterated in other places of the Holy Book. It is to be noted that Islam makes no distinction between secular and religious duties; also, that in Islamic law a woman has an independent juridical personality. She has to be respected as a person.

When then, and how, did inequality creep in?

The answer to this question lies in the psycho-sociological totality that prevailed for centuries in most societies including Indian, and still does, and which can be summed up as a system of values and social practices that became and remain embedded in economy and culture and are referred to as *patriarchy*. Details, of course, vary from society to society; its overall impact was and remains a lessoning of the equal status of women.

Thus, the equality bestowed by faith was diluted or denied by tradition and practice and replaced by subordination. An obvious result of this was overt or covert misogyny so vividly reflected in proverbs relating to women in most languages in use in Muslim societies.

III

This state of affairs is clearly contrary to tenets of faith. It is unethical and is harmful to the individuals and the community. It must change. Only then can women, as equal partners participate in the creation of a society that is humane. This requires meaningful correctives in social practices.

I asked a lady some time ago about empowerment of women. She said: 'We are born empowered; life is created within us, through us.'

The validity of her response is evident. A child's first lessons in life are received from the mother. Despite this, the fact remains that deep-rooted social handicaps diminish the full impact of this relationship. The conscious or sub-conscious perception in many segments of society is that the girl child is a burden, even a misfortune, on account of social evils like insistence on dowry, outlawed though it is, and many beliefs and practices associated with the institution of marriage.

Our present effort, through affirmative action initiatives of the government, or through voluntary initiatives, is to produce equity of varying intensity rather than substantive equality. It is clearly inadequate.

The challenge is to produce substantive gender equality so that women become active and equal partners in the creation of a humane society.

The first step in this direction is to be taken with the girl child, with her nourishment, education and inculcation of a sense of equality. Each of these has to be given adequate weight. The principal responsibility for this lies with the parents but for this to happen meaningfully, the social ambiance and the attitude of the husband has to change accordingly. The traditional societal bias towards a patriarchal relationship in the family unit has thus to give way to a relationship of equal partners.

The next step is at the nursery, primary and secondary school level where gender equality has to be practiced and be a part of the curricula. A supportive but essential element in this is obligatory physical training and yoga and encouragement to participate in sports of choice. The human potential for learning and excellence has no gender and class ceiling and experience shows that given opportunity the most deprived in both sexes can scale the heights.

Alongside is the question of preparing the younger generation for participation in the workforce and for requisite career planning. At present, according to World Bank data, it is only 27 per cent for India as against 51 in Indonesia, 49 in Malaysia, 43 in Bangladesh, 30 in Sri Lanka and 25 in Pakistan. Muslim women's share of this 27 per cent is barely 10 per cent.

There is, surely, considerable room for improvement. Such an improvement would be in consonance with requirements of faith and necessitates individual and community effort since 'Verily never will god change the condition of a people until they change it themselves' (s xiii.11).

This indeed is an imperative need of our times.

27

India and the Muslim World

Historically, a terminological predecessor of the expression *Muslim World* is Christendom, a church-State entity that emerged after the dissolution of the Roman Empire. 'Muslim World' itself has a genealogy in political and academic literature. In January 1911 the Hartford Seminary in the United States commenced publication of a journal by this name. It was dedicated to the promotion and dissemination of scholarly research on Islam and Muslim societies and on historical and current aspects of Muslim-Christian relations. Its editorial in the first issue referred to the need to supplement information on 'the Moslem problem politically' and was intended to be an aid to Christian missionaries in the 'Moslem world'. A century later a special issue of the journal on the decade after 9/11 focused on 'the need for a new paradigm of interfaith dialogue'.

Its origins and history apart, and given globalization in all its dimensions, the need for a dialogue with interlocutors in societies everywhere is evident.

The term 'Muslim World' is used variously depending on occasion and context. It means (a) the totality of global population professing the Islamic faith; (b) countries the majority of whose populations profess to be Muslims; (c) countries that have formally declared themselves to be Islamic and use faith as the source of legislation; and (d) nations that are members of the OIC (Organization of Islamic Conference) an international organization founded in 1969, consisting of fifty-seven member states, with a total population of over 1.8 billion (in 2015) with forty-nine of them being Muslim-majority and declared to be 'the collective voice of the Muslim world and professing to safeguard and protect the interests of the Muslim world in the spirit of promoting international peace and harmony'.

In the first meaning of the term, therefore, India could be considered part of the Muslim world.

In demographic terms, according to Pew, people of Muslim faith number around 1.8 billion or 24.1 per cent of the global population. Of these 1.2 billion or 66.7 per cent are in Asia principally in Indonesia, Bangladesh, Pakistan and India.

A look at the map is helpful. India as a geographical entity was not terra incognita to the Arabian Peninsula and other lands of western Asia where Islam had its first followers. This was particularly true of contacts of the trading communities of the coastal regions of western and southern India; Records show that established trade routes existed well before the advent of Islam; so was the presence of Indian trading communities in those lands.

For the purpose of this essay, it is relevant to locate India and Indian interests in the Muslim world in a proper context.

II

India is justly proud of its diversity. One of its many dimensions is Muslim. India has the third largest Muslim community in the world that has, over centuries, made its contributions to Islamic civilization just as Muslims in India have contributed to Indian civilization. This is a continuing process.

The historical context of the relationship is unique and relevant. India's experience and interaction with Muslims and Muslim lands is not that of European societies. India was a known land, sought for its prosperity and trading skills and respected for its attainments in different branches of knowledge. Arab geographers in the 9th to 11th centuries were aware of its location long before the advent of Muslim conquerors. Alberuni in the early 11th century studied Indian religion, philosophy, sciences, manners and customs and produced a virtual encyclopedia remarkable for its detail and objectivity; particularly instructive is its chapter entitled 'On the belief of Hindus in God.'

The new faith came to India through diverse channels—through traders in the south and through conquerors and travellers in north-west. Historians have noted that the vast majority of Indian Muslims are converts and that the main agency for conversions was the mystics, principally in the 15th and 16th centuries. Another historian depicts Indian culture as

synthetic in character: It comprehends ideas of different orders. It embraces in its orbit beliefs, customs, rites, institutions, arts, religions and philosophies belonging to society in different stages of development. It eternally seeks to find a unity for the heterogeneous elements which make up its totality. At worst its attempts end in mechanical juxtaposition, at best they succeed in evolving an organic system.[1]

Heterogeneity was the core of this process. It was a characteristic of the social, cultural and philosophical landscape. Interaction with its own people who had opted for a new faith produced a variety of responses, conscious and sub-conscious. One aspect was formal and political, another was social and intellectual. The first adapted to the ground reality, benefited from it and in turn induced the second.

Over time, the imprint of the structure of Indian society was visible and so was adaptability. Professor Richard Eaton has observed that 'the Indo-Islamic traditions that grew and flourished between 711 and 1750 served both to shape Islam to the regional cultures of South Asia and to connect Muslims in those cultures to a worldwide faith community'. He adds that 'it is precisely this double movement between local cultures of South Asia and the universal norms of Islam that makes the study of Indian Islamic traditions so rewarding'.[2]

Adaptability and accommodation, and attendant creativity, can thus be depicted as two dimensions of Muslim culture as it developed and flourished in the Indian subcontinent. This was reflected on a wide canvas in many segments of social life, particularly in statecraft, social life, creative arts and the broad realm of spirituality whose liberal principles restrained orthodox Muslims in their attitude and encouraged many Muslim rulers to pursue a tolerant attitude to their non-Muslim subjects. An instance of this is a mid-17th-century work, *Dabistan-e-Mazahib*, described by a scholar as the greatest book ever written in India on comparative religion.

This manifestation of Muslim life and thought in India over many centuries depicts adaptability, creativity and diversity. It is sui generis. This situation underwent a drastic and traumatic change with the advent of British rule and brought forth a multiplicity of responses from social groups and religious leaders ranging from religious reform to militancy. Resistance to creeping foreign control took the shape of a series of peasant revolts in different regions. The theologian Shah Abdul Aziz proclaimed resistance as religiously valid. The uprising of 1857 was thus the culmination of a process in whose aftermath serious introspection about the Muslim condition took divergent routes,

Politically, Muslim reactions to British rule in India after 1857 ranged between general allegiance (to seek some modest benefits), to protestations on specific issues and occasional resort to revolutionary language and behaviour. There also was much empathy for movements against foreign dominance in other Muslim countries. Half a century after 1857, the Indian Muslims had a salient cause to rally around: this took the shape of Indian Medical Mission to Turkey in 1912–1913 Balkan Wars.

After World War I Mahatma Gandhi's effort to forge a broad Hindu-Muslim front by linking and supporting the Khilafat Movement with the Non-Cooperation Movement met with some success but could not be sustained. The record shows that in the late 1920s and 1930s leaders of the freedom movement with varying viewpoints struggled with competing impulses on political and societal challenges confronting them. Scrutiny shows that a lesser dose of cultural bias and a greater element of cultural accommodation may have brought forth more harmony and, perhaps, prevented the tragic happening of 1947.

Ten years after that cataclysmic event, the resulting situation was graphically expressed by the McGill scholar Wilfred Cantwell Smith:

> The Indo-Muslim community, battered by outward circumstances and gripped inwardly by dismay, has stood disconcerted, inhibited by effective self-recognition and from active vitality. And yet not only is the welfare of that community at stake, now and for future generations. Also the histories of both India and Islam will in part turn on the success or failure of this community in solving its present problems, on its skill and wisdom in meeting the challenge of today.

Three factors, he observed, would impact on this response: size, past tradition and involvement in 'the transcending complex of India'.[3]

The process of recovery from the trauma has been gradual and uneven, at times painful, and continues to be influenced by three impulses: autonomous initiatives, policy correctives and stated or unstated impulses to discriminate.

Indian Muslims have hesitatingly sought to tend their wounds, face the challenges and seek to develop response patterns. Success has been achieved in some measure; much however remains to be done. Educational levels remain below the national average and are particularly noticeable in regard to women where the slow pace of social reforms also results in low social mobility and workforce participation.

It is evident from the compendium of official and civil society reports that the principal problems confronting India's Muslims relate to (a) identity and security, (b) education and empowerment, (c) equitable share in the largesse of the state, and (d) fair share in decision-making. Each of these is a right of the citizen in terms of the plural, secular and democratic dimensions of the Indian polity. The defaults by the State are therefore to be corrected at policy and implementation stages by the State at the federal and state levels. Political sagacity, the imperative of social peace and an informed and educated public opinion play an important role in this.

Communal commotions against Muslims are not of recent origin and sufficient literature on it is available in the public domain. The Sachar Report (2006) stated that 'lack of sense of security and discriminatory towards Muslims is felt widely' and that 'the government's action in bringing to book perpetrators of communal violence has been a sore point for the community'.[4]

To what extent is the constitutional definition of Muslims as a minority ingrained in the collective psyche of the community? This question was sought to be addressed in a study published in 2014. The answer then was that

> Muslim narratives recorded here do not suggest any cementing of boundaries or fixity of ideas. They flout treading a singular trajectory and in doing so, underscore the imperative to talk in terms of a plurality of Muslim subjectivities—not necessarily in harmony with each other.[5]

The derailment in State policy and practice reflected in recent legislation at central and state levels are manifestations of 'majoritarianism' and 'Islamophobia'. They reflect changing ground realities. This is witnessed by the outside world including its Muslim segment.

The emotional bonds of oneness among co-religionists, reinforced by adherence to a basic doctrine and obligatory rituals including the annual *Haj*, and notwithstanding sectarian divides, and have been an existential reality in Muslim ranks the world over. History records that these bonds are invoked whenever misfortune befalls any segment of the *ummah*. Modern information technology quickens the process and is reflected in cases of such happenings anywhere in recent decades.

III

Independent India crafted its policy towards Muslim countries under multiple impulses: of age old cultural and commercial ties and religious affinities of an important segment of its citizen body; of recollections of the freedom movement and struggle against colonialism, and of more recent solidarity emanating from the Non-Aligned Movement. Notwithstanding these affinities, however, a common policy towards them could not be crafted because of divergence in a range of other interests. What was done was to identify, and address apart from geo-political questions, those concerns in which Non-Aligned solidarity and Muslim sentiments could be evoked in relation to India and its citizens. This focused on the well-being of the Muslim minority, on expressions of concern regarding its security and status and on efforts to redress those grievances to the extent possible.

Since Muslim States and their interests are not identical, a common policy towards them cannot be crafted. What can be done is to identify and address those concerns in which Muslim sentiments are evoked in relation to India. This focuses on the question of security, status and welfare of the Muslim minority. It is aggravated in times of stress and impacts adversely on the official efforts to promote better relations.

Prior to the Rabat Conference of 1969, the Muslim world did not have an organizational existence at governmental level. India's relationship with those countries can therefore be traced through broad foreign policy orientations. The principal political crises of 1950s and 1960s— Iran's nationalization of the Anglo Iranian Oil Company and Egypt's nationalization of the Suez Canal—were essentially directed at dealings with vestiges of European colonialism and had no religious overtones. The Indian responses to both were emphatically clear in terms of known policies. Similar was the position in 1967 at the time of the Six-Day War. Our support was for forces of Arab nationalism and for non-alignment. For the same reason, we opposed Western initiatives like the Central Treaty Organization (CENTO) and the Southeast Asia Treaty Organization (SEATO). We maintained correct and ostensibly cordial relations with Muslim countries but with a discernible warmth towards those who in dealings with the outside world were not inclined towards Western alliances.

In the 1950s and 1960s Iran and Saudi Arabia explored areas of political and intelligence cooperation. One result of it was the Safari Club in 1974; it consisted of Iran, Saudi Arabia, France, Egypt and Morocco and ceased to function after the Iranian Revolution.[6]

The Al Aqsa Mosque incident in August 1969 provided the opportunity for convening the First Islamic Summit Conference at Rabat in September 1969. A unanimous invitation was extended to India at the instance of King Faisal of Saudi Arabia and, pending the arrival of a ministerial level delegation, our ambassador in Morocco attended and spoke in the plenary session. The next day however Pakistani threats of a walkout resulted in the obstruction of our delegation's attendance at subsequent sessions and the distortion of our mention in the final communiqué.

The OIC's interest in matters Indian resurfaced in the wake of the insurgency in Kashmir in 1990–1991 and Pakistan's effort to focus attention on it in the councils of the UN. A Contact Group was formed but efforts to galvanize support through a resolution in UNHRC were unsuccessful. Thereafter, and until very recently, Kashmir-related matters seem to disappear from the agenda of international bodies. Despite this, Pakistan's efforts would nevertheless resurface as long as discontent festers in Kashmir. The same would hold for matters relating to Muslim minorities. Here, a certain deftness is noticeable; an OIC decision to prepare a report on the status of Muslim minorities in the world remains unimplemented after several decades.

Specific proposals for intensifying the projection of the Indian image in Muslim countries should be based on the requirements of each destination depending upon the intensity of its knowledge/interaction with India or lack thereof—and cannot be generalized.

In terms of practical statecraft there is need to shift away from policies of 'containment' and 'appeasement' and to generate genuine trust-building on the basis of a truly secular agenda that sees minorities as assets rather than liabilities. This would necessitate correcting certain perceptions and stereotypes developed over time and reiterating in practice principles of justice, equality and fraternity within the framework of a plural, democratic and secular Indian State.

Image building in Muslim countries would go hand in hand with, and strengthen, the ongoing projection of India as an emerging economic power with a vast market potential and capacity to export technology and technology-related services to both developed and developing countries. Good evidence is to be found recently in some of the GCC (Gulf Cooperation Council) States to avail of investment opportunities in India. The success stories in this area are the arrangements arrived by Reliance Industries with Saudi Arabian Oil Company (Saudi Aramco) and of Abu Dhabi National Oil Company (ADNOC) in the UAE. In both instances, these inputs are reflecting changed perceptions on matters relating to our core interests.

India–Pakistan questions are political problems between neighbours. Muslim states should continue to be sensitized to the damaging impact of attempts to make these into Muslim questions. An observation by a senior Saudi official many years ago that he viewed problems between India and Pakistan as between two friends and not between a friend and an enemy is relevant in this context.

Muslim countries and societies have been in recent decades psychologically besieged on account of the post-9/11 Western onslaught on them. India, given its long association with these societies, projects a better understanding of their individual developmental compulsions and subscribes to the view that while social change and political evolution is an essential ingredient of modernization, the content and pace of this change should be left to individual societies. India also holds the view that India in terms of its Constitutional principles offers an alternate working model of pluralism in thought and action with its three ingredients of a plural society, a secular polity and a democratic State structure.

While the security requirements of the State are to be fully met, it is essential to correct the dominant discourse in some quarters of equating terrorism with Islam or with Muslims since it impacts adversely on public perceptions of Muslims and Muslim States.

In a wider perspective, there is a need to shift away from the perspectives of 'containment' and 'appeasement' and to generate genuine trust-building on the basis of a truly secular agenda that sees minorities as assets rather than as liabilities. This would necessitate correcting certain perceptions and stereotypes developed over time and etched, albeit unevenly, in popular (and, at times, official) imagery.

IV

Given the totality of existential factors, India's interaction with the Muslim world cannot be separated or segregated from our very large community of Muslim citizens. Wisdom and statecraft both desire a mutually beneficial modus vivendi within the ambit of rule of law. Citizens of the State, irrespective of their identity, cannot be viewed as liabilities.

There is instead a requirement for sharply focused affirmative action by the State, in terms of the accepted norms of human development and human security, to address the socio-economic and educational backwardness of the overwhelming majority of Muslims and to enable them to play a fuller role in national life, including interaction with the Muslim world (where the paucity of Indian Muslim talent at professional levels is sometimes adversely commented upon). Some of this would have a beneficial impact on the debate on social reforms.

Is this being done in sufficient measure in word and deed? There are questions in the minds of many citizens about it, about our commitment to the core values of pluralism and secularism, about our capacity to resist the onslaught of ideas and practices that militate against values of justice, liberty, equality and fraternity prescribed for us by the Constitution.

The urgency of giving this a practical shape at national, state and local levels through various suggestions in the public domain is highlighted by enhanced apprehensions of insecurity amongst segments of our citizen body, particularly Dalits, Muslims and Christians. The objective of various groups indulging in strong-arm tactics 'is to make minorities feel unsafe and insecure, to force them to become furtive and fearful while practicing their faith or celebrating their festivals and thereby destroy India's pluralist heritage.'[7] These, along with other manifestations of distress in different social segments and regions, tend to suggest that we are perhaps a polity at war with itself in which the process of emotional integration has faltered and is in dire need of reinvigoration.

This rejuvenation is unavoidable given Indian society's living experience of diversity and plurality, tolerance and coexistence. The challenge today is to educate opinion about the consequences of intolerance, of narrow nationalism and of illiberal democracy and to ensure that it does not become pervasive by associating with fellow citizens who wish to retain secular principles and practices.

The Muslims of India, inheritors of a rich legacy, cannot but be a part of this process as actors and as beneficiaries. They recall with pride Abul Kalam Azad's advice to them in October 1947 on the morrow of the Partition: 'come, let us vow that this is our land, we are for it, and that basic decisions about its destiny will remain incomplete without our voice'. They are committed to the Constitution and to the constitutional procedures for redress of grievance. They are concerned over rising incidents of intolerance and violence but there is no inclination in their ranks to opt for ideologies and practices of violence. This is reflective of their moorings in a composite society and their non-alienation. They retain and reiterate their claim of being citizens, endowed with rights and duties bestowed on them by the Constitution, and 'a form of citizenship that is marked neither by a universalism generated by complete homogenization, nor by particularism of self identical and closed communities'.[8]

Despite some shortcomings and occasional aberrations, the Indian model of accommodation of diversity in a country with a complex societal make up remains a relevant example for a globalizing world that requires all members of its citizen-body to go beyond mere tolerance to acceptance of diversity in all aspects of life. Imperatives of ultra-nationalism and geopolitics in recent decades have resulted in projecting the Muslim as 'the new Other' and this Otherness is being perceived as a spectre haunting the world very much like radical ideologies of earlier ages. This drift into apprehension and intolerance has to be resisted and reversed; sanity demands that all of us pull back from the precipice and anchor thought and action on civic virtues national and global. It is particularly so in India, justly proud of its diversity, a societal trait that has developed over millennia.

Acknowledgements

I place on record my thanks to Shri Premanka Goswami of Penguin Random House India for the arrangements of the publication of this book and also Ms Ranjana Sengupta and Binita Roy for their strenuous efforts in editing the text at various levels. The assistance of my colleague Shri Anil Kaushik was invaluable.

Notes

Introduction

1. *An Agenda for Peace*: Report of the UN Secretary General pursuant to the statement adopted by the Security Council on 31 January 1992.
2. Said Amir Arjomand (ed.), *The Political Dimensions of Religion* (New York, 1993), p. 2.
3. Gregory Gause III, 'Should We Stay or Should We Go? The United States and the Middle East', *Survival*, September 2019; Anthony H. Cordesman, 'The Changing Security Dynamics of the MENA Region', Center for Strategic & International Studies, Washington, 22 March 2021; and Rory Stewart, 'The Last Days of Intervention', *Foreign Affairs*, November/December 2021.
4. Upendra Baxi, 'The Rule of Law in India', *International Journal of Human Rights*, Issue 6, 2007.
5. Ananya Vajpeyi, *Righteous Republic: The Political Foundations of Modern India* (Harvard, 2012), p. 250.
6. Rasheeduddin Khan, *Bewildered India: Identity, Pluralism, Discord* (New Delhi, 1995), p. 295.
7. Richard M. Eaton has dwelt on its ramifications in *India in the Persianate Age 1000–1765* (2019).
8. Goolam E. Vahanvati, 'Rule of Law: The Sieges Within', in *Human Rights and the Rule of Law* edited by Mool Chand Sharma and Raju Ramachandran (2005), pp. 165–176.
9. Shiv Visvanathan, 'Prisoners of Conscience', *The Telegraph* (Kolkata), 24 February 2021. Another expression of the same perception was made a few years earlier by T.K. Oommen: 'The empirical reality of India does not suit the institution of nation-state which relentlessly pursues cultural homogenization in the name of national consolidation' (*Social Inclusion in Independent India: Dimensions and Approaches* [New Delhi, 2014], p. 15).

10. Suhas Palshikar, 'Towards Hegemony: The BJP Beyond Electoral Dominance', in *Majoritarian State: How Hindu Nationalism Is Changing India* edited by Angana P. Chatterjee, Thomas Blom Hansen and Christophe Jaffrelot (New Delhi, 2019), pp. 103–104.

11. My lecture at the Australian National University, Canberra in March 2018 dealt with this in some detail.

12. 'Social, Economic and Educational Status of the Muslim Community in India: The Sachar Committee Report, 2006' (2006), p. 243 and 'Report on the Expert Group on Diversity Index' (2008), pp. vii–viii.

13. Speech of 29 November 1949.

14. 'Punishing Process', Editorial in *The Indian Express*, 28 April 2021, p. 8.

15. See https://www.marxists.org/archive/trotsky/1930/hrr/ch00.htm.

16. A. Kaaiyarasan et al., 'A Mirror to the Future of Tamil Nadu and India', *The Hindu*, 3 May 2021.

17. The UN Charter prescribes the rights and duties of States in the international system. It also, through Article 55, suggests standards implemented through a series of special covenants that States should follow to ensure human rights and fundamental freedoms for their peoples.

18. Joseph E. Stiglitz, *The Price of Inequality* (2012), p. 142.

19. Ajay Gudavarthy, *Maoism, Democracy and Globalisation* (New Delhi, 2014), p. 25. 'Human rights are the new universal language that allows societies that are differently placed, in terms of economic development, political systems and cultural orientations, to speak to each other. They have allowed a complementary and utterly essential political language to the process of globalization' (pp. 25–26).

20. T.K. Oommen. *Social Inclusion in Independent India: Dimensions and Approaches* (2014), pp. 285–287.

21. See http://hdr.undp.org/en/2015-report and the following years.

22. Amartya Sen and Jean Drèze, *An Uncertain Glory: India and Its Contradictions* (2013), p. 8.

23. B.G. Verghese, *Rage, Reconciliation and Security: Managing India's Diversities* (2008), p. xiv.

24. Ibid.

25. M.N. Srinivas (ed.), *Caste: Its Twentieth Century Avatar* (1996), pp. xxv–xxvi.

26. Balachandra Mungekar, Preface to the Second Edition, *Dr. Babasaheb Ambedkar* (reprint, 2011 [1944]), pp. 4–5.

27. *Indian Express*, 27 July 2021. This was repeated in the Supreme Court on 23 September (*The Hindu*, 24 September) where the government described it as 'administratively difficult and cumbersome'. On the other hand, it has been pointed out by Yogendra Yadav (*Indian Express*, 25 August 2021) that the

Indra Sawhaney judgment of the Supreme Court in 1992 had required that evidence of caste-based reservations be collected every ten years to screen out the privileged castes from the benefits of reservations.

28. Yael Tamir, *Liberal Nationalism* (Princeton, 1993), pp. 79, 83, 90, 95. The author's views have been attenuated in a subsequent work (*Why Nationalism*, 2019), arguing for 'a new and caring nationalism' since 'it would be a tragedy if nationalism—with its tremendous creative and productive powers—were left in the hands of the extremists' (pp. 178–182).

29. Christophe Jaffrelot, 'India's Democracy at 70: Towards a Hindu State?' *Journal of Democracy*, volume 28, number 3 (3 July 2017), pp. 52–63, citing Smooha, who defines ten conditions that can lead to the establishment of an ethnic democracy.

30. Indrajit Roy, 'The Hindu Vote, an Emerging Ethnocracy', *The Hindu*, 7 October 2021: 'An ethnocracy has taken root in India since 2014 . . . Indeed, the BJP has been so successful creating an ethnocracy in India that its rivals are increasingly emulating it.'

SECTION ONE: HUMAN RIGHTS AND GROUP RIGHTS

Chapter 1: Annual Conference of the National Minorities Commission

1. Address of the President to the Joint Session of Parliament, 25 February 2005: 'Government would recast the present programme for the welfare of minorities.'

Chapter 2: India and the Contemporary International Norms on Group Rights

1. J.J. Rousseau, *The Social Contract or Principles of Political Right* translated by H.J. Tozer, 3rd ed. (London, 1948), p. 99.
2. John Rawls, *A Theory of Justice* (Cambridge, Mass. Rev. ed., 1999), pp. 3–4.
3. Kautilya, *The Arthashastra*, translated by L.N. Rangarajan (New Delhi, 1992), 7.5.26–28.
4. *The Laws of Manu* (New Delhi, 1991), 7. 10, 8. 12–19.
5. Aristotle, *Politics* (London, 1948), III.1.6.
6. Qu'ran, IV.58 and Mohammad Hashim Kamali, *Principles of Islamic Jurisprudence* (Cambridge, 1991), p. 348.
7. Otto Gierke, *Political Theories of the Middle Age* (Cambridge, 1958), p. 37.
8. Guido De Ruggario, *The History of European Liberalism* (Boston, 1959), pp. 1–2.

9. John Locke, *Two Treatises of Civil Government* (London, 1949), II.190.

10. Yael Tamir, *Liberal Nationalism* (Princeton, 1993), p. 144.

11. Neera Chandoke, *Beyond Secularism: The Rights of Religious Minorities* (New Delhi, 1999), p. 277, citing *Readings on Minorities: Perspectives and Documents* edited by Iqbal A. Ansari (New Delhi, 1996), Vol. I, p. xvi.

12. *The United Nations and Human Rights 1945–1995* (New York, 1995), p. 239.

13. Ibid., p. 451.

14. Human Rights Committee, CCPR/C/21/Rev.1/Add 5, General Comment 23, 08/04/1994, and Ansari, Op. cit., pp. 251–281, citing from Francesco Capotorti's Report.

15. E/CN.4/Sub.2/AC.5/2001/2, 2 April 2001, Commission on Human Rights, Sub-Commission on the Promotion and Protection of Human Rights. Final text of Commentary on the 1992 Declaration by Ashjorn Eide, Chairperson of the Working Group on Minorities, paragraphs 21–29.

16. Ibid., paragraphs 41–49. These are based on the Lund Recommendations on the Effective Participation of National Minorities in Public Life (September 1999), finalized in the CSCE framework.

17. Commission on Human Rights, E/CN.4/2006/74, 6 January 2006, Special Groups and Individuals: Minorities, Report of the Independent Expert on Minority Issues, Gay McDougall.

18. Ansari, Op. cit., pp. 131–133 for the text.

19. Ibid., pp. 167–168 for the text.

20. Mushirul Hasan (ed.), *India's Partition: Process, Strategy and Mobilisation* (New Delhi, 1994), p. 61.

21. Ansari, Op. cit., pp. 214–333. The debate on the Report heard Mahavir Tyagi asserting that 'before a minority there is only one alternative: it is to be loyal to the majority and cooperate and gain the confidence of the majority. There are also other alternatives—which of course I do not advocate, nor support—according to these, minorities become extinct'. Govind Ballabh Pant, urging the minorities to give up the right of separate representation, said, 'Your safety lies in making yourself an integral part of the organic whole which forms the real genuine State'. Ibid., pp. 289 and 294.

22. Chandoke, Op. cit., pp. 59–61.

23. Ibid., pp. 364, 368–370 and 403.

24. Mushirul Hasan, *Legacy of a Divided Nation: India's Muslims since Independence* (New Delhi, 1997), p. 144, citing *Selected Works of Jawaharlal Nehru*, Vol. 8, p. 804.

25. CCPR/C/76/Add.6, 17 July 1996, Human Rights Commission, Third periodic report states parties due in 1992: India 17 July 1996, paragraphs 3, 5, pp. 125–129. It is understood that subsequent reports have yet to be made.

26. Harold J. Laski, *A Grammar of Politics* (London, 1951, reprint of 4th ed.), pp. 104, 100–101.

27. Soli J. Sorabji, 'Minorities: National and International Protection', in Ansari, Op. cit., p. 169. Judge Cordozo's observation is relevant: 'We may try to see things as objectively as we please. None the less we can never see them with any eyes except our own' as also Laski's caution that 'those responsible for judicial interpretation [of constitutions] must always be careful lest they mistake their private prejudice for eternal truth' (Op. cit., p. 545).

28. Lloyd Rudolph and Susanne Rudolph. *In Pursuit of Lakshmi* (New Delhi, 1987), p. 47.

29. Some details, relating to the Muslim minority, are available in Abusaleh Shariff and Mehtabul Alam, *Economic Empowerment of Muslims in India* (New Delhi, 2004). Legislation on 'religious conversion' in different States is seen by the Christians as assault on their freedom, under Article 25, to propagate religion. Administrative regulations and discontinuance of grants-in-aid are disrupting Christian educational activities. Data suggests that the weaker sections of the minorities do not benefit equitably from welfare programmes of the State.

30. The Report for 1996–1997 was tabled in July 2006. The delay makes the recommendations irrelevant.

31. Commission on Human Rights, E/CN/4/Sub.2/AC.5/2005/4, 26 May 2005, Report on the Subregional Seminar on Minority Rights: Cultural Diversity and Development in South Asia (Kandy, Sri Lanka, 21–24 November 2004, paragraph 7).

32. Speech by Congress President Sonia Gandhi at the inauguration of the India Islamic Centre, New Delhi, 12 July 2006. The Prime Minister's New 15-Point Programme for Welfare of Minorities (August 2006) addresses specific socio-economic problems and speaks of 'equitable share in economic activity and employment' and in 'rural housing schemes'. Its implementation, however, would depend on the approach of the States. Relevant in this context are the Prime Minister's (Manmohan Singh's) speech of 5 September 2006 and his letter of 10 September to the Chief Ministers. Both signal awareness of the dimensions of the problem. However, the question of the inadequacy of minority representation in elected bodies, at all levels, has not been touched upon in the Programme.

33. Chandoke, Op. cit., pp 92–96.

Chapter 5: International Human Rights Day

1. Antonio Cassese, *Human Rights in a Changing World* (Philadelphia: Temple University Press, 1990).

2. Compilation prepared by the Office of the High Commissioner for Human Rights in accordance with paragraph 5 of the annex to Human Rights Council resolution 16/21; Human Rights Council, Working Group on Universal Periodic Review, Thirteenth session, 21 May–4 June 2012.
3. See https://www.globalcitizen.org/en/partners/the-country-global-citizenship-report-card-project/.
4. See https://www.hrw.org/asia/india#_blank.
5. Amnesty International Report, 2014/15, 'The State of the World's Human Rights', p. 178. See amnesty.org/en/countries/asia-and-the-pacific/india/report-india.

SECTION TWO: INDIAN POLITY, IDENTITY, DIVERSITY AND CITIZENSHIP

Chapter 6: Nehru's Vision for India as a Major Power

1. Judith M. Brown, *Nehru: A Political Life* (New Delhi: Oxford University Press, 2003), p. 345; Benjamin Zachariah, *Nehru* (London, 2004), p. xxiii.
2. Hedley Bull, *The Anarchical Society: A Study of Order in World Politics*, 2nd ed. (London: Macmillian, 1995), p. 200. For Ranke's definition, see p. 316n3.
3. Henry Kissinger, *Diplomacy* (London: Simon and Schuster, 1995), pp. 396–397.
4. Baldev Raj Nayar and T.V. Paul, *India in the World Order: Searching for Major-Power Status* (Cambridge: Cambridge University Press, 2003), p. 31, citing Kim's paper on China in *Current History* (September 1997).
5. Ibid., p. 32.
6. Sarvepalli Gopal, *Jawaharlal Nehru: A Biography* (New Delhi: Oxford University Press, 1979), Vol. II, p. 43, referring to an interview reported in *The New York Times*, 1 September 1946. The term 'national interest' has lent itself to many definitions. Nehru might have agreed with John Rawls's view that it is 'defined by the principles of justice' to which a state subscribes (*A Theory of Justice*, p. 333). On the other hand, he may also have endorsed the Nixon–Kissinger theorem on national interest: 'Our objective, in the first instance, is to support our interests over the long run with a sound foreign policy. The more that policy is based on a realistic assessment of our and others' interest, the more effective our role in the world can be. We are not involved in the world because we have commitments; we have commitments because we are involved. Our interests must shape our commitments, rather than the other way around' (Kissinger, Op. cit., pp. 711–712).
7. Gopal, Op. cit., Vol. I, p. 336. Over the next few years, Soviet perceptions of India were generally negative. Nehru, on his part, was 'wary of the Soviet

Union' and leaning towards the United States and the United Kingdom (Vol. II, pp. 63–64).

8.   Speech in the Constituent Assembly (8 March 1949), cited in Gopal, Op. cit., Vol. II, p. 300.
9.   US Department of State, *Foreign Relations of the United States, 1950* (Washington, 1978), Vol. V, p. 1499. The remark occurs in a secret Department of State policy paper on Pakistan and is dated 3 April 1950. In the context of this assessment of India, the paper opines that 'a desirable balance of power in South Asia' could be achieved 'through a strong Muslim block under the leadership of Pakistan'.
10. Broadcast over All India Radio, Delhi, 31 December 1952.
11. Speech in the House of Representatives and the Senate, Washington, 13 October 1949.
12. Jawaharlal Nehru, *Ends and Means* (17 October 1949), address to Columbia University.
13. Gopal, Op. cit., Vol. II, pp. 60–63.
14. Ibid., p. 59 (7 November 1952) citing a letter from Krishna Menon to Nehru.
15. Ibid. (2 October 1949) quoting letter to chief ministers.
16. Baldev Raj Nayar and T.V. Paul, *India in the World Order: Searching for Major-Power Status* (Cambridge University Press, 2003), p. 156, citing letter by A.P. Saxena, 'Nehru and the Bomb', *Times of India*, New Delhi, 8 July 1998.
17. Nayar and Paul, Op. cit., pp. 156–157.
18. Gopal, Op. cit., Vol. II, p. 43, citing an interview reported in *National Herald*, 1 September 1946. The practical implications of this remark, and its imprint on the conduct of policy, have been insufficiently analysed by most commentators.
19. *Jawaharlal Nehru's Speeches* (New Delhi, 1954), pp. 320–338, speech of 16 February 1953. This approach was repeated in another speech, on 18 February 1953 (pp. 338–355): 'If you demand peace, you must work for it peacefully . . . the incursion of the military mentality in the chancelleries of the world is a dangerous development.'
20. Gopal, Op. cit., Vol. II, pp. 44–45.
21. J.N. Dixit, *India's Foreign Policy and Its Neighbours* (New Delhi: Gyan Publishers, 2001), p. 25.
22. Gopal, Op. cit., Vol. II, p. 128.
23. Jawaharlal Nehru, *Letters to Chief Ministers*, Vol. 3, 1952–1954 (New Delhi, 1987), letter of 5 July 1952, pp. 49–50: 'India occupies a very special position in regard to Nepal. We acknowledge, of course, the position and we do not approve of other foreign powers interfering in Nepal. I have also

stated in Parliament that from the point of view of the defence of India, the Himalayas are our frontier in the north and the north-east. We have no desire to interfere internally in Nepal.'

24. Gopal, Op. cit., Vol. II, p. 176, statement in Parliament, 20 November 1950. A generation later, the Indian State is less categorical in the matter.

25. Gopal, Op. cit., Vol. III, p. 237, citing report of press conference of 9 October 1963.

26. Nehru, *Letters*, Vol. 3, pp. 263–264.

27. Ibid., p. 33, letter of 2 July 1953.

28. Ibid., p. 145, letter of 30 October 1952.

29. Gopal, Op. cit., p.192, citing Nehru's instructions of 21 October 1958 to the Ambassador Chagla in Washington.

30. Nehru, *Letters*, Vol. 3, p. 416, letter of 6 November 1953.

31. Gopal, Op. cit., Vol. II, p. 278, citing 29 July 1956 instructions to the Foreign Secretary.

32. Ibid., p. 285. Gopal's assessment is noteworthy: 'The Suez crisis had brought the best in Nehru . . . he had combined . . . firmness with a genuine desire to protect British interest', p. 290.

33. Ibid., p. 291, citing the note of 2 November 1956 to the Prime Minister from the Secretary General of the Ministry of External Affairs.

34. Ibid., p. 292, citing Nehru's telegram of 5 November 1956.

35. Ibid., pp. 292–293.

36. Ibid., pp. 296–297. It would be useful to compare the Indian response pattern to another act of the Soviet State when it sent its armed forces into Afghanistan in December 1979.

Chapter 7: Identity and Citizenship: An Indian Perspective

1. Manuel Castells, *The Power of Identity*, 2nd ed. (Wiley-Blackwell, 2010), p. 6.

2. Amartya Sen, *Identity and Violence: The Illusion of Destiny* (London, 2006), p. 169.

3. Abdolkarim Soroush, *Reason, Freedom and Democracy in Islam* (Oxford, 2000), p. 156.

4. Jeremy Waldron, 'Cultural Identity and Civic Responsibility', in *Citizenship in Diverse Societies* edited by Will Kymlica and Wayne Norman (Oxford, 2000), p. 157.

5. Ramachandra Guha, *India After Gandhi: The History of the World's Largest Democracy* (London, 2007), pp. ix–xx.

6. Tara Chand, *The Influence of Islam on Indian Culture* (Allahabad, 1922), p. i.

7. B.G. Verghese, *Race, Reconciliation and Security: Managing India's Diversities* (New Delhi, 2008), p. 216.

8. Kautilya, *The Arthashastra*, edited by L.N. Rangarajan (Penguin, 1992), p. 140.

9. Niraja Gopal Jayal, *Citizenship and Its Discontents: An Indian History* (New Delhi, 2013), pp. 16 and 273–275. Also, B. Shiva Rao (ed.), *The Framing of India's Constitution—A Study*, 2nd revised ed. (2012), p. 150.

10. Ernest Barker, *Principles of Social and Political Theory* (Oxford, 1951), p. vi.

11. *Constituent Assembly Debates*, Volume X, p. 979, 25 November 1949.

12. Rajni Kothari, *Rethinking Democracy* (New Delhi, 2005), p. 98.

13. Prabhat Patnaik, 'Independent India at Sixty-Five', in *Social Scientist* (New Delhi), Vol. 41, Nos 1–2, January–February 2013, pp. 5–15.

14. Amy Gutmann, *Identity in Democracy* (Princeton, 2003), pp. 3–7, 37.

15. Rajni Kothari, 'Rise of the *Dalits* and Renewed Debate on Caste', in *State and Politics in India* edited by Partha Chatterjee (Oxford 1999), p. 444.

16. Apoorvanand, 'Democratisation of Communalism', *DNA*, 23 September 2013.

17. V.P. Menon, *The Story of the Integration of Indian States* (New Delhi, 1956), p. 469.

18. Rasheeduddin Khan, *Bewildered India: Identity, Pluralism, Discord* (New Delhi, 1995), p. 295.

19. *Report of the Expert Group on Diversity Index* (Submitted to Ministry of Minority Affairs, Government of India, 2008), pp. vii–viii.

20. Will Kymlica, *Multiculturalism: Success, Failure and the Future* (Minority Policy Institute, Europe, February 2012), pp. 1–2.

21. Gurpreet Mahajan, *The Multicultural Path: Issues of Diversity and Discrimination in Democracy* (New Delhi, 2002), pp. 15, 17, 217–218.

22. Ramachandra Guha, 'Politicians and Pluralism: The Inclusive Ideals of the Republic Must Not Be Lost Sight of', *The Telegraph*, 7 September 2013.

Chapter 8: Cohesion, Fragility and the Challenge of Our Times

1. Edward W. Said, *Orientalism* (New York, 1978), p. 78.

2. V.P. Menon, *The Story of the Integration of the Indian States* (Orient Longman, 1956), p. 490. Many years later, in October 1961, the first National Integration Conference said in its concluding statement that 'national integration cannot be built by brick and mortar, by chisel and hammer. It has to grow silently in the minds and hearts of men'.

3. Rajni Kothari, *Rethinking Democracy* (New Delhi, 2005), p. 1.

4. B.G. Verghese, *Rage, Reconciliation and Security: Managing India's Diversities* (New Delhi, 2008), pp. 6 and 239.

5. Amartya Sen and Jean Drèze, *An Uncertain Glory: India and Its Contradictions* (New Delhi, 2013), pp. 8 and 11.

6. Response to address presented by All India Depressed Classes Conference, Nagpur, 20 July 1942, in *Dr. Babasaheb Ambedkar: Writings and Speeches* (Mumbai, 2003), Volume 17, Part Three, p. 276.
7. Sunil K. Khilnani, *The Idea of India* (London, 1997), p. 203.
8. Ananya Vajpeyi, *Righteous Republic: The Political Foundations of Modern India* (Harvard, 2012), p. 248.
9. B.R. Ambedkar, 'Conditions Precedent for the Successful Working of Democracy', 22 December 1952, Op. cit., pp. 473-486.
10. Pratap Bhanu Mehta, *The Burden of Democracy* (New Delhi, 2003), p. 17.
11. Speech in Constituent Assembly, 25 November 1949.
12. John Rawls, *A Theory of Justice* (Harvard, 1971), pp. 3–4.
13. Amartya Sen, *The Idea of Justice* (London, 2009), pp. 68–69.
14. *R.C. Podyal* v *Union of India*, 1994 Supp(1) SCC 325.
15. Law Commission of India—Report No. 255, March 2015, pp. 80–82.
16. Association for Democratic Reforms: Lok Sabha Election Watch, 2014, pp. 5, 34–35 and Election Commission of India: Turnout Trends over the Years.
17. The Departmentally Related Standing Committees (DRSC), established in 1993, have improved matters but reference of proposed legislation to them is not obligatory and is often dispensed with. Furthermore, attendance by members leaves much to be desired.
18. Granville Austin, *Working a Democratic Constitution: A History of the Indian Experience* (New Delhi, 1999), pp. 5, 10, 11.
19. Ibid., pp. 561, 570.
20. Commission on Centre–State Relations: Report, Part I, 1988, p. 18.
21. Op-ed by Kalaignar Karunanidhi in *The Hindu*, 15 August 2007.
22. Editorial, *The Telegraph*, Kolkata, 24 August 2016.
23. Niraja Gopal Jayal, 'Unity in Diversity: An Indian Perspective' in Unity in Diversity: Learning from Each Other—4th International Conference on Federalism, 2007, New Delhi, organized by the Inter State Council Secretariat, p. 31.
24. Shiv Visvanathan, *Theatres of Democracy* (New Delhi, 2016), pp. 135–138.
25. Louise Tillin, 'Asymmetrical Federalism', in *The Oxford Handbook of the Indian Constitution* edited by Sujit Choudhry, Madhav Khosla, Pratap Bhanu Mehta (New Delhi, 2016), pp. 541–549 and Rekha Saxena, 'Is India a Case of Asymmetrical Federalism?' *Economic and Political Weekly*, volume 47, number 2 (14 January 2012), pp. 70–75.
26. Govind Bhattacharjee, 'Asymmetric Solution I & II', in *The Statesman*, 7 and 8 September 2016, wherein the pattern in federal structure in other countries has been carefully traced.

27.   Sonalde B. Desai, Amaresh Dubey, Brij Lal Joshi, Mitali Sen, Abusaleh Shariff and Reeve Vanneman, *Human Development in India: Challenges For A Society in Transition* (New Delhi, 2010), pp. 206–207.

28.   Ajay Gudavarthy, *Maoism, Democracy and Globalisation: Cross Currents in Indian Politics* (New Delhi, 2014), p. 7.

29.   Rajeev Bhargava in Rajeev Bhargava and Vipul Mudgal (eds), *Claiming India from Below: Activism and Democratic Transformation* (New Delhi, 2016), pp. xix–xx.

30.   Atishi Merlena, Prashant Bhushan and Reena Gupta, 'Initiatives and Referendums—The Next Step in Indian Democracy', in *Claiming India from Below: Activism and Democratic Transformation* edited by Rajeev Bhargava and Vipul Mudgal (New Delhi, 2016).

Chapter 9: Religion, Religiosity and World Order

1.   Cited in Christophe Jaffrelot, 'Indian Democracy at 70: Towards a Hindu State?', *Journal of Democracy*, volume 28, number 3 (July 2017), pp. 59–60. The author apprehends that 'India is on the path of becoming an ethnic democracy' for which the 'bulk of conditions' mentioned by Smooha exist.

2.   Cesare Merlini, 'A Post-Secular World?', *Survival*, volume 53, number 2 (2011), pp. 117–130.

3.   Monica Duffy Toft, Daniel Philpott and Timothy Samuel Shah, *God's Century: Resurgent Religion and Global Politics* (New York, 2011), p. 127.

4.   Abdel Bari Atwan, *Islamic State: The Digital Caliphate* (London, 2015), pp. 15–31 and 218.

5.   Headley Bull, *The Anarchical Society: A Study of Order in World Politics* (London, 1977), pp. 19 and 22.

6.   Henry Kissinger, *World Order: Reflections on the Character of Nations and the Course of History* (London, 2014), p. 3.

7.   Edward Gibbon, *The Decline and Fall of the Roman Empire* (New York, 1952), Vol. 1, p. 12. It was somewhat similar in early Hindu polity—cf. Narayan Chandra Bandyopadhyaya, *Development of Hindu Polity and Political Theories* (New Delhi, 1980), pp. 420–421. The same approach was advocated by the Moghul Emperor Akbar in his homily to Shah Abbas of Persia.

8.   Martin E. Marty and R. Scott Appleby, *The Fundamentalism Project*, Vol. 4, *Accounting for Fundamentalisms* (Chicago, 1994), p. 1. This study covers Christian, Jewish, Islamic, Hindu and Buddhist fundamentalist movements in different countries and regions.

9.   Ibid., p. 7.

10. Michael Barkun, 'Religious Violence and the Myth of Fundamentalism', *Politics, Religion and Ideology*, volume 4, number 3 (Winter 2003), Special Issue: Religious Fundamentalism and Political Extremism.

11. Anthony H. Cordesman, *Global Trends in Terrorism 1970–2016* (Center for Strategic & International Studies, Washington D.C., 2016), Executive Summary, p. 3. In this sense, a sharper focus is developed in our own categorization of internal security threat into (i) terrorism in the hinterland of the country; (ii) left wing extremism in certain areas; (iii) cross-border terrorism in Jammu & Kashmir and (iv) insurgency in the North-Eastern states (Annual Report of the Ministry of Home Affairs, 2017–2018, paragraph 2.2).

12. Rick Gladstone, 'What Is Terrorism? Attacks in Canada and Belgium Reflect Uncertain Definition', the *New York Times*, 31 May 2018.

13. Said Amir Arjumand (ed.), *The Political Dimensions of Religion* (New York, 1993), pp. 1–2.

14. Ibid., p. 5. Some specific instances of this are cited by the author.

15. Marty and Appleby, Op. cit, p. 20; Robert Wuthnow and Mattew P. Lawson, 'Sources of Christian Fundamentalism in the United States'.

16. Youssef M. Choueiri, *Islamic Fundamentalism* (Boston, 1990), passim.

17. Wilfred Cantwell Smith, *Islam in Modern History* (Princeton, 1957). 'The fundamental *malaise* of modern Islam is a sense that something had gone wrong with Islamic history. The fundamental problem of modern Muslims is how to rehabilitate that history: to set it going again in full vigour so that Islamic society can once again flourish as a divinely guided society should and must. The fundamental spiritual crisis of Islam in the twentieth century stems from an awareness that something is awry between the religion that God has appointed and the historical development of the world which He controls' (pp. 47–48).

18. Odd Arne Westad, *The Cold War: A World History* (New York, 2017), p. 472.

19. David Menashri, *Post-Revolution Politics in Iran: Religion, Society and Power* (London, 2001), pp. 1–3.

20. Martin Kramer (ed.), *The Islamism Debate* (Tel Aviv: Dayan Center Papers 129, 1997), p. 7.

21. Tariq Ramadan, *Islam and the Arab Awakening* (New York, 2012). He focuses on the need in Arab societies of 'a thoroughgoing intellectual revolution that will open the door to economic change, and o spiritual, cultural, and artistic liberation—and to the empowerment of women' (p. 14).

22. Sadik Al-Azm, 'Arab Nationalism, Islamism and the Arab Uprising', in *The New Middle East: Protest and Revolution in the Arab World* edited by Fawaz A. Gerges (Cambridge, 2014), p. 273.

23. Fawaz A. Gerges, *ISIS: A History* (Princeton, 2016), pp. 199, 219.
24. Jason Burke, *The New Threat from Islamic Militancy* (London, 2015), p. 20.
25. Ayesha Jalal, *Partisans of Allah: Jihad in South Asia* (New Delhi, 2008), p. 19.
26. Rabindranath Tagore, *Nationalism*, in *Indian Nationalism: The Essential Writings*, edited by S. Irfan Habib (New Delhi, 2017), pp. 119–133.
27. Sunanda Datta-Ray, *Business Standard*, 26 May 2018, p. 8.
28. Vinayak Damodar Savarkar, *Hindutva* (New Delhi: Hindi Sahitya Sadan, 2003), p. 19.
29. M.S. Golwalkar, *M.S. Golwalkar: His Vision and Mission* (Kochi, 2008), p. 42.
30. M.S. Golwalkar, *Bunch of Thoughts* (Bangalore, 1968), pp. 437–438.
31. D.L. Sheth and Ashis Nandy (eds), *The Multiverse of Democracy: Essays in Honour of Rajni Kothari* (New Delhi, 1996), p. 23.
32. Meghnad Desai, *The Raisina Model* (New Delhi, 2017), pp. 53–54.
33. Dhirendra K. Jha, *Shadow Armies: Fringe Organizations and Foot Soldiers of Hindutva* (New Delhi, 2017). Eight organizations depicted as 'communal eddies generated by the powerful currents of Hindutva politics' have been studied in the book. The 2018 Annual Report of US Commission for International Religious Freedom (USCIRF) has observed that 'in 2017, religious freedom conditions continued a downward trend in India. India's history as a multicultural and multireligious society remained threatened by an increasingly exclusionary conception of national identity based on religion'.
34. John Dayal, Leena Dabiru and Shabnam Hashmi (eds), *Dismantling India: A 4 Year Report* (New Delhi, 2018).
35. Marty and Appleby, Op. cit, p. 603.
36. Rahul Sagar, 'Jiski Lathi, Uski Bhains: The Hindu Nationalist View of International Politics', in *India's Grand Strategy* edited by Kanti Bajpai, Saira Basit and V. Krishnappa (New Delhi, 2014), pp. 253–254.
37. Philpott, Toft and Shah, Op. cit, p. 129.
38. Karen Armstrong, *A History of God* (New York, 1993), p. 399.
39. Philip Bobbitt, *The Shield of Achilles* (New York, 2002), p. 816.

Chapter 10: Indira Gandhi: A Vision for Global Justice and Social Democracy

1. See https://meaindia.nic.in/cdgeneva/?pdf0590?000.
2. Ibid.
3. See https://openthemagazine.com/essay/farewell-fidel/.
4. See https://www.thehindu.com/opinion/op-ed//article62118809.ece.
5. See https://www.princeton.edu/~kohli/docs/UNRISD.pdf.

6. See https://books.google.co.in/books?id=E4zAhxHdW3sC&pg=PT15&l pg=PT15&dq=Amartya+Sen,+%E2%80%98has+to+be+judged+not+just+ by+the+institutions+that+formally+exist+but+by+the+extent+to+which+d ifferent+voices+from+diverse+sections+of+the+people+can+actually+be+h eard.%E2%80%99&source=bl&ots=0mczXnxuJU&sig=ACfU3U17vg3S WEcjoEoai9HB5EQLcC7Y5A&hl=en&sa=X&ved=2ahUKEwi3yofYn rP3AhWYS2wGHZYKDnEQ6AF6BAgDEAM#v=onepage&q=Amart ya%20Sen%2C%20%E2%80%98has%20to%20be%20judged%20not%20 just%20by%20the%20institutions%20that%20formally%20exist%20but%20 by%20the%20extent%20to%20which%20different%20voices%20from%20 diverse%20sections%20of%20the%20people%20can%20actually%20be%20 heard.%E2%80%99&f=false.

Chapter 11: Two Obligatory Isms: Why Pluralism and Secularism Are Essential for Our Democracy

1. John Rawls, *A Theory of Justice* (Harvard, 2001), pp. 3–4.
2. Cited in Neera Chandoke, *Contested Secessions* (New Delhi, 2012), p. 44.
3. Aziz Al-Azmeh, 'Pluralism in Muslim Societies', lecture delivered on 29 January 2005 at the India International Centre (IIC), New Delhi.
4. Niraja Gopal Jayal, *Citizenship and Its Discontent: An Indian History* (New Delhi, 2013), p. 255. More recently, the author has observed that 'while jus soli remains the governing principle of citizenship in India, citizenship law and jurisprudence have come to be manifestly inflected by elements of jus sanguinis' ('Citizenship' in *The Oxford Handbook of the Indian Constitution* [New Delhi, 2016], p. 179).
5. Sunil Khilnani, *The Idea of India* (London, 1997), p. 175.
6. Charles Taylor, 'Democratic Exclusion (and Its Remedies?)', in *Multiculturalism, Liberalism and Democracy*, edited by Rajeev Bhargava, A.K. Bagchi and R. Sundaram (New Delhi, 2007), pp. 139–163.
7. Alain Touraine, *What Is Democracy?* (Boulder, Colorado, 1997), p. 190.
8. Rajeev Bhargava (ed.), *Secularism and Its Critics* (New Delhi, 1998); Akeel Bilgrami, 'Secularism—Its Contents and Context', *Economic and Political Weekly*, volume 47, number 4 (28 January 2012), pp. 89–100. Also, Mohita Bhatia, 'Secularism and Secularisation: A Bibliographical Essay', *Economic and Political Weekly*, volume 48, number 50 (14 December 2013), pp. 103–110.
9. *S.R. Bommai* v *Union of India* (1994) 3 SCC (Jour) 1, 11 March 1994, para 252. Also, paras 153(viii), 176, 177, 304, 434(10).
10. *Manohar Joshi* v *Nitin Bhaurao Patil* (1996), AIR SC 796.

11. V.M. Tarkunde, 'Supreme Court Judgment: A Blow to Secular Democracy', 19 January 1996, *PUCL Bulletin*, February 1996.

12. S.K. Ghosh, 'Charge of the Cow Brigade', *The Statesman*, 18 May 2017, New Delhi.

13. Shabnum Tejani, *Indian Secularism—A Social and Intellectual History* (New Delhi, 2007), p. 265.

14. Brenda Cossman and Ratna Kapur, *Secularism's Last Sigh? Hindutva and the (Mis)Rule of Law* (New Delhi, 1999), pp. 139–140.

15. Pratap Bhanu Mehta, *The Burden of Democracy* (New Delhi, 2003), pp. 16–17.

16. Rasheeduddin Khan, *Bewildered India: Identity, Pluralism, Discord* (New Delhi, 1995), p. 295.

17. T.K. Oommen, *Social Inclusion in Independent India: Dimensions and Approaches* (New Delhi, 2014), p. 269.

18. Upendra Baxi, 'The Rule of Law in India', *Sur, Rev. int direitos human*, volume 4, number 6 (Sao Paulo, 2007)

19. Zoya Hasan, *Democracy and the Crisis of Inequality* (New Delhi, 2014), p. 4.

20. Association for Democratic Reform (ADR), National Election Watch. The Law Commission of India indicated in March 2015 (Report No. 255, pp. 80–82) that the winning candidate wins only 20–30 per cent of the votes.

21. Pratap Bhanu Mehta, Op. cit., p. 161.

22. B.L. Shankar and Valerian Rodrigues, *The Indian Parliament: A Democracy at Work* (New Delhi, 2011), p. 336. The situation has worsened in recent years.

23. Davish Kapur and Pratap Bhanu Mehta, 'The Indian Parliament as an Instrument of Accountability', UN Research Institute for Social Development: Democracy, Governance and Human Rights Programme, Paper No. 23, January 2006.

24. Atisi Merlena, Prashant Bhushan and Reena Gupta, 'Initiatives and Referendums: The Next Step in Indian Democracy', in *Claiming India from Below: Activism and Democratic Transformation* edited by Rajeev Bhargava and Vipul Mudgal (New Delhi, 2016), p. 323.

25. Report of the Expert Group on Diversity Index submitted to the Ministry of Minority Affairs, Government of India, 2008, pp. vii–viii.

26. Sanghamitra Padhy, 'Secularism and Justice: A Review of Indian Supreme Court Judgments', *Economic and Political Weekly*, volume 39, numbers 46/47 (20–26 November 2004), pp. 5027–5032.

27. Granville Austin, 'The Supreme Court and the Struggle for the Custody of the Constitution', in *Supreme but Not Infallible: Essays in Honour of the Supreme Court of India* (New Delhi, 2000), p. 13.

28. Amartya Sen, *The Argumentative Indian* (New Delhi, 2005), p. 108.

29. M. Hamid Ansari, 'Cohesion, Fragility and the Challenge of Our Times', Indira Gandhi Memorial Lecture, The Asiatic Society, Kolkata, 3 October 2016.

30. Sudipta Kaviraj, 'Nationalism', in *The Oxford Companion to Politics in India* edited by Niraja Gopal Jayal and Pratap Bhanu Mehta (New Delhi, 2013), p. 325.

31. Rabindranath Tagore, 'Nationalism in India', in *Nationalism* (New Delhi, 2012), pp. 85–116.

32. 'Use This Law More Selectively', Editorial in *Hindustan Times*, 22 June 2017.

33. Kaushik Basu, 'Resisting the Moral Retreat', *Indian Express*, 22 June 2017.

34. Andrew J. Bacevich, *The New American Militarism: How Americans Are Seduced by War* (New York, 2005), p. 224.

35. Yael Tamir, *Liberal Nationalism* (Princeton, 1993), pp. 79, 83, 90, 95.

Chapter 12: Democracy and the Perils of Bending Reality

1. B.R. Ambedkar, *Speeches and Writings*, Vol. 17, Part Three (1979), pp. 473–486.

2. Walter Lippman, *The Phantom Public* (New York, 1993), pp. 141 and 160.

3. Khasa Subba Rao, 'Preserving the Freedom of the Press', *Swarajya*, Annual Number 1072, in Nirmala Lakshman, *Writing a Nation—An Anthology of Indian Journalism* (New Delhi, 2007), p. 179.

4. *Rangarajan Etc* v *P. Jagjivan Ram* on 30 March 1989, SCR (2) 204, 1989 SCC (2) 574.

5. 'Vice President Presents IPI India Award for Excellence in Journalism 2007 to Outlook', https://pib.gov.in/newsite/erelcontent.aspx?relid=34133.

6. Alan Rusbridger, *Breaking News: The Remaking of Journalism and Why It Matters Now* (Edinburgh, 2018), pp. xxiii–iv and 179.

7. Dan Gillmor, *We the Media: Grassroot Journalism, by the People, for the People* (2004), p. xiii.

8. Kurian Joseph, 'Idea Exchange', *The Sunday Express*, 9 December 2018, p. 10.

9. In the 1987 Meerut riots, forty-five suspects were gunned down by the Provincial Armed Constabulary (PAC) on the banks of a canal. The decision in the prolonged court proceedings was given in March 2015.

10. Karan Thapar, 'Why the Indian Media Can't Emulate the US Media', *Hindustan Times*, 25 November 2018.

11. O.P. Rawat, Interview with Devesh K. Pandey, *The Hindu*, 1 December 2018, p. 8.

12. Ajit Prakash Shah, 'Dissent under Siege', *The Indian Express*, 21 April 2017.

Chapter 13: The Ethics of Gandhi and the Dead Weight of Statecraft

1. ↙ See http://www.drbrambedkarcollege.ac.in/sites/default/files/M.K.Gandhi %20Eng.pdf.
2. See https://www.mkgandhi.org/momgandhi/chap18.htm.
3. Mervyn Jones, 'International Law and Politics', *Transactions of the Grotius Society*, volume 41 (1955), pp. 5–23, http://www.jstor.org/stable/743287.
4. Goolam E. Vahanvati in *Constitutionalism, Human Rights and the Rule of Law* edited by Mool Chand Sharma (2005), p. 168.
5. See https://pib.gov.in/newsite/PrintRelease.aspx?relid=138871.

Chapter 15: Some Thoughts on the Dichotomies of Our Times: The Philosophy of Guru Nanak

1. Zbigniew Brzezinski, *Out of Control: Global Turmoil on the Eve of the 21st Century* (Touchstone, 1995).
2. Rabindranath Tagore, 'Nationalism in the West' (1917), reprinted in Rabindranath Tagore and Mohit K. Ray, *Essays* (2007), p. 465.
3. Interview with George Viereck, *Saturday Evening Post*, 1929.
4. Dan Rather on *BBC Newsnight*, 2002.

Chapter 16: Sins and Sinners: Where Did It Go Wrong?

1. Ananya Vajpeyi, *Righteous Republic: The Political Foundations of Modern India* (Harvard, 2012), p. 250.
2. Scroll, 14 June 2017.
3. Niraja Gopal Jayal, *Re-Forming India: The Nation Today* (New Delhi, 2019), p. xxxix.
4. Angana P. Chatterji, Thomas Blom Hansen and Christophe Jaffrelot, *Majoritarian State: How Hindu Nationalism Is Changing India* (New Delhi, 2019), p. 1.
5. Goolam E. Vahanvati, 'Rule of Law: The Siege Within', in *Constitutionalism, Human Rights & the Rule of Law* edited by Mool Chand Sharma and Raju Ramachandran (New Delhi, 2005), p. 168.
6. *The Economist*, 'The Global Crisis in Conservatism', https://www.economist.com/leaders/2019/07/04/the-global-crisis-in-conservatism.

Chapter 17: Journalism in Times of Strident Nationalism

1. B.G. Verghese, *Rage, Reconciliation and Security: Managing India's Diversities* (New Delhi, 2008), p. xiv.

2. Khasa Subba Rao, 'Preserving the Freedom of the Press', *Swarajya*, Annual Number 1072, in Nirmala Lakshman, *Writing A Nation—An Anthology of Indian Journalism* (New Delhi, 2007), p. 179.

3. *Rangarajan Etc* v *P. Jagjivan Ram* on 30 March 1989, SCR (2) 204, 1989 SCC (2) 574.

4. Kurian Joseph, 'Idea Exchange', *The Sunday Express*, 9 December 2018, p. 10.

5. See https://www.orwellfoundation.com/the-orwell-foundation/orwell/essays-and-other-works/notes-on-nationalism/.

6. Andreas Wimmer, 'Why Nationalism Works and Why It Isn't Going Away', *Foreign Affairs* (New York, March/April 1919).

7. M.K. Gandhi, 'Nationalism and Internationalism', https://www.mkgandhi.org/voiceoftruth/nationalism.htm.

8. The Print, 'Veer Savarkar: The Man Credited with Creating Hindutva Didn't Want It Restricted to Hindus', https://theprint.in/pageturner/excerpt/veer-savarkar-hindutva-india/38073/.

9. D.L. Sheth and Ashis Nandy (eds), *The Multiverse of Democracy: Essays in Honour of Rajni Kothari* (New Delhi, 1996), p. 23.

10. Chrisophe Jaffrelot, 'Towards a Hindu State?' *Journal of Democracy*, July 2017, pp. 59–60. Smooha's paper 'The Model of Ethnic Democracy: Israel as a Jewish and Democratic State' was published in *Nations and Nationalism*, 8 October 2002, pp. 475–503.

11. Hamid Ansari, '*Citizenship*', *Seminar*, number 713, January 2019, p. 4, note 9. It should also be mentioned that even after the passing of the bill and the lapse of the statutory time of three months, enactment is still pending.

12. Karan Thapar, 'Why the Indian Media Can't Emulate the US Media', *Hindustan Times*, 25 November 2018.

13. O.P. Rawat, interview with Devesh K. Pandey, *The Hindu*, 1 December 2018, p. 8.

14. T.N. Ninan, 'The Week's Takeaways', *Business Standard*, 2 March 2019.

15. Vidya Subramaniam, 'Fatal, Not Funny: Nationalist Outrage and Journalists against Journalist', The Hindu Centre for Politics and Public Policy, 5 March 2019.

16. Shiv Visvanathan, 'Think Like a Civilisation', *The Hindu*, 28 February 2012.

17. Ramachandra Guha, 'After Pulwama, a Writer's Dilemma', *The Telegraph*, 2 March 2019.

18. Ravish Kumar, The Wire Dialogue, 24 February 2019.

Chapter 18: Citizenship

1. See https://www.uvm.edu/~jbailly/courses/clas158/notes/aristotlePolitics III.html.

2.   Niraja Gopal Jayal, *Citizenship and Its Discontents: An Indian History* (New Delhi, 2013), pp. 52–53 and 80.

3.   Niraja Gopal Jayal, 'Citizenship', in *The Oxford Handbook of the Indian Constitution* (New Delhi, 2016), p. 166.

4.   Valerian Rodrigues, 'Citizenship and the Indian Constitution', in *Politics and Ethics of the Indian Constitution* edited by Rajeev Bhargava (New Delhi, 2009), pp. 174–175.

5.   Jayal, Op. cit. (2016), p. 175.

6.   Lovish Garg, 'If India Wants to Remain Secular, the New Citizenship Bill Isn't the Way to Go', The Wire, 21 September 2016.

7.   *Report of the High Level Committee on Indian Diaspora* (2003), p. 180.

8.   Jayanti Ghosh, 'More Equal Than Others', *Frontline*, volume 19, issue 2 (19 January–1 February 2002).

9.   L.K. Advani, 'PM's Ill-Advised Announcement on Dual Citizenship', BJP press release, 12 January 2005.

10. 'This is not a Jewish state only because most of the inhabitants are Jews. It is a state for the Jews wherever they may be, and for any Jew who wishes to be here', said PM Ben Gurion when this was debated in the Israeli Parliament in 1950 (Shlomo Sand: *The Invention of the Jewish People* [London, 2009], p. 287).

11. Apurva Thakur, 'Why the Citizenship Amendment Bill Goes against the Basic Tenets of the Constitution', *Economic and Political Weekly*, volume 53, number 13 (31 March 2018).

12. Jayal, Op. cit. (2016), p. 179. The use of the term 'diaspora' is now metaphoric in social science literature, as pointed out by William Safran in 'Diasporas in Modern Societies: Myths of Homeland and Return', *Diaspora: A Journal of Transnational Studies*, volume 1, number 1 (Spring 1991), pp. 83–99.

Chapter 19: Reimagining Parliament: Hopes and Perils

1.   Mint, 'BR Ambedkar: In His Own Words', https://www.livemint.com/Home-Page/JHyUYYjoMzBFWSKuptd8LK/BR-Ambedkara-man-of-many-parts.html.

2.   *Outlook*, 'The Grammar of Anarchy', https://www.outlookindia.com/website/story/the-grammar-of-anarchy/289235.

3.   See https://indiankanoon.org/doc/906726/?type=print.

4.   Apocryphally, British PMs have occasionally felt in need of a sip of brandy before facing Question Hour (Chris Bryant, *Parliament: The Biography*, Volume 2: *Reform* (2014), p. 203).

5.   Christophe Jaffrelot and Sanjay Kumar, *Rise of the Plebians? The Changing Face of Indian Legislative Assemblies* (New Delhi, 2009), pp. 5–9.

6.   Niraja Gopal Jayal, 'The Rival Representative Claims of Parliament and Civil Society in India', in *The Indian Parliament: A Critical Appraisal* edited by Sudha Pai and Avinash Kumar (New Delhi, 2014), pp. 334–340.

7.   Chris Bryant, *Parliament: The Biography*, Volume 2: *Reform*, (London, 2014) p. 372.

SECTION THREE: INDIAN MUSLIM PERCEPTIONS AND THE INDIAN CONTRIBUTION TO THE CULTURE OF ISLAM

Chapter 20: Militant Islam

1.   Ira M. Lapidus, *The History of Islamic Societies* (Cambridge, 1988), pp. xx, 551–53, 882–883.

2.   Ibrahim M. Abu-Rabi, *Intellectual Origins of Islamic Resurgence in the Modern Arab World* (Albany SUNY, 1996), p. 61.

3.   Aziz Al-Azmeh, *Islam and Modernities* (London, 1993), pp. 24–26.

4.   John Esposito, *The Islamic Threat: Myth or Reality?* (New York, 1992), p. 8.

5.   Roy Oliver, *The Failure of Political Islam* (Cambridge, Massachusetts, 1994), passim.

6.   Laura Guazzone, *The Islamist Dilemma* (Ithaca Press, 1995), p. 4.

7.   Youssef M. Choueiri, *Islamic Fundamentalism* (Boston, 1990), p. 9.

8.   Saad Eddin Ibrahim, *Egypt, Islam and Democracy* (Cairo, 1996), p. 69.

9.   Yusuf Al Qaradawi, *State in Islam* (Cairo, 1998), p. 126.

10. Wilfred Cantwell Smith, *Islam in Modern History* (Princeton, 1957), pp. 47–48.

11. Fouad Ajami, *The Arab Predicament* (New York, 1981), p. 12.

12. Ibrahim, Op. cit., p. 5.

13. Abu Rabi, Op. cit., p. 64.

14. Hasan Al Banna, *Six Tracts* (Kuwait, n.d.), p. 31.

15. Ibid., pp. 63–66.

16. Ibid., pp. 217–219.

17. Ibid., pp. 260–261.

18. Ibid., pp. 234–236.

19. Sayyid Qutb, *Milestones* (Kuwait, 1978), pp. 7–14.

20. Ibid., pp. 16–17.

21. Ibid., pp. 234–236.

22. Ibid., pp. 105–106.

23. Ibid., pp. 109–110.

24. Ibid., p. 139.

25. Abul Hasan Ali Nadwi, *Islam and the World* (English translation, Lucknow, 1967), p. 3. Arab commentators like Abu Rabi (Op. cit., p. 139) regard as

secondary the external intellectual influences on Qutb of Islamist thinkers like Nadwi and Maudoodi. The parallelism, however, has been carefully traced by Ahmad S. Moussalli in *Moderate and Radical Islamic Fundamentalism* (University of California Press, 1999).

26. Ajami, Op. cit., p. 61.

27. Nazih Ayyubi, *Political Islam* (London, 1991), pp. 72–77.

28. Ibrahim, Op. cit., pp. 15–19.

29. Geneive Abdo, *No God but God: Egypt and the Triumph of Islam* (Oxford, 2000), pp. 10–11.

30. Ahmad Jouadjia, 'Discourse and Strategy of the Algerian Islamist Movement (1986–1992)' in L. Guazzone, Op. cit., pp. 74–75.

31. Ibid., p. 81.

32. Ibid., p. 96.

33. Esposito and Voll, *Islam and Democracy* (Oxford, 1996), p. 166.

34. Ibid., p. 167.

35. Leon Trotsky, *The History of the Russian Revolution* (London, 1932), volume I, p. 16.

36. Cited in Fred Halliday, *Islam and the Myth of Confrontation* (London, 1996), p. 69.

37. Farida Adelkhah, *Being Modern in Iran* (London, 1999), pp. ix–x.

38. Halliday, Op. cit., p. 67.

39. Sya'ban H. Muhammad, *Islam in Indonesian Politics* (New Delhi, 1999), p. 93.

40. Ibid., p. 105.

41. Ibid., p. 20.

42. Yusuf al Qaradawi, *Islamic Awakening between Rejection and Extremism*, 3rd ed. (International Institute of Islamic Thought, Herndon, Virginia, USA, 1995), pp. 21–22.

43. Ibid., pp. 33–46.

44. Ibid., p. 60.

45. Ibid., p. 67.

46. Bernard Lewis, *Islam and the West* (Oxford, 1993), p. 123.

47. Ibid., p. 154.

48. Fouad Ajami, *The Dream Palace of the Arabs* (New York, 1998), pp. xi–xii.

49. Yusuf al Qaradawi, *Priorities of the Islamic Movement in the Coming Phase* (Cairo, 1992), p. 209.

50. Rachid al Ghannouchi, 'Secularism in the Arab Maghrib', in *Islam and Secularism in the Middle East* edited by Azzam Tamimi and John Esposito (London, 2000), pp. 97–123. Ghannouchi asserts that 'a democratic secular government is less evil than a despotic system of government that claims to be Islamic'.

51. Qaradwi, Op. cit., p. 277.

Chapter 21: Islam and the Democratic Principle

1. Muhammad ibn Jarir al-Tabari, *The History of al Tabari* (Albany, 1989), volume I, pp. 249–257.
2. Daniel Brown, *Rethinking Tradition in Modern Islamic Thought* (Cambridge, 1996), p. 3.
3. Ibn Ishaq, *Sira Rasul Allah*, English translation by A. Guillaume (Karachi, 1980), p. 232.
4. Ibn Hisham, Op. cit., pp. 682–687. Tabari, Op. cit., volume IX, pp. 185–201, volume X, pp. 1–16. Outlining his approach to governance, Abu Bakr said, 'I am only a follower, not an innovator. If I am upright, then follow me; but if I deviate, then straighten me out'. He also prescribed ten principles for the conduct of the Muslim army.
5. Tabari, Ibid., volume XI, p. 148.
6. Ibid., volume XIV, pp. 143–148.
7. Ibid., volume X, pp. 2–16 and volume XI, pp. 148–150 for Abu Bakr and volume XI, pp. 158–159 for Omar. The latter corresponded regularly with his Governors and field commanders; Tabari has reported details. Noteworthy are his instructions for the preservation of churches in Jerusalem (volume XII, pp. 191–192). Ali's Sermon on the mutuality of rights and obligations between the ruler and his subjects and his Instrument of Instructions to the Governor of Egypt, covering virtually every aspect of administrative activity, are given in Nahjul Balagha (Qum, 1975), pp. 437–440 and pp. 529–554 respectively.
8. W. Montgomery Watt, *Muhammad at Mecca* (Oxford, 1953), p. 22.
9. Tabari, Op. cit., volume XVIII, p. 5.
10. A.K.S. Lambton, *State and Government in Medieval Islam* (Oxford, 1981), p. 62.
11. Ibid., pp. 208–209.
12. M.A. Shaban, *Islamic History: A New Interpretation*, volumes 1 and 2 (Cambridge, 1971 and 1976). 'The use of military power (in the period after Muawiyah) became the main basis of government and armed revolt the only means of opposition. This was the result of the failure of the Arabs to develop their political institutions in response to new circumstances' (volume 1, p. 166).
13. Aziz Al-Azmeh, *Muslim Kingship: Power and the Sacred in Muslim, Christian and Pagan Polities* (London, 1997), p. 79.
14. Shaban, Op. cit., pp. 89–90, and Wilfred Madelung, *The Succession to Mohammad: A Study of the Early Caliphate* (Cambridge, 1997), p. 326. The substantive changes in the style of governance have been traced in detail by Abul Ala Maudoodi, *Khilafat wa Malookiat* (Lahore, 1987), pp. 157–205.
15. Lambton, Op. cit., p. 45.

16. Shaban, Op cit., volume II, pp. 89 and 115.
17. Al-Mawardi, *The Ordinances of Government* (Reading, UK, 1996), pp. 3–22. According to Hamid Enayat, *Modern Islamic Political Thought* (London, 1982), the influence of al-Mawardi can be seen in the early writings of Maulana Abul Kalam Azad (p. 59).
18. Lambton, Op. cit., pp. 110–111.
19. Ibid., pp. 183–185.
20. Ibid.
21. Muhammad Asad, *The Principles of State and Government in Islam* (Berkeley, California, 1961), p. 93. The book puts together, on pages 69–94, the relevant texts.
22. S.H.M. Jafri, *The Origins and Early Development of Shia Islam* (Beirut, 1976, reprinted in Qum n.d.), p. 235.
23. Ibid., pp. 281 and 289–292.
24. For details of the three schools, see Lambton, Op. cit., pp. 28–33 and 219–263. Lambton concludes that both the Sunni and the Imami theory led to 'political quietism'.
25. Said Amir Arjomand, *The Shadow of God and the Hidden Imam: Religion, Political Order, and Societal Change in Shi'ite Iran from the Beginning to 1890* (Chicago, 1984), pp. 171–187. The concept of Imamate as 'spiritual sovereignty' permitted the acceptance of temporal authority.
26. Albert Hourani, *Arabic Thought in the Liberal Age 1798–1939* (Cambridge 1983), pp. 184–188. Also, L. Binder, *Islamic Liberalism* (Chicago, 1988), pp. 129–158.
27. Cited in Hamid Enayat, Op cit., p. 65.
28. Yahia H. Zoubir, 'Democracy and Islam in Malek Bennabi's Thought', *The American Journal of Islamic Social Sciences*, volume 15, number 1 (1998), pp. 107–112. Also, Azzam Tamimi, 'Democracy in Islamic Political Thought', *Encounters: Journal of Inter-Cultural Perspectives*, volume 3, number 1 (March 1997), pp. 37–41.
29. Azzam Tamimi, 'Democracy: The Religious and the Political in Contemporary Islamic Debate', *Encounters: Journal of Inter-Cultural Perspectives*, volume 4, number 1 (1998), pp. 36–64.
30. Rachid Al Ghannouchi, 'Secularism in the Arab Maghreb', in *Islam and Secularism in the Middle East* edited by Azzam Tamimi and John Esposito (London, 2000), pp. 97–123.
31. Fazlur Rahman, 'The Principle of Shura and the Role of the Ummah in Islam', in *State and Politics in Islam* edited by Mumtaz Ahmad (Washington, 1986), pp. 90–91, 95.
32. Vennesa Martin, *Creating an Islamic State: Khomeini and the Making of a New Iran* (London, 2003), pp. 117 and 122.

33. Asghar Schirazi, *The Constitution of Iran: Politics and the State in the Islamic Republic* (London, 1997), p. 1.
34. Lecture at the Oxford Centre for Islamic Studies, 16 April 1996.
35. The occasion was the summit conference of the OIC in Tehran, 9–10 December 1997.
36. Seyed Mohammad Khatami, *Islam, Dialogue and Civil Society* (New Delhi, 2003), pp. 96–97.
37. Remarks to a correspondent of the Australian Broadcasting Corporation, 14 April 2002.
38. Abdullah Laroui wrote in *The Crisis of the Arab Intellectual: Traditionalism or Historicism* (1974), 'The cardinal problem of the Arabs: their historical retardation.'
39. David Held, *Political Theory and the Modern State* (Stanford, 1989), pp. 182–183.
40. Fazlur Rahman, Op. cit., p. 250.
41. Mohammad Iqbal, *The Reconstruction of Religious Thought in Islam* (Lahore, 1982 reprint), p. 157.
42. Kung Chuan Hsiao, *Political Pluralism: A Study of Contemporary Political Theory* (New York, 1927), passim. This characterized the debate throughout the 20th century. In the last decade of the century, the Secretary General of the United Nations could proclaim without fear of contradiction: 'The time of absolute and exclusive sovereignty, however, has passed; its theory was never matched by reality' (*An Agenda for Peace* [New York, 1992], p. 9).
43. Bassam Tibi, *The Crisis of Modern Islam: A Preindustrial Culture in the Scientific-Technological Age* (Salt Lake City, 1988), p. 81.
44. Fazlur Rahman, Op. cit., p. 240.
45. John L. Esposito and John O. Voll, *Islam and Democracy* (New York, 1996), p. 3.
46. Mohammad Hashim Kamali, 'The Islamic State: Origins, Definition and Salient Attributes', in *Islam in Southeast Asia: Political, Social and Strategic Challenges for the 21st Century* edited by K.S. Nathan and M.H. Kamali (Singapore, 2005), p. 292.
47. Mohammad Hashim Kamali, *Principle of Islamic Jurisprudence* (Cambridge, 1991), pp. 348–350.
48. Abdulhamid A. Abusulaiman, *Crisis in the Muslim Mind* (Herndon, Virginia, 1993), p. 28.
49. Ibid., pp. 3–4.

Chapter 22: Convocation Address at the Jamia Millia Islamia University

1. Akbar S. Ahmad, *Postmodernism Islam: Predicament and Problems* (1992).
2. Sachar Committee Report on Social Economic and Educational Status of the Muslim Community in India: A Report of the Cabinet Secretariat.

Chapter 23: Convocation Address at the Aligarh Muslim University

1. Bertrand Russell, *The Basic Writings of Bertrand Russell* (Routledge, 2009).
2. Will Kymlicka, *Multicultural Odysseys: Navigating the New International Politics of Diversity* (Oxford University Press, 2009).

Chapter 24: Indian Muslims: Quest for Justice

1. Preface, Report of the Expert Group on Diversity Index, Government of India, 2008.
2. Amitabh Kundu, Post Sachar Evaluation Committee—Final Report (Presented to the Ministry of Minority Affairs, Government of India, 29 September 2014), pp. 170–181.
3. A.G. Noorani, *The Muslims of India* (New Delhi, 2003), p. 13.
4. Mohammed Arkoun, *Rethinking Islam: Common Questions, Uncommon Answers* (Boulder, Colorado, 1994), p. 13.
5. The Qu'ran, s xiii.11.

Chapter 25: India and Islamic Civilization: Contributions and Challenges

1. Ibn Hisham, *The Life of Mohammad* translated by A. Guillaume (Karachi, 1967), p. 646.
2. Mohammad Mujeeb, *The Indian Muslims* (London, 1967), pp. 20–22.
3. Tara Chand, *Influence of Islam on Indian Culture* (Allahabad, 1922), p. i.
4. Richard M. Eaton (ed.), *India's Islamic Traditions* (New Delhi, 2003), p. 6.
5. Iqtidar Alam Khan, 'State in Mughal India', *Social Scientist*, volume 29, number 1 (2001), p. 35. Many other instances to substantiate the point are cited in this paper including text of a letter from Emperor Aurangzeb to Rana Raj Singh of Mewar stating that the rulers are bound to ensure 'that men belonging to various communities and different religions should live in the vale of peace and pass their days in prosperity', and 'no one should interfere in the affairs of another (and that) the kings who resorted to intolerance become the cause of dispute and conflict and of harm to the people at large (and this) is a habit deserving to be rejected and cast off' (p. 31). This, however, underwent a change in the last 20 years of his reign (pp. 31–32).
6. Iqtidar Alam Khan, Ibid., p. 30: 'In this new situation the Turanis were reduced to a minority in the total strength as well as among high echelons. While, on the other hand, the strength of the nobles of Indian origin, i.e., Rajputs, other Hindus and Indian Muslims put together rose to nearly 44 per cent in the total strength. Their large representation in the nobility

tended to make them aspire for establishing their sway in the empire after sidelining the Turanis and Iran.' The changing percentages of different ethnic communities in the employ of the State make interesting reading.

7. Mohammad Habib, 'Life and Thoughts of Ziauddin Barani', in *Politics and Society During the Early Medieval Period* edited by K.A. Nizami (New Delhi, 1981), pp. 361–362.

8. Iqtidar Alam Khan, 'Medieval Indian Notions of Secular Statecraft in Retrospect', *Social Scientist*, volume 14, number 1 (January 1996), p. 5.

9. Mansura Haider, *Mukatabat-i-Allami* (New Delhi, 1998), p. 97. Letter of 14 December 1594.

10. Iftikhar Alam Khan (1986), Op. cit., p. 8.

11. H.K. Sherwani, *History of the Qutb Shahi Dynasty* (New Delhi, 1974), pp. 198 and 300.

12. Satish Chandra, 'Secularism and Composite Culture in a Pluralistic Society', in *Composite Culture in a Multicultural Society* edited by Bipen Chandra and Sucheta Mahajan (New Delhi, 2007), p. 177.

13. Kanwar Muhammad Ashraf, *Life and Conditions of the People of Hindustan* (Delhi, 1959), p. 107.

14. Mujeeb, Op. cit. pp. 354–388, where a detailed account of social life is given and a distinction made (p. 379) between political and social analysis: 'We find that while the Muslim proclaimed his mission and trumpeted his intentions, hindu influences, moving silently and and unobtrusively like waters of a flood, surrounded him from all sides, leaving only small islands where the flag of Islam flew high—and defenceless.'

15. Marcus Hattstein and Peter Delius (eds), *Islam; Art and Architecture* (2004), p. 456.

16. Irfan Habib, *Medieval India: The Study of a Civilization* (New Delhi, 2007), p. 144.

17. Ashin Das Gupta, 'Trade and Politics in Eighteenth Century India', in *The Moghul State 1526–1750* edited by Muzaffar Alam and Sanjay Subrahmanyan (Delhi, 1998), p. 361.

18. A.N.D. Haksar, *India's Forgotten Heritage: Cultural Intermingling and Harmony in Sanskrit Literature* (IIC Occasional Publication 79, New Delhi, November 1916).

19. Mujeeb, Op. cit., p. 306.

20. The similarities and parallelism in mystic teachings in Iraq, Iran, Khurasan, Turkey and India were the subject of a lecture given by me at the Mevlana University, Konya (Turkey), on 12 October 2011.

21. Mujeeb, Ibid., pp. 116 and 167.

22. Percival Spear, *Islam in South Asia* edited by Mushirul Hasan (New Delhi, 2010), volume VI, p. 153.

23. Aziz Ahmad, *Studies in Islamic Culture in the Indian Environment* (London, 1964), p. 163.

24. Ishwar Dayal Gaur, *Society, Religion and Patriarchy: Exploring Medieval Punjab Through Hir Waris* (New Delhi, 2009), p. 20.

25. Barbara Daly Metcalf, *Islamic Revival in British India: Deoband 1860–1900* (1982), pp. 7–9.

26. Mushirul Hasan, *A Moral Reckoning: Muslim Intellectuals in Nineteenth Century Delhi* (New Delhi, 2005), p. 249.

27. Maulana Hussain Ahmad Madani, *Composite Nationalism and Islam* (1938 English translation, New Delhi, 2005).

28. Wilfred Cantwell Smith, *Islam in Modern History* (Princeton, 1957), p. 261.

29. Ibid., p. 259.

30. *Report of the Prime Minister's High Level Committee on Social, Economic and Educational Status of the Muslim Community of India*, New Delhi, 17 November 2006.

31. Amitabh Kundu, 'Post Sachar Evaluation Committee—Final Report Presented to the Ministry of Minority affairs, Government of India, September 29, 2014', pp. 170–181.

32. Manini Chatterjee, 'Shadowed Christmas: Attack on Christians Are Central to *Hindutva* Ideology', *The Telegraph*, Kolkata, 25 December 2017.

33. Gurpreet Mahajan, *The Multicultural Path: Issues of Diversity and Discrimination in Democracy* (New Delhi, 2002), pp. 217–218.

Chapter 26: The Role of Women in Making a Humane Society

1. See https://www.unwomen.org/en/news/in-focus/commission-on-the-status-of-women-2012/facts-and-figures.

Chapter 27: India and the Muslim World

1. Tara Chand, *Influence of Islam on Indian Culture* (Allahabad, 1922), p. i.

2. Richard M. Eaton, *India's Islamic Traditions, 711–1750* (New Delhi, 2003), p. 6.

3. Wilfred Cantwell Smith, *Islam in Modern History* (New York, 1957), p. 261.

4. 'Social, Economic and Educational Status of the Muslim Community in India', 2006, p. 13, available at https://journals.sagepub.com/doi/abs/10.1177/0973184913411149?journalCode=ceda#:~:text=Muslim%20participation%20in%20higher%20education,per%20cent%20among%20the%20Muslims.

5. Tanweer Fazl, 'Being Muslim in Contemporary India', in *Being Muslim in South Asia: Diversity in Daily Life* edited by Robin Jeffry and Ronojoy Sen (New Delhi, 2014), pp. 216, 223.

6. Saeed M. Baddeb, *Saudi-Iranian Relations 1932–1982* (London, 1993), pp. 130–132.

7. Manini Chaterjee, 'Shadow Christmas: Attacks on Christians Are Central to Hindutva Ideology', *The Telegraph*, Kolkata, 25 December 2017.

8. Gurpeet Mahajan, *The Multicultural Path: Issues of Diversity and Discrimination in Democracy* (New Delhi, 2002), pp. 217–218

Index